SHERLOCK HOLMES
THE PAINFUL PREDICAMENT OF ALICE FAULKNER

ISBN: 9781934985175
Sherlock Holmes and the Painful
Predicament of Alice Faulkner
Volume 1
2009 First Printing

(c.) 2009 Bret M. Herholz
www.herbertzohl.webs.com

From the 1899 play "SHERLOCK HOLMES" by William Gillette based upon the characters originally created by Sir Arthur Conan Doyle.

published by Alterna Comics
www.alternacomics.com

Bret M. Herholz
Script & Art

Rori Shapiro
Cover colorist & Graytones

Jared D'Orr Wicklund
Copyeditor

Peter Simeti & Erin Kohut
Co-editors

6047

Also by Bret M. Herholz:

From Alterna Comics:

Diary of the Black Widow

Confessions of a Peculiar Boy...And Other Stories

The Spaghetti Strand Murder

The Adventures of Polly and Handgraves: A Sinister Aura

From the Undercoverfish Group Anthology:

The Big Sleep

Detour

103 in the Shade

Burned with the Leaves

Tales from the Boneyard

At my Chamber Door

Detour #9

Detour #10

It Fell from the Sky

Friends and Monsters

COMING SOON!!

Six Miles from Cockainge written by Joshua Michael Stewart

Romance with a Croquet Mallet (or a plausibly stirring afternoon at Sloughshire Manor)

An Introduction from Paul Magrs

I always knew that Holmes lived in a very dark world. In my imagination it's only rarely that he ventures out into the daylight. A ramble across the occasional blasted moor or an infrequent trot through Regent's Park. And, when he is seen in the daytime, he looks rather peaky and has these terrible shadows under his eyes.

In Bret M. Herholz's graphic novel we find the ultimate expression of this nocturnal dandy. He hovers at the edges of the underworld, enmeshed in a fury of subfusc cross-hatching. In Herholz's graphic world evil feels like a darkly palpable thing. A web built by spiders who weave very rationally in the form of millions of tiny oblongs. It is against this velvety backdrop that we find our new Holmes, Watson and Moriarty. They are like pale dolls in some Gothic paper puppet theatre. The reader gives a rather tense cheer, as each familiar character slides into view, as each new clue clicks into place.

I love the languid elegance of this Holmes. He who has such 'hypernatural powers' that he even knows 'what the rats are thinking in the cellars.' He can't help but remind the reader of Jeremy Brett's unparalleled performance in the 80s / 90s Granada TV series (filmed a mere two miles from where I sit writing this, in Manchester in the North of England!) This is a Holmes filled with pent-up energy and a Holmes who feels mortality coming. He smokes fiercely, speaks tersely, has no time for fools but surprises himself with sudden twinges of tenderness, not least that felt for the eponymous heroine in this particular case. Like the other creatures who touch upon Moriarty's nefarious web, he casts these wonderful sidelong glances in almost every frame he appears. He's catching glimpses of terrible things around every corner.

This is the world Herholz delights in. Darkness and dismay. A world of lissom girls with haunted eyes and rather epicene gentlemen with side partings and curiously pointed fingers, smoking enigmatically in the dark.

Comics these days are so action-packed and annoying. So overly busy and boistrous. I'm so glad to be ushered into these sinister drawing rooms, where characters stand still to ponder and exclaim, as a great feeling of dread wells up all around them, drawing the reader in.

Paul Magrs has just published 'Hell's Belles', the fourth of his Brenda and Effie Mystery novels with Headline Review. His new collection of short fiction, 'Twelve Stories' is out with Salt Publishing, and BBC Audio have recently brought out his five part audiobook serial, 'Doctor Who – Hornets' Nest', starring Tom Baker. He lives in Manchester, England.

Dedicated in memory of

Patrick W. Welch
1965-2008

Artist, teacher, Micromentalist,
mentor and my friend.

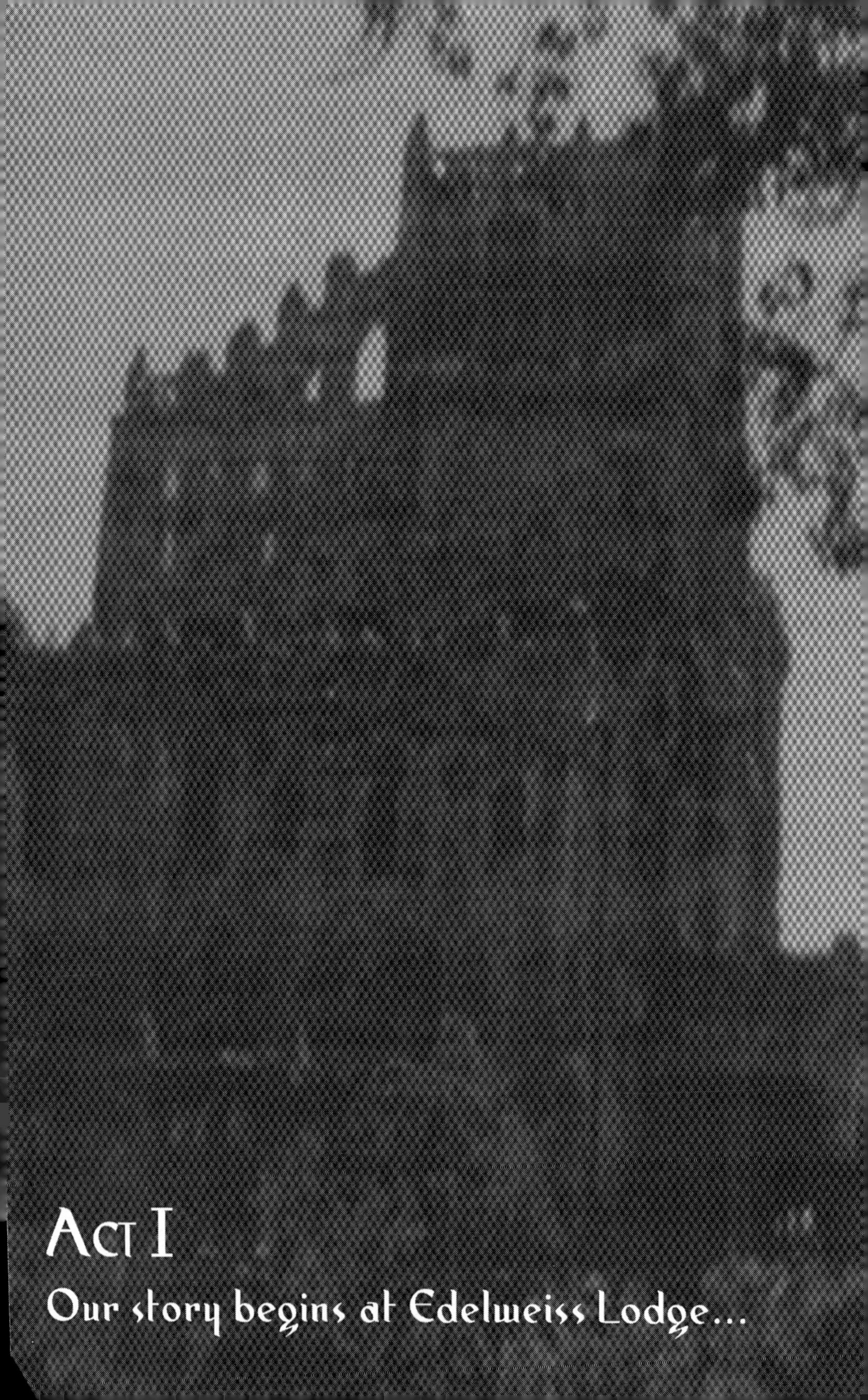

Act I

Our story begins at Edelweiss Lodge...

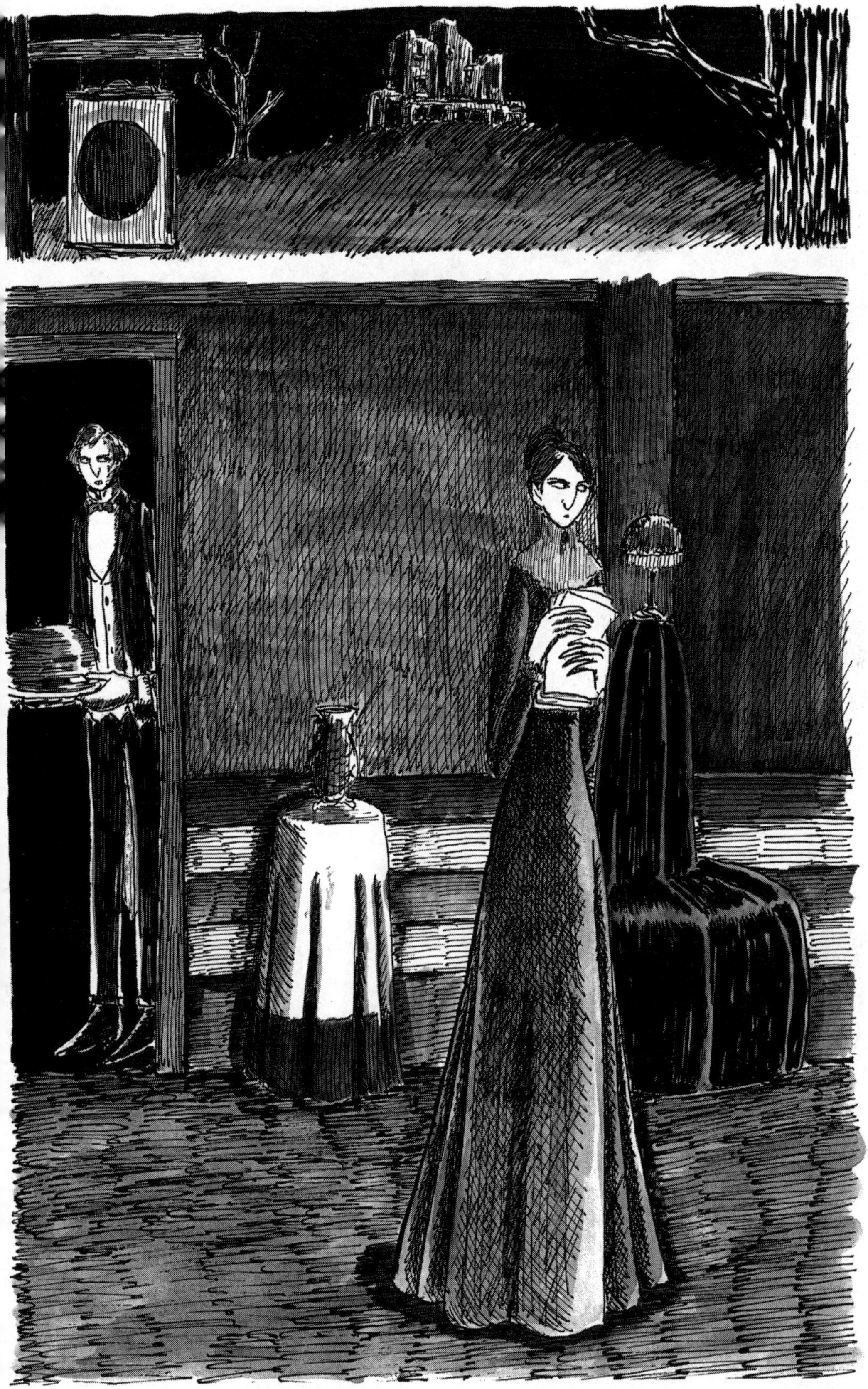

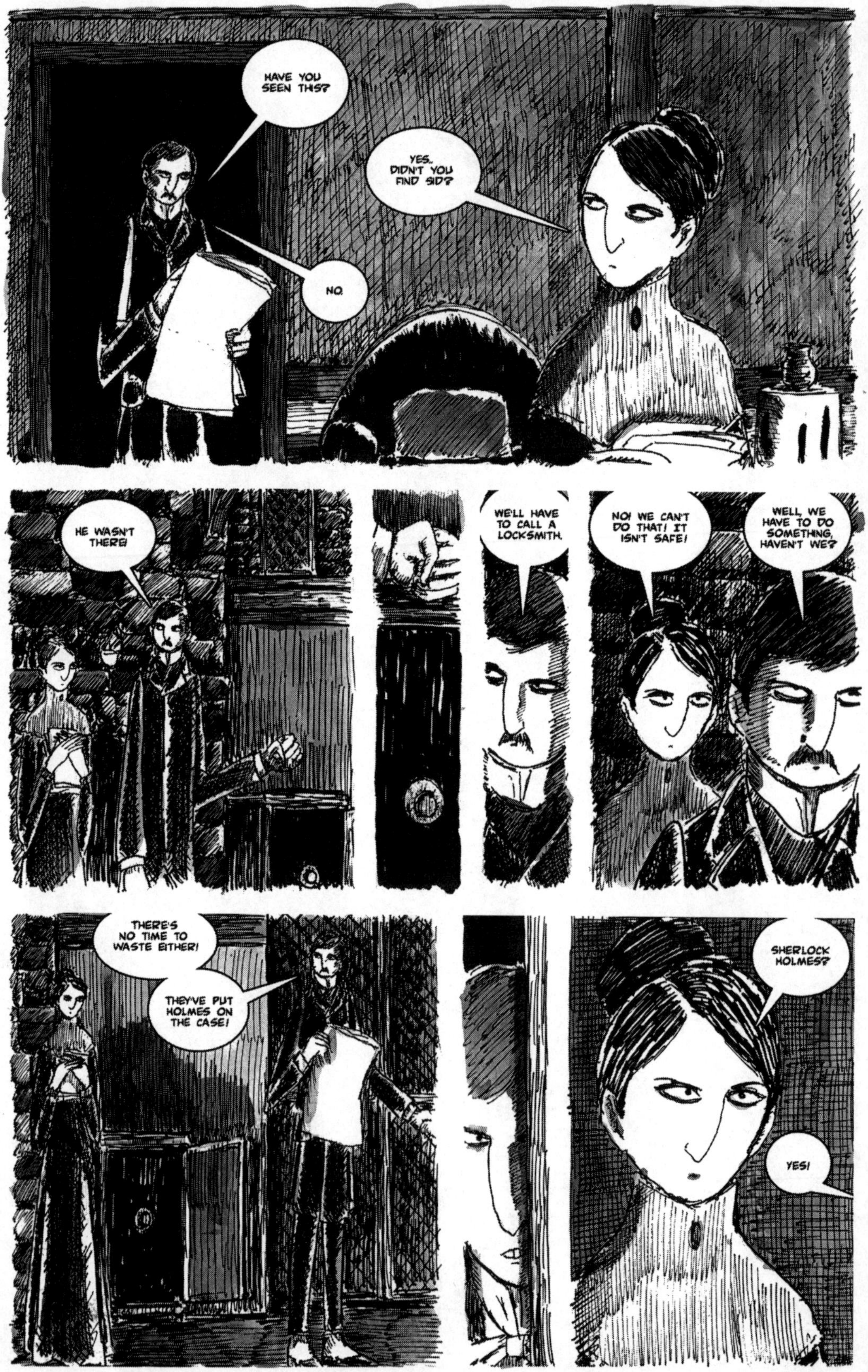
HAVE YOU SEEN THIS?
YES.. DIDN'T YOU FIND SID?
NO.
HE WASN'T THERE!
WE'LL HAVE TO CALL A LOCKSMITH.
NO! WE CAN'T DO THAT! IT ISN'T SAFE!
WELL, WE HAVE TO DO SOMETHING, HAVEN'T WE?
THERE'S NO TIME TO WASTE EITHER!
THEY'VE PUT HOLMES ON THE CASE!
SHERLOCK HOLMES?
YES!

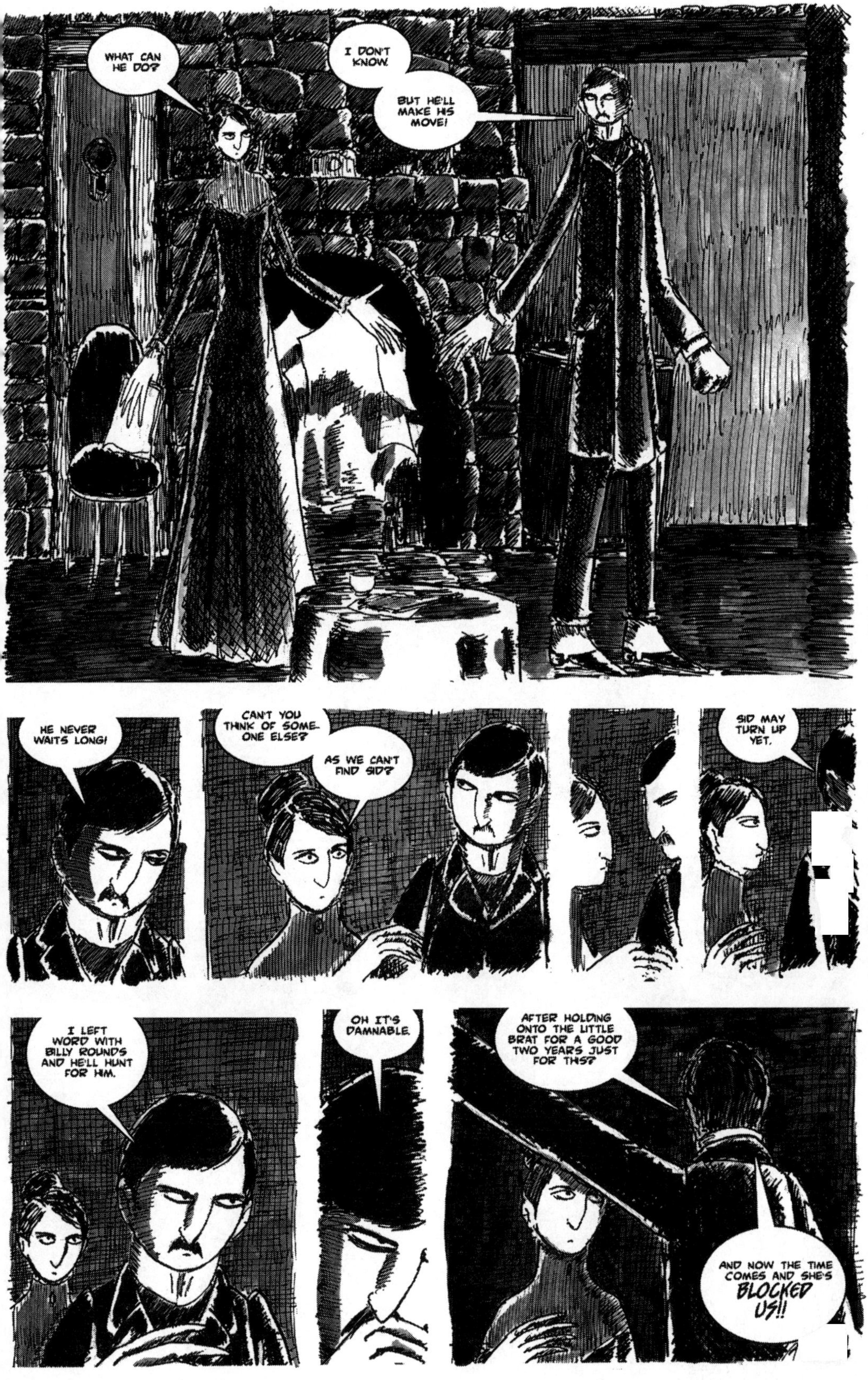
WHAT CAN HE DO?
I DON'T KNOW.
BUT HE'LL MAKE HIS MOVE!
HE NEVER WAITS LONG!
CAN'T YOU THINK OF SOME-ONE ELSE?
AS WE CAN'T FIND SID?
SID MAY TURN UP YET.
I LEFT WORD WITH BILLY ROUNDS AND HE'LL HUNT FOR HIM.
OH IT'S DAMNABLE.
AFTER HOLDING ONTO THE LITTLE BRAT FOR A GOOD TWO YEARS JUST FOR THIS?
AND NOW THE TIME COMES AND SHE'S BLOCKED US!!

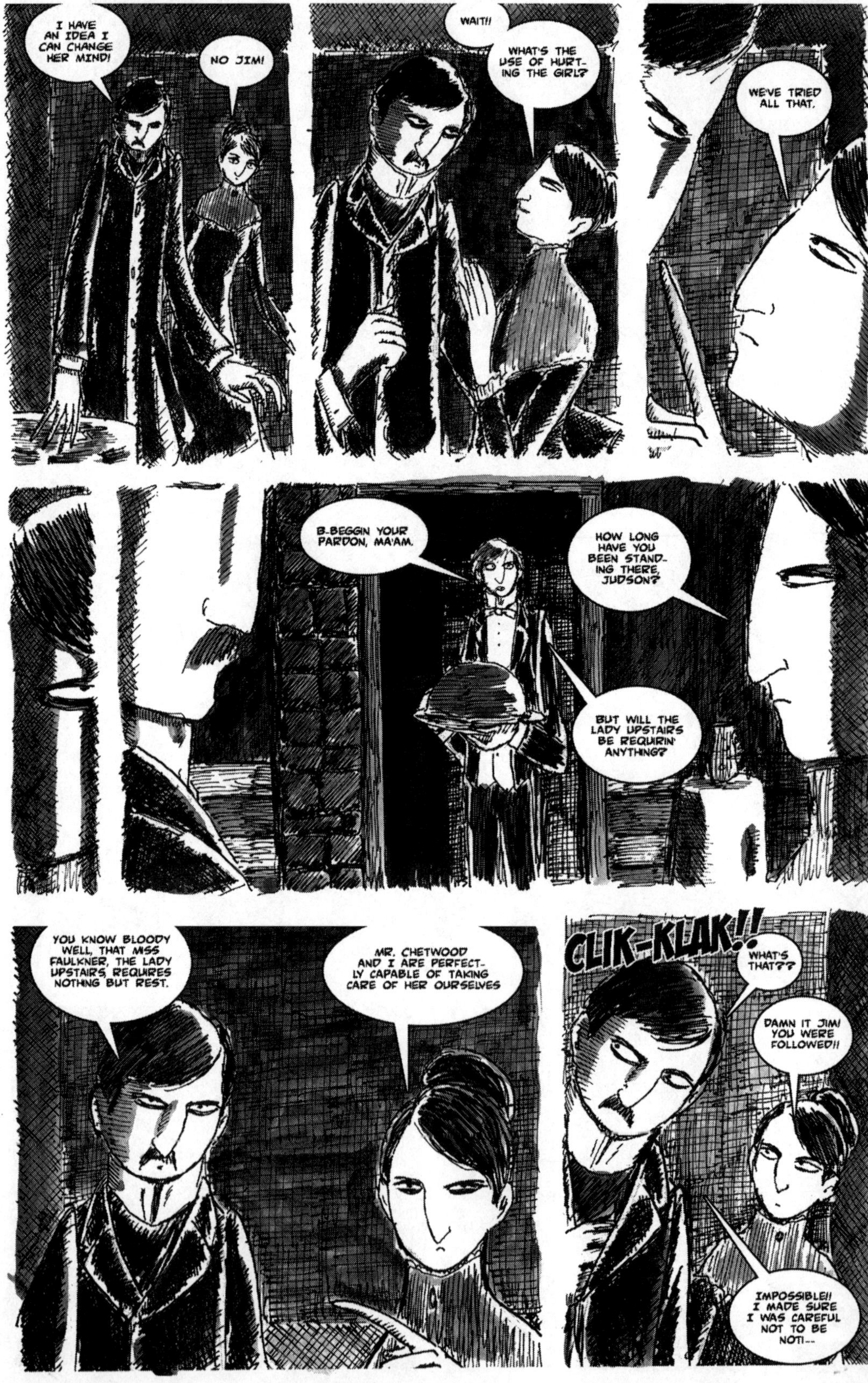
I HAVE AN IDEA I CAN CHANGE HER MIND!
NO JIM!
WAIT!!
WHAT'S THE USE OF HURT-ING THE GIRL?
WE'VE TRIED ALL THAT.
B-BEGGIN YOUR PARDON, MA'AM.
HOW LONG HAVE YOU BEEN STAND-ING THERE, JUDSON?
BUT WILL THE LADY UPSTAIRS BE REQUIRIN' ANYTHING?
YOU KNOW BLOODY WELL, THAT MISS FAULKNER, THE LADY UPSTAIRS, REQUIRES NOTHING BUT REST.
MR. CHETWOOD AND I ARE PERFECT-LY CAPABLE OF TAKING CARE OF HER OURSELVES
CLIK-KLAK!!
WHAT'S THAT??
DAMN IT JIM! YOU WERE FOLLOWED!!
IMPOSSIBLE!! I MADE SURE I WAS CAREFUL NOT TO BE NOT!--

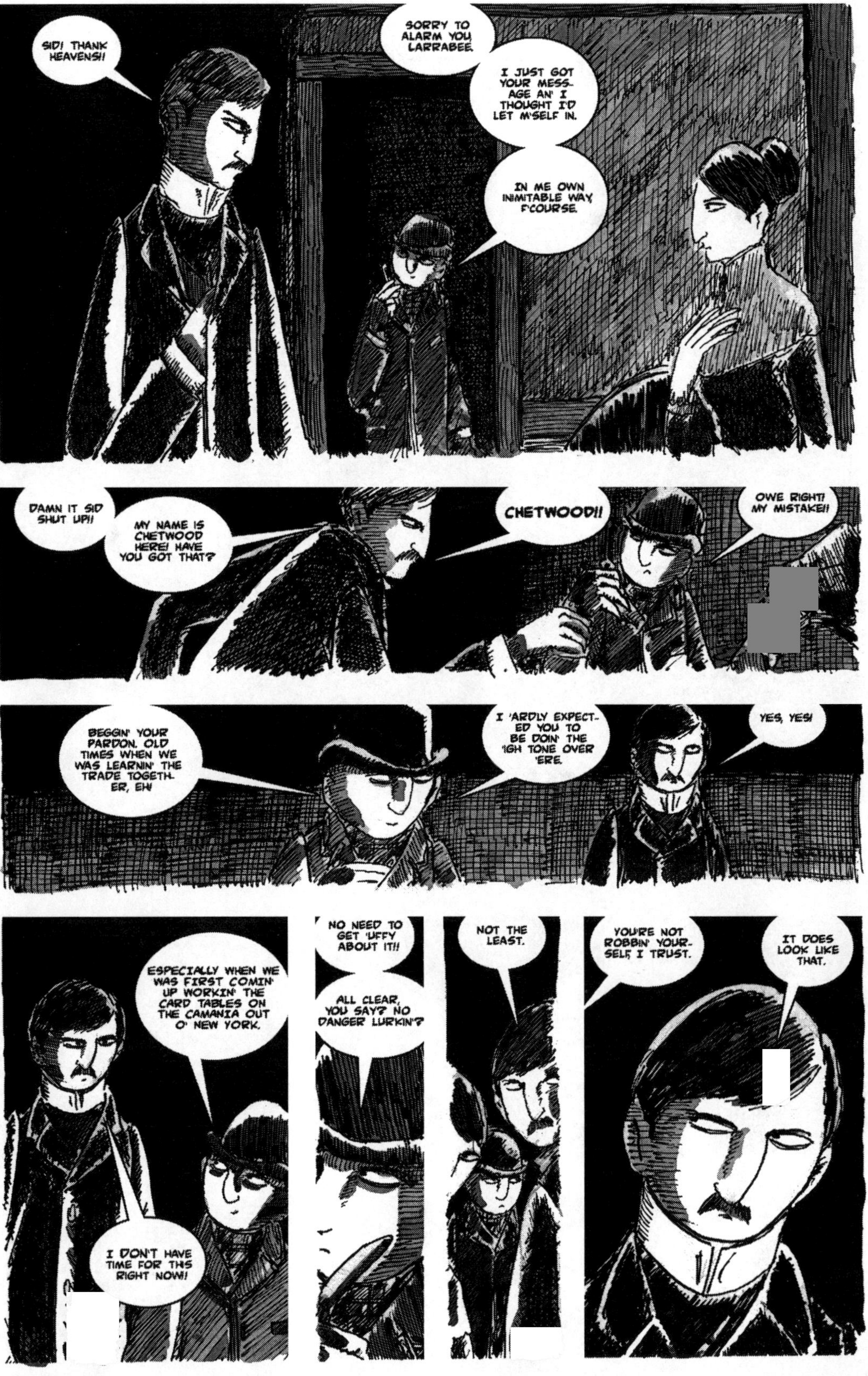
SID! THANK HEAVENS!!
SORRY TO ALARM YOU, LARRABEE.
I JUST GOT YOUR MESS-AGE AN' I THOUGHT I'D LET M'SELF IN.
IN ME OWN INIMITABLE WAY, F'COURSE.
DAMN IT SID SHUT UP!!
MY NAME IS CHETWOOD HERE! HAVE YOU GOT THAT?
CHETWOOD!!
OWE RIGHT! MY MISTAKE!!
BEGGIN' YOUR PARDON. OLD TIMES WHEN WE WAS LEARNIN' THE TRADE TOGETH-ER, EH!
I 'ARDLY EXPECT-ED YOU TO BE DOIN' THE 'IGH TONE OVER 'ERE.
YES, YES!
ESPECIALLY WHEN WE WAS FIRST COMIN' UP WORKIN' THE CARD TABLES ON THE CAMANIA OUT O' NEW YORK.
I DON'T HAVE TIME FOR THIS RIGHT NOW!
NO NEED TO GET 'UFFY ABOUT IT!!
ALL CLEAR, YOU SAY? NO DANGER LURKIN'?
NOT THE LEAST.
YOU'RE NOT ROBBIN' YOUR-SELF, I TRUST.
IT DOES LOOK LIKE THAT.

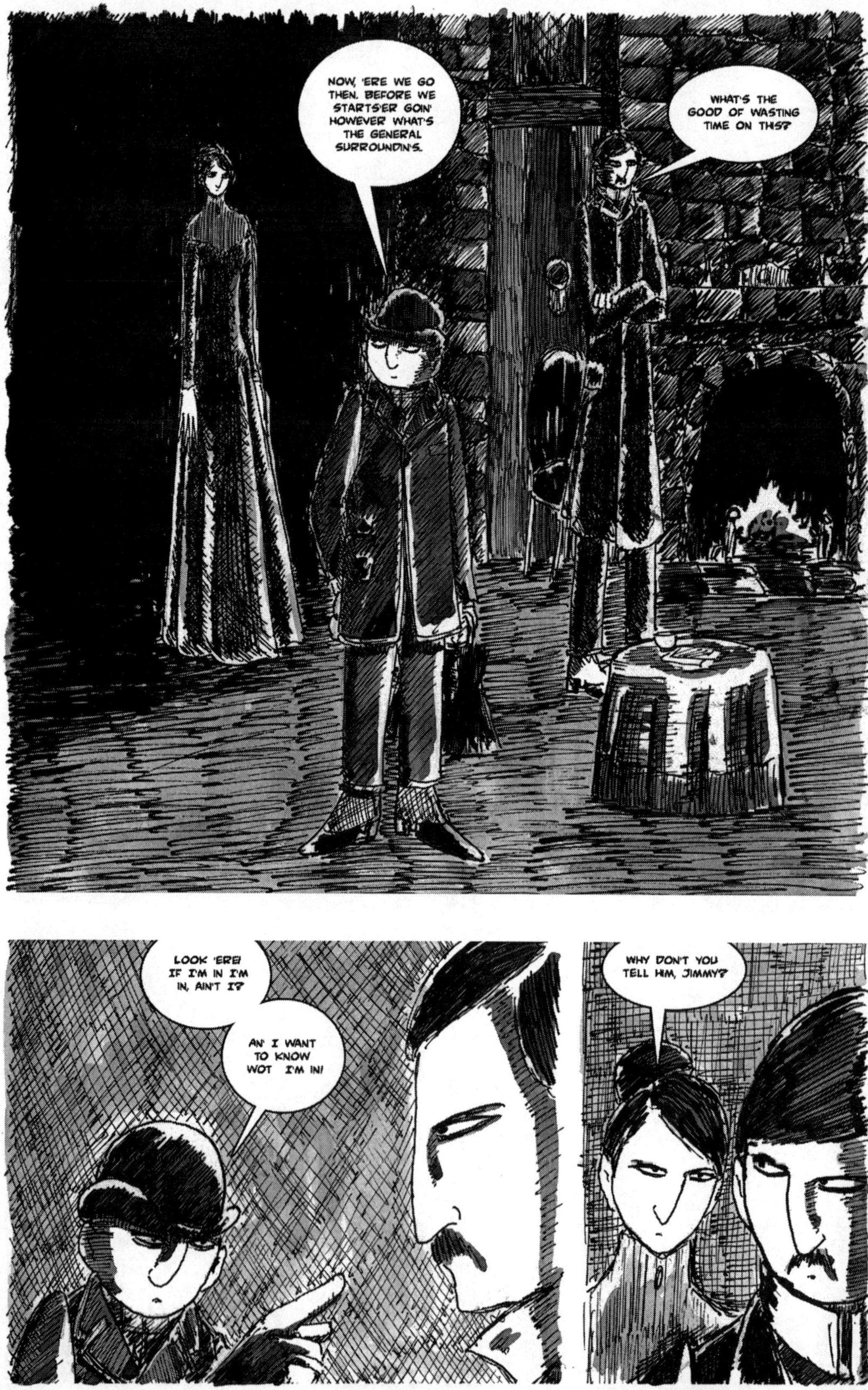
NOW, 'ERE WE GO THEN. BEFORE WE STARTS'ER GOIN' HOWEVER WHAT'S THE GENERAL SURROUNDIN'S.
WHAT'S THE GOOD OF WASTING TIME ON THIS?
LOOK 'ERE! IF I'M IN I'M IN, AIN'T I?
AN' I WANT TO KNOW WOT I'M IN!
WHY DON'T YOU TELL HIM, JIMMY?

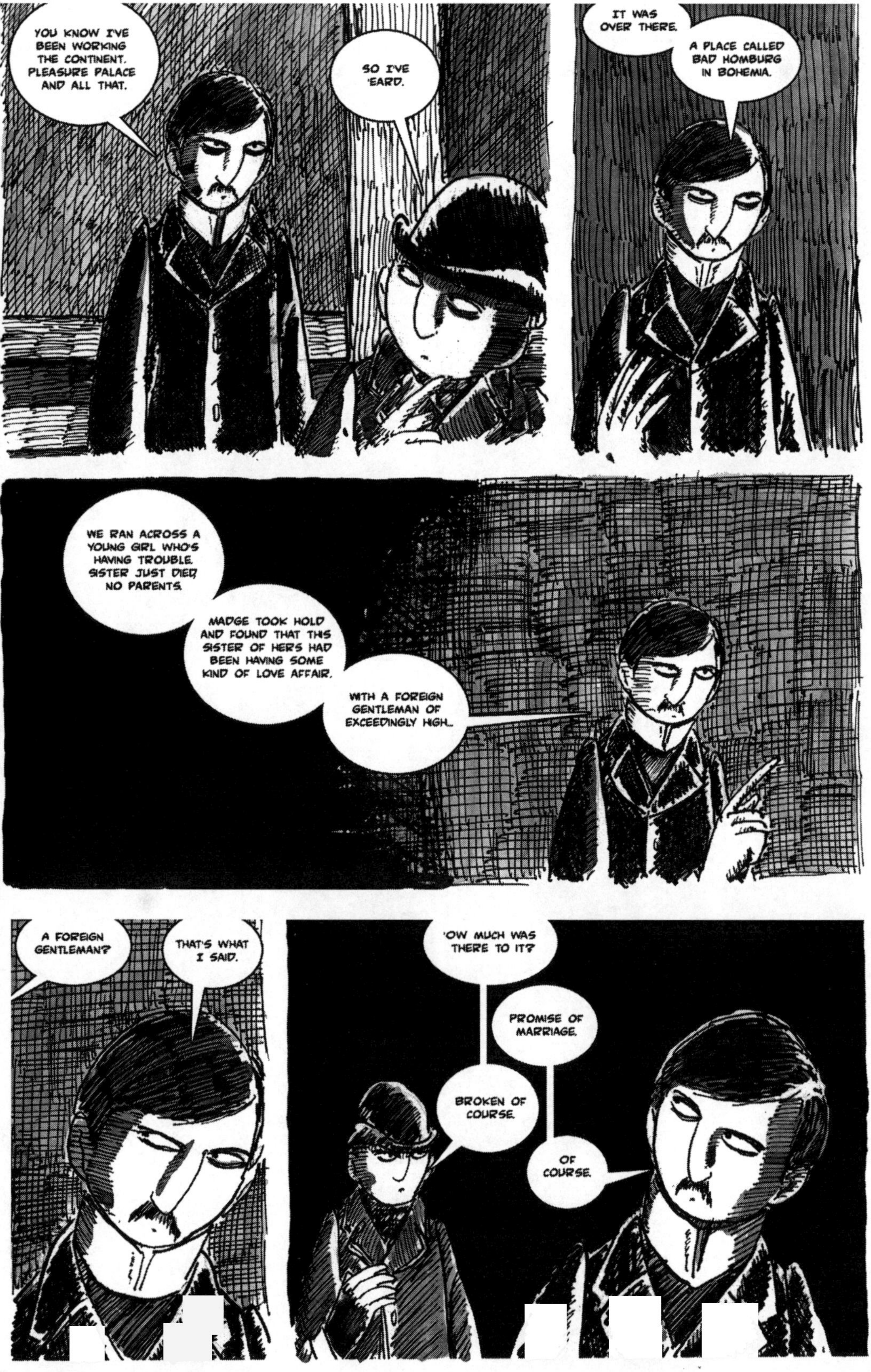
YOU KNOW I'VE BEEN WORKING THE CONTINENT. PLEASURE PALACE AND ALL THAT.
SO I'VE 'EARD.
IT WAS OVER THERE.
A PLACE CALLED BAD HOMBURG IN BOHEMIA.
WE RAN ACROSS A YOUNG GIRL WHO'S HAVING TROUBLE. SISTER JUST DIED. NO PARENTS.
MADGE TOOK HOLD AND FOUND THAT THIS SISTER OF HERS HAD BEEN HAVING SOME KIND OF LOVE AFFAIR.
WITH A FOREIGN GENTLEMAN OF EXCEEDINGLY HIGH...
A FOREIGN GENTLEMAN?
THAT'S WHAT I SAID.
'OW MUCH WAS THERE TO IT?
PROMISE OF MARRIAGE.
BROKEN OF COURSE.
OF COURSE.

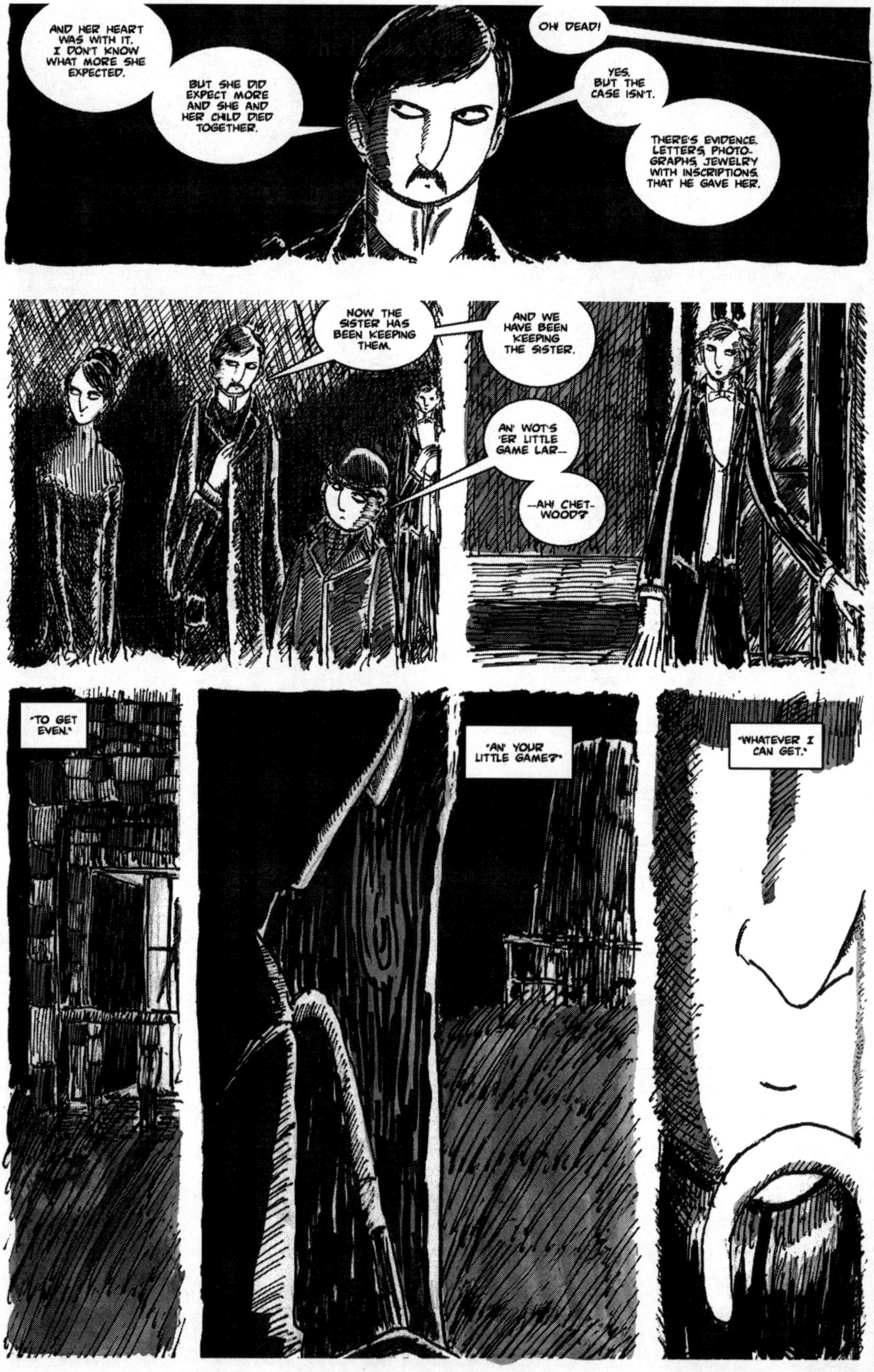
AND HER HEART WAS WITH IT. I DON'T KNOW WHAT MORE SHE EXPECTED.
BUT SHE DID EXPECT MORE AND SHE AND HER CHILD DIED TOGETHER.
OH! DEAD!
YES. BUT THE CASE ISN'T.
THERE'S EVIDENCE. LETTERS, PHOTOGRAPHS, JEWELRY WITH INSCRIPTIONS THAT HE GAVE HER.
NOW THE SISTER HAS BEEN KEEPING THEM.
AND WE HAVE BEEN KEEPING THE SISTER.
AN' WOT'S 'ER LITTLE GAME LAR--
--AH! CHETWOOD?
"TO GET EVEN."
"AN' YOUR LITTLE GAME?"
"WHATEVER I CAN GET."

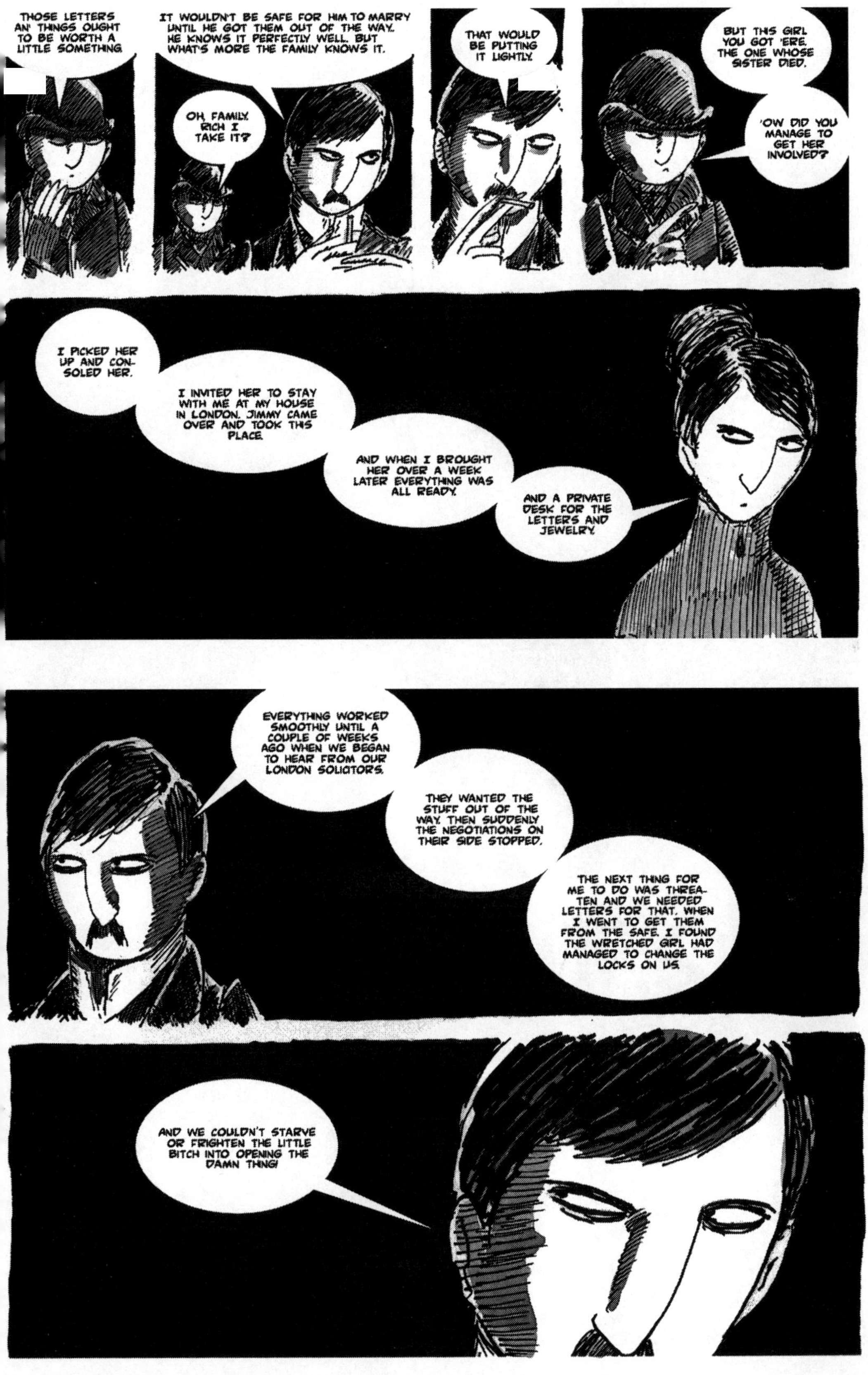
THOSE LETTERS AN' THINGS OUGHT TO BE WORTH A LITTLE SOMETHING.
IT WOULDN'T BE SAFE FOR HIM TO MARRY UNTIL HE GOT THEM OUT OF THE WAY. HE KNOWS IT PERFECTLY WELL. BUT WHAT'S MORE THE FAMILY KNOWS IT.
OH, FAMILY. RICH I TAKE IT?
THAT WOULD BE PUTTING IT LIGHTLY.
BUT THIS GIRL YOU GOT 'ERE. THE ONE WHOSE SISTER DIED.
'OW DID YOU MANAGE TO GET HER INVOLVED?
I PICKED HER UP AND CON-SOLED HER.
I INVITED HER TO STAY WITH ME AT MY HOUSE IN LONDON. JIMMY CAME OVER AND TOOK THIS PLACE.
AND WHEN I BROUGHT HER OVER A WEEK LATER EVERYTHING WAS ALL READY.
AND A PRIVATE DESK FOR THE LETTERS AND JEWELRY.
EVERYTHING WORKED SMOOTHLY UNTIL A COUPLE OF WEEKS AGO WHEN WE BEGAN TO HEAR FROM OUR LONDON SOLICITORS.
THEY WANTED THE STUFF OUT OF THE WAY. THEN SUDDENLY THE NEGOTIATIONS ON THEIR SIDE STOPPED.
THE NEXT THING FOR ME TO DO WAS THREA-TEN AND WE NEEDED LETTERS FOR THAT. WHEN I WENT TO GET THEM FROM THE SAFE. I FOUND THE WRETCHED GIRL HAD MANAGED TO CHANGE THE LOCKS ON US.
AND WE COULDN'T STARVE OR FRIGHTEN THE LITTLE BITCH INTO OPENING THE DAMN THING!

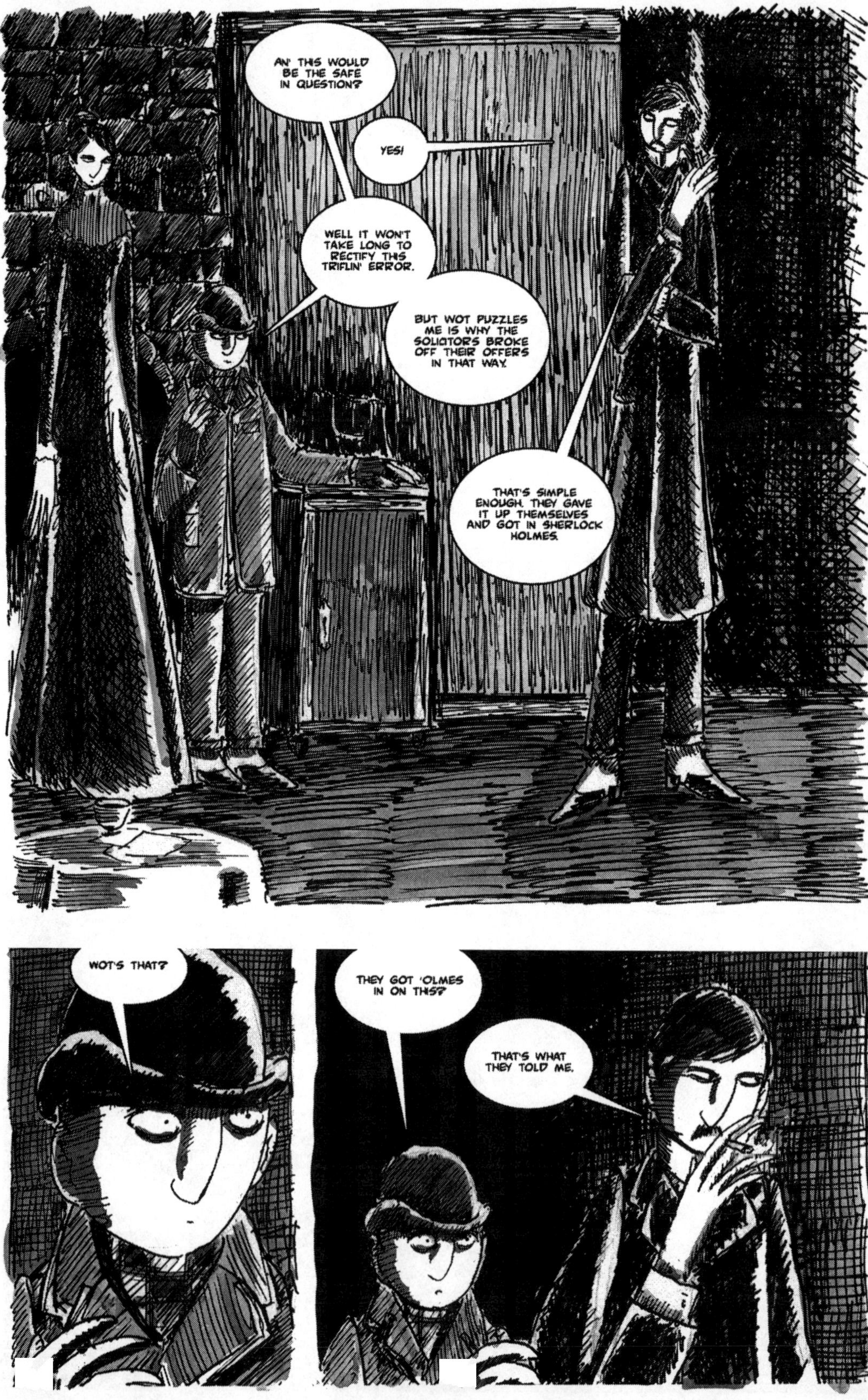
AN' THIS WOULD BE THE SAFE IN QUESTION?
YES!
WELL IT WON'T TAKE LONG TO RECTIFY THIS TRIFLIN' ERROR.
BUT WOT PUZZLES ME IS WHY THE SOLICITORS BROKE OFF THEIR OFFERS IN THAT WAY.
THAT'S SIMPLE ENOUGH. THEY GAVE IT UP THEMSELVES AND GOT IN SHERLOCK HOLMES.
WOT'S THAT?
THEY GOT 'OLMES IN ON THIS?
THAT'S WHAT THEY TOLD ME.

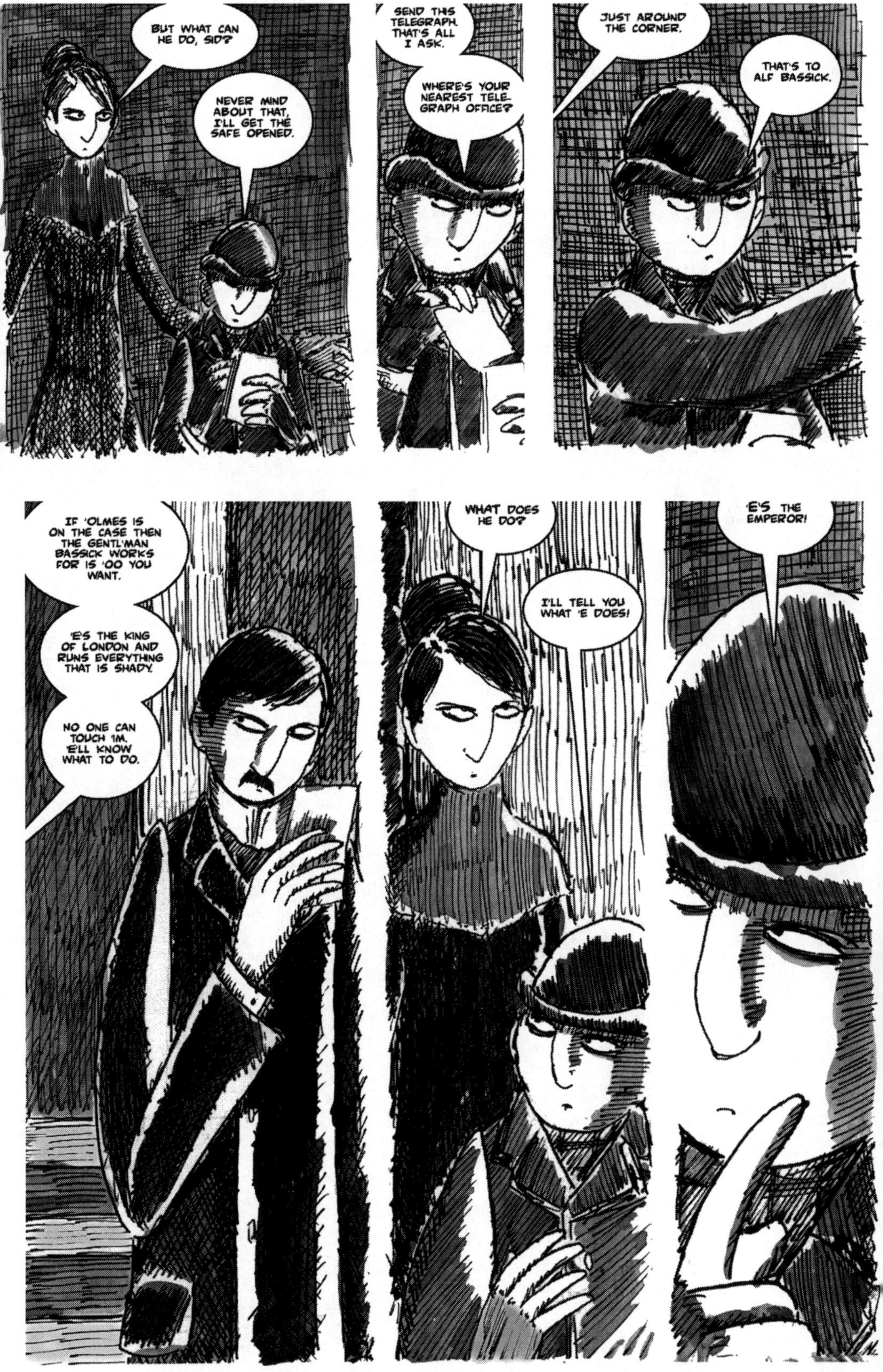
BUT WHAT CAN HE DO, SID?
NEVER MIND ABOUT THAT, I'LL GET THE SAFE OPENED.
SEND THIS TELEGRAPH. THAT'S ALL I ASK.
WHERE'S YOUR NEAREST TELEGRAPH OFFICE?
JUST AROUND THE CORNER.
THAT'S TO ALF BASSICK.
IF 'OLMES IS ON THE CASE THEN THE GENTL'MAN BASSICK WORKS FOR IS 'OO YOU WANT.
'E'S THE KING OF LONDON AND RUNS EVERYTHING THAT IS SHADY.
NO ONE CAN TOUCH 'IM. 'E'LL KNOW WHAT TO DO.
WHAT DOES HE DO?
I'LL TELL YOU WHAT 'E DOES!
'E'S THE EMPEROR!

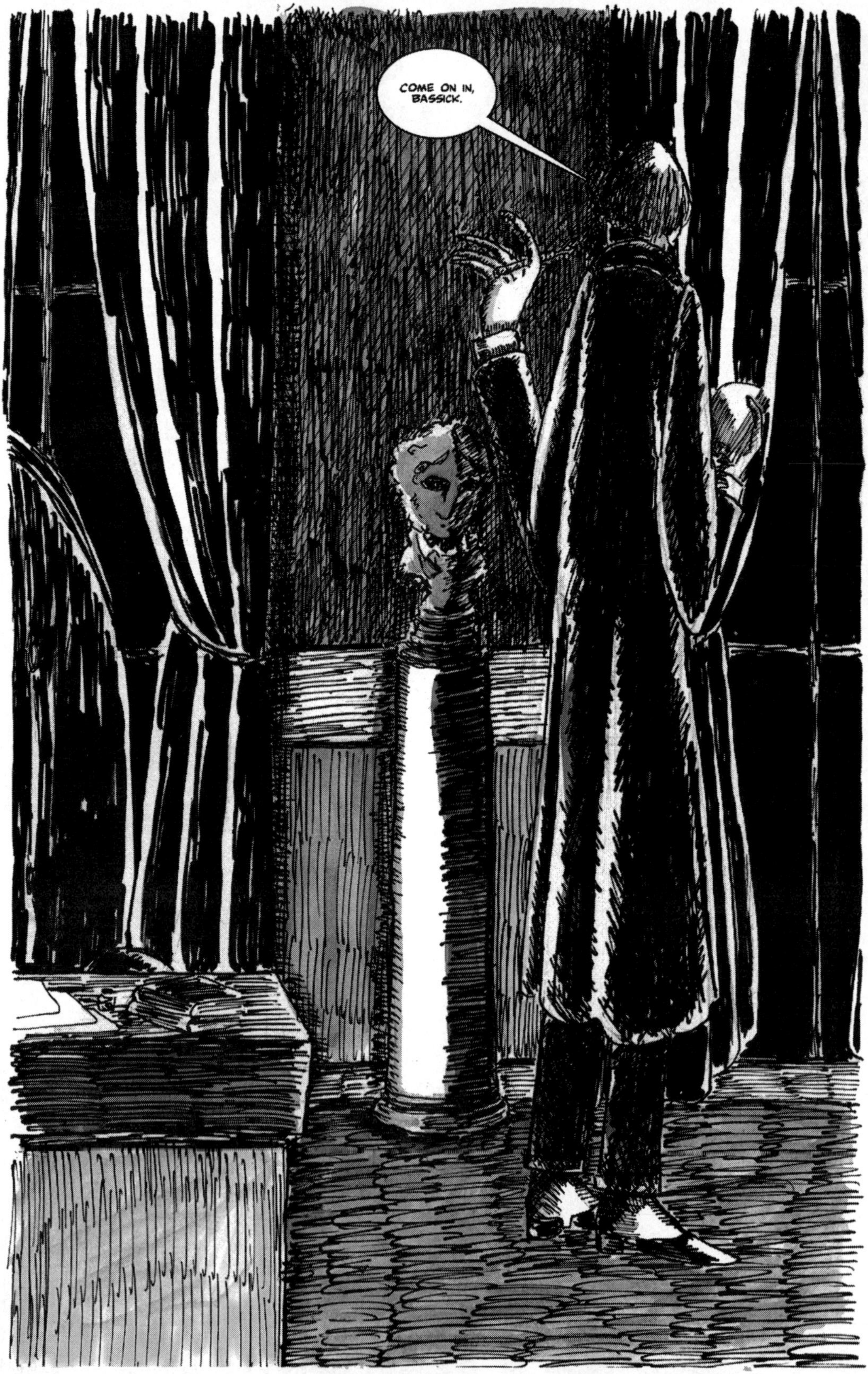
COME ON IN, BASSICK.

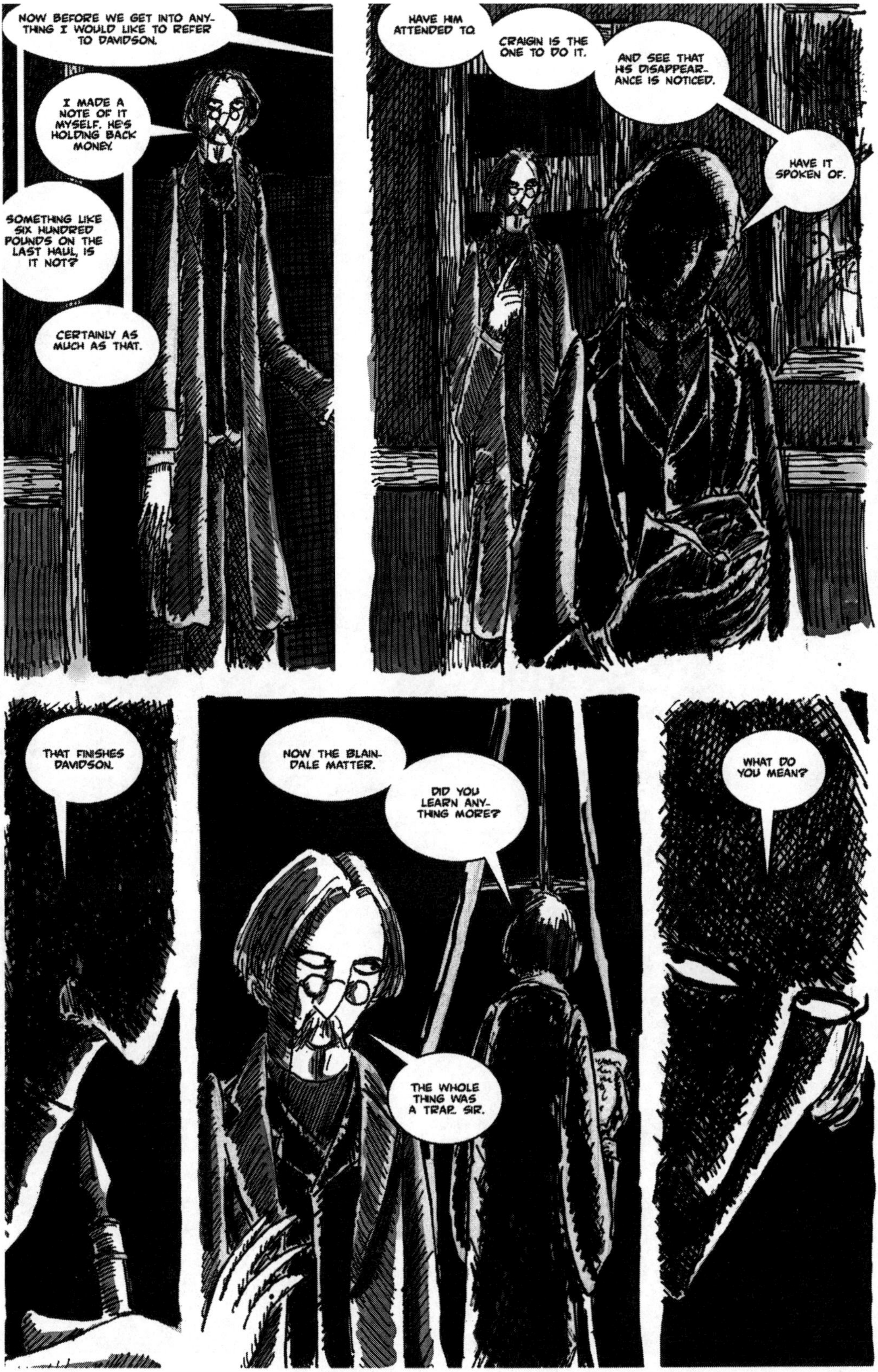
NOW BEFORE WE GET INTO ANY-THING I WOULD LIKE TO REFER TO DAVIDSON.
I MADE A NOTE OF IT MYSELF. HE'S HOLDING BACK MONEY.
SOMETHING LIKE SIX HUNDRED POUNDS ON THE LAST HAUL, IS IT NOT?
CERTAINLY AS MUCH AS THAT.
HAVE HIM ATTENDED TO.
CRAIGIN IS THE ONE TO DO IT.
AND SEE THAT HIS DISAPPEAR-ANCE IS NOTICED.
HAVE IT SPOKEN OF.
THAT FINISHES DAVIDSON.
NOW THE BLAIN-DALE MATTER.
DID YOU LEARN ANY-THING MORE?
THE WHOLE THING WAS A TRAP, SIR.
WHAT DO YOU MEAN?

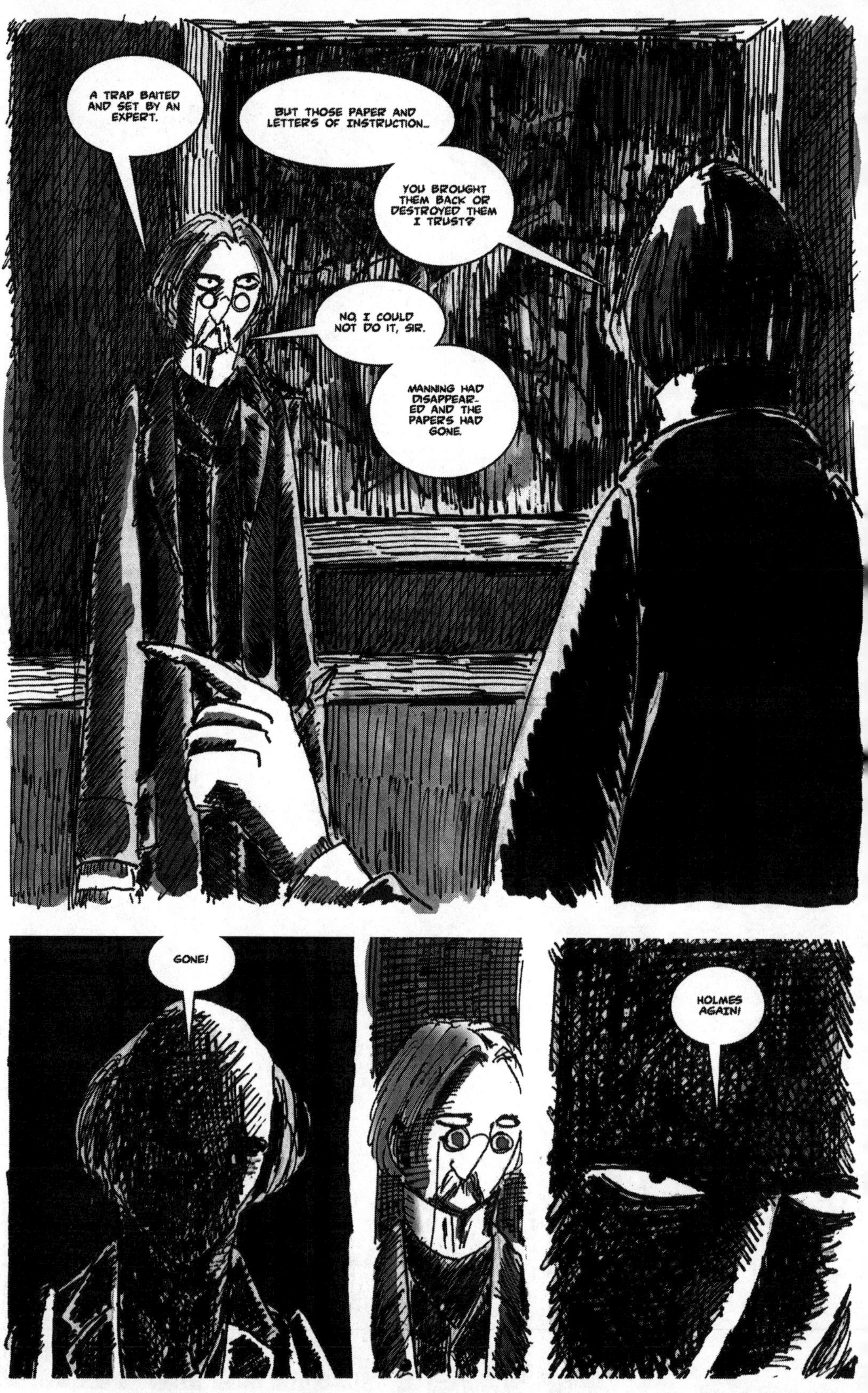
A TRAP BAITED AND SET BY AN EXPERT.
BUT THOSE PAPER AND LETTERS OF INSTRUCTION...
YOU BROUGHT THEM BACK OR DESTROYED THEM I TRUST?
NO, I COULD NOT DO IT, SIR.
MANNING HAD DISAPPEAR-ED AND THE PAPERS HAD GONE.
GONE!
HOLMES AGAIN!

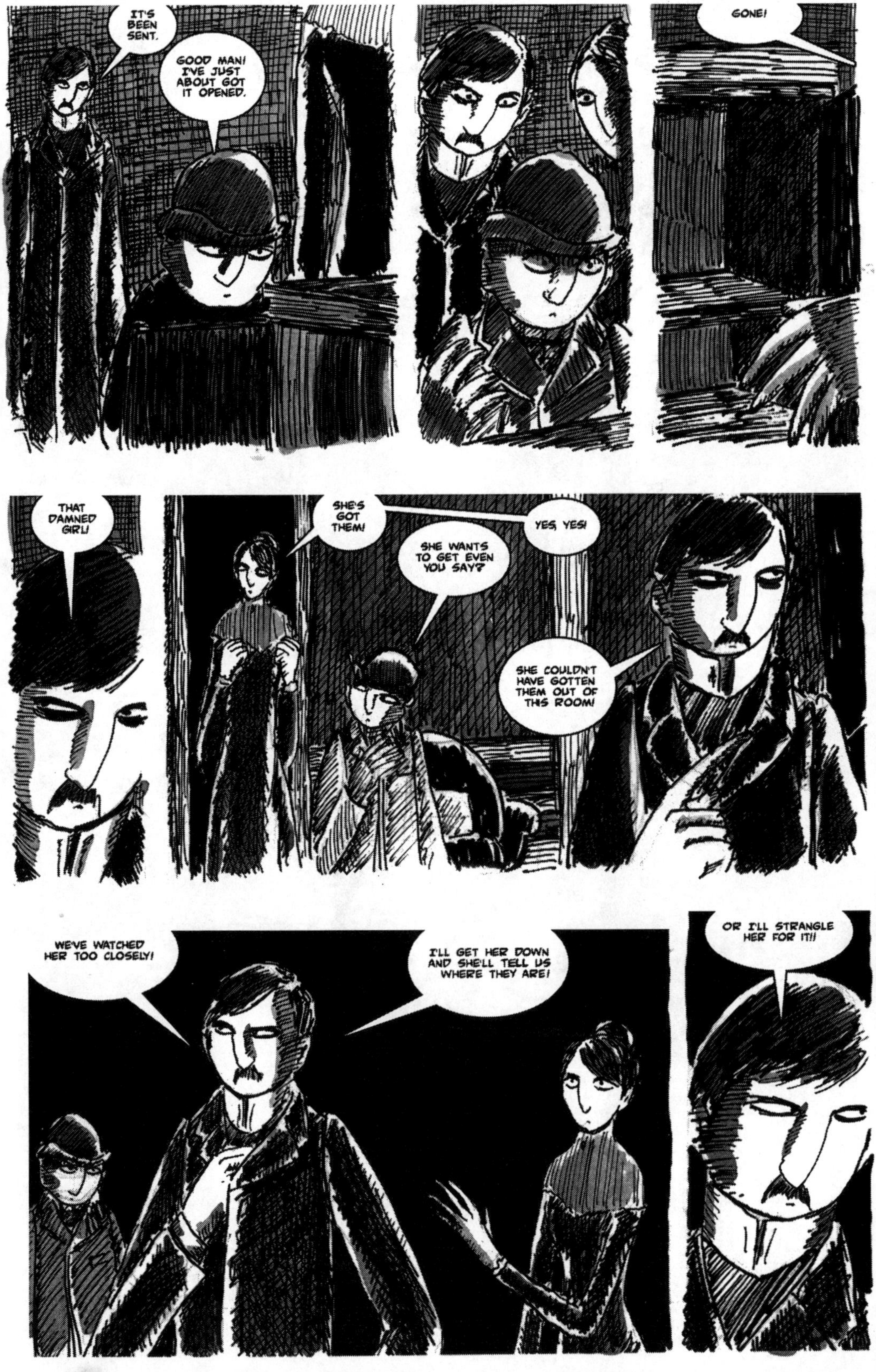
IT'S BEEN SENT.
GOOD MAN! I'VE JUST ABOUT GOT IT OPENED.
GONE!
THAT DAMNED GIRL!
SHE'S GOT THEM!
YES, YES!
SHE WANTS TO GET EVEN YOU SAY?
SHE COULDN'T HAVE GOTTEN THEM OUT OF THIS ROOM!
WE'VE WATCHED HER TOO CLOSELY!
I'LL GET HER DOWN AND SHE'LL TELL US WHERE THEY ARE!
OR I'LL STRANGLE HER FOR IT!!

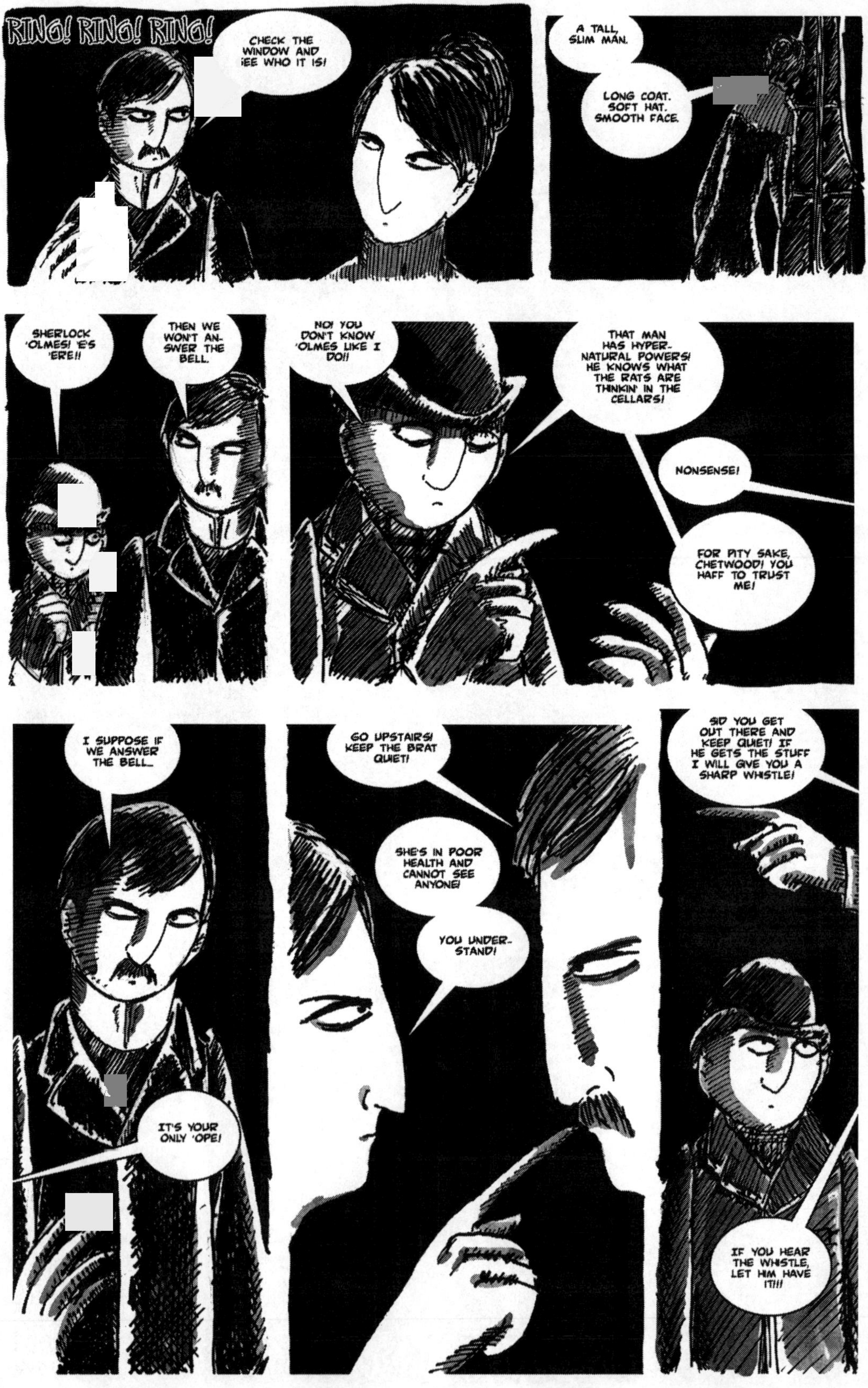
RING! RING! RING!
CHECK THE WINDOW AND SEE WHO IT IS!
A TALL, SLIM MAN.
LONG COAT. SOFT HAT. SMOOTH FACE.
SHERLOCK 'OLMES! 'E'S 'ERE!!
THEN WE WON'T AN-SWER THE BELL.
NO! YOU DON'T KNOW 'OLMES LIKE I DO!!
THAT MAN HAS HYPER-NATURAL POWERS! HE KNOWS WHAT THE RATS ARE THINKIN' IN THE CELLARS!
NONSENSE!
FOR PITY SAKE, CHETWOOD! YOU HAFF TO TRUST ME!
I SUPPOSE IF WE ANSWER THE BELL...
IT'S YOUR ONLY 'OPE!
GO UPSTAIRS! KEEP THE BRAT QUIET!
SHE'S IN POOR HEALTH AND CANNOT SEE ANYONE!
YOU UNDER-STAND!
SID YOU GET OUT THERE AND KEEP QUIET! IF HE GETS THE STUFF I WILL GIVE YOU A SHARP WHISTLE!
IF YOU HEAR THE WHISTLE, LET HIM HAVE IT!!!

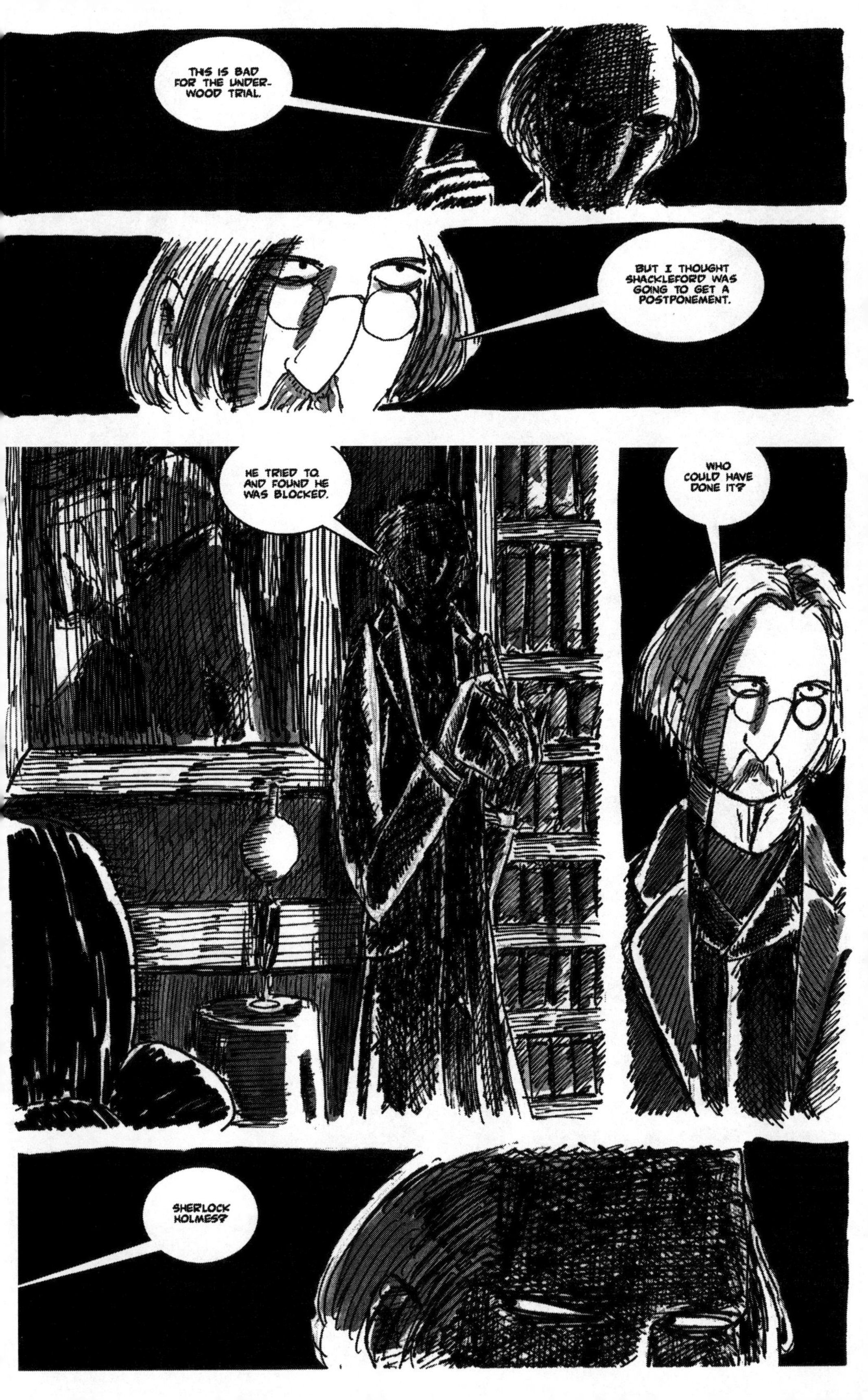
THIS IS BAD FOR THE UNDER-WOOD TRIAL.
BUT I THOUGHT SHACKLEFORD WAS GOING TO GET A POSTPONEMENT.
HE TRIED TO, AND FOUND HE WAS BLOCKED.
WHO COULD HAVE DONE IT?
SHERLOCK HOLMES?

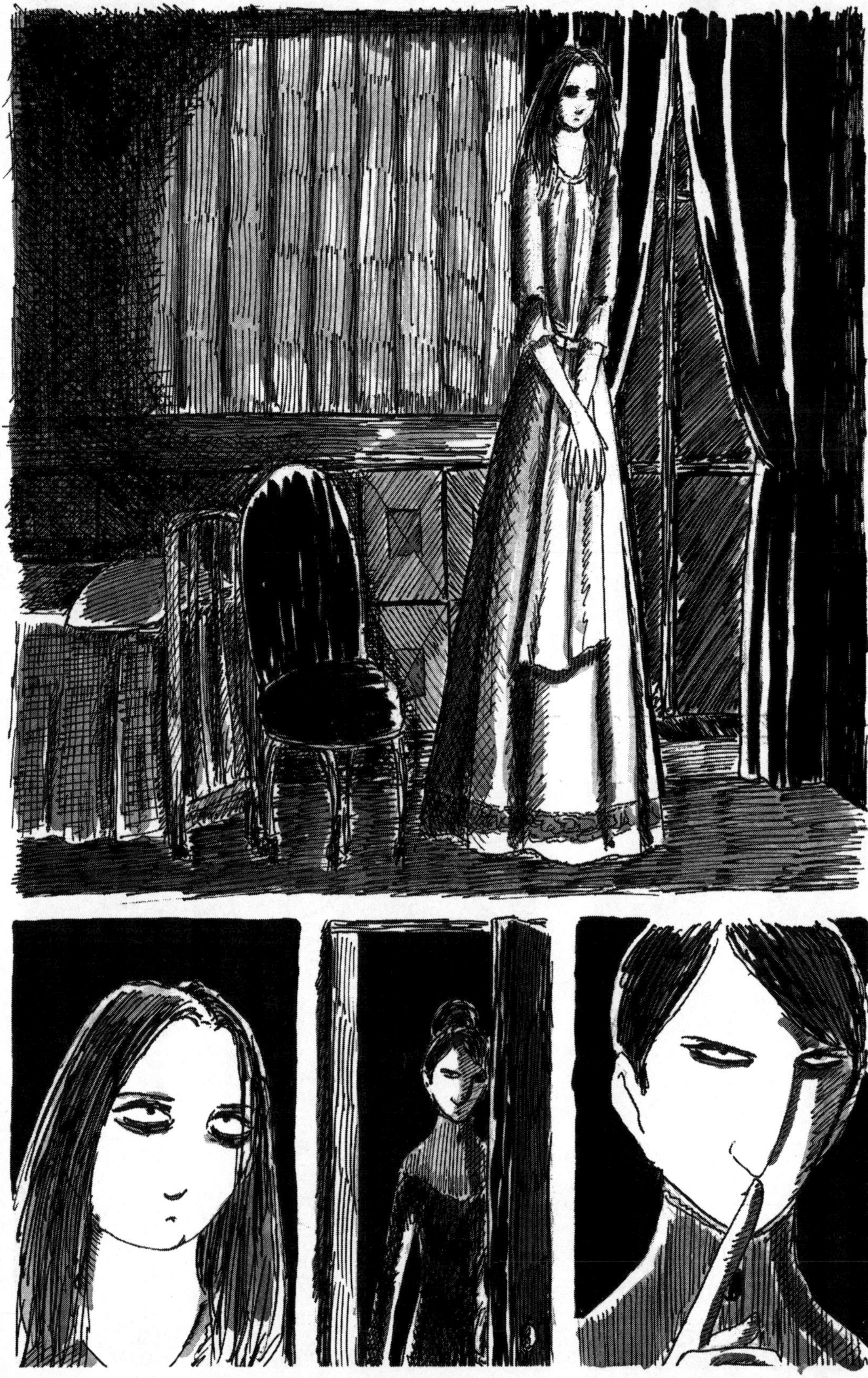

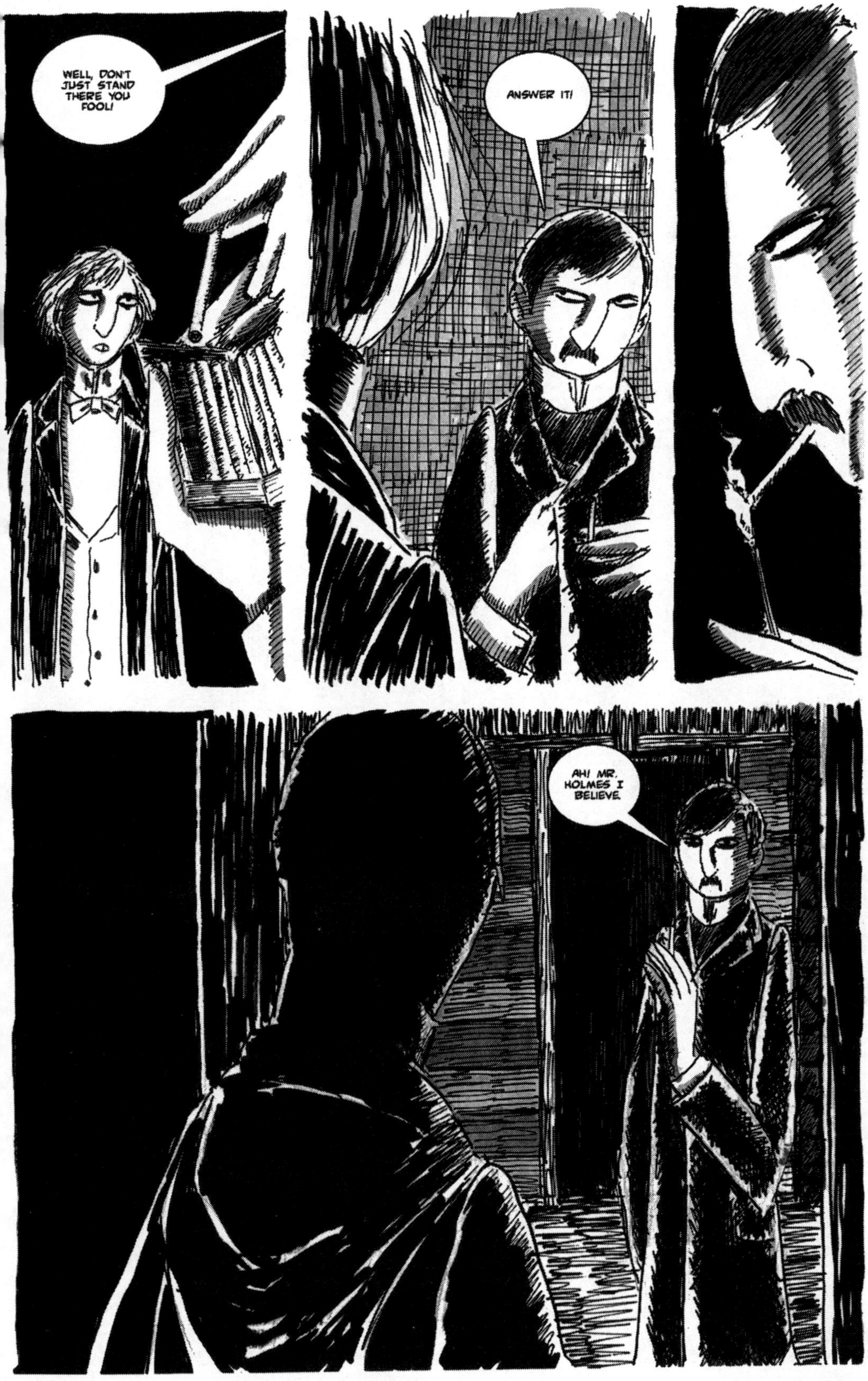
WELL, DON'T JUST STAND THERE YOU FOOL!
ANSWER IT!
AH! MR. HOLMES I BELIEVE.

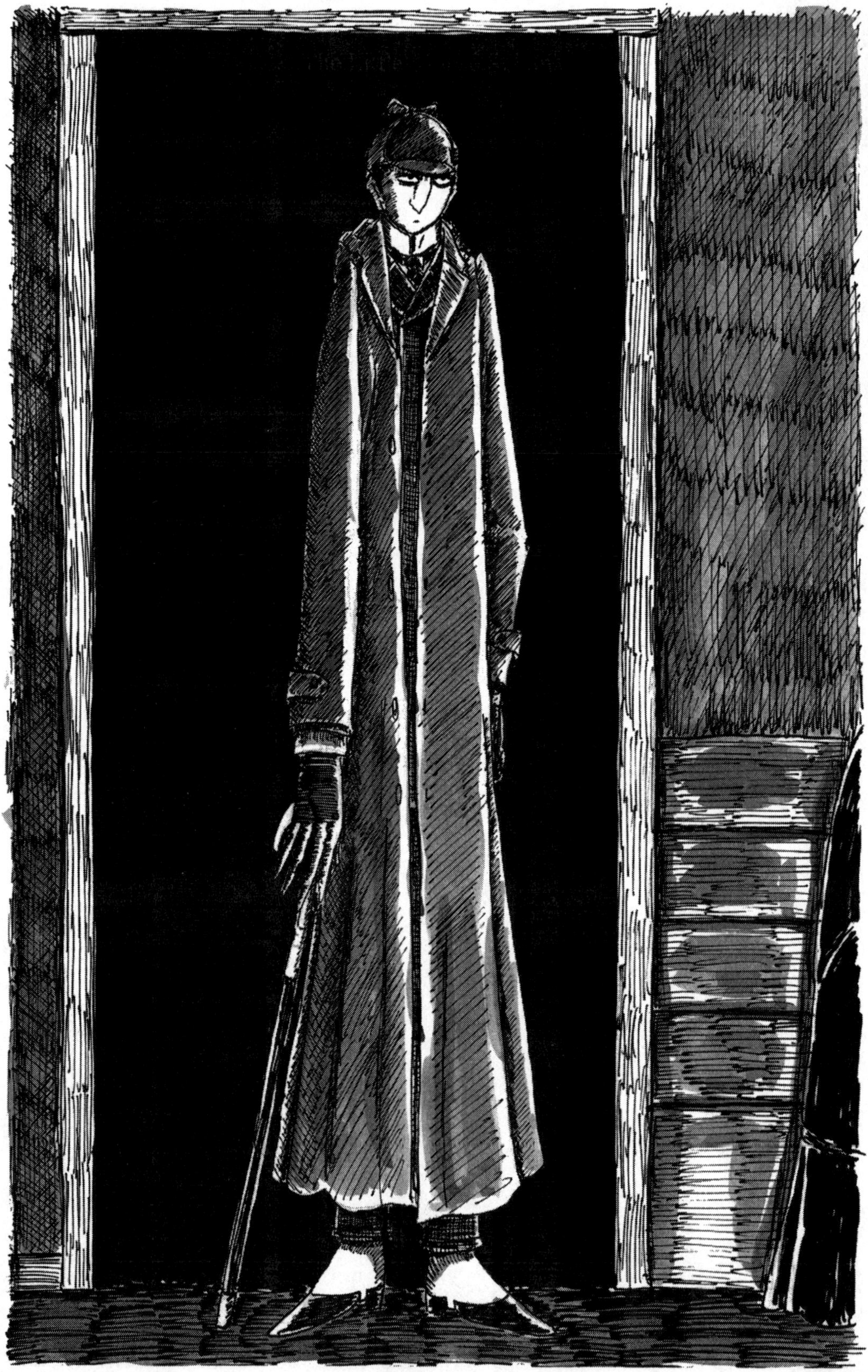

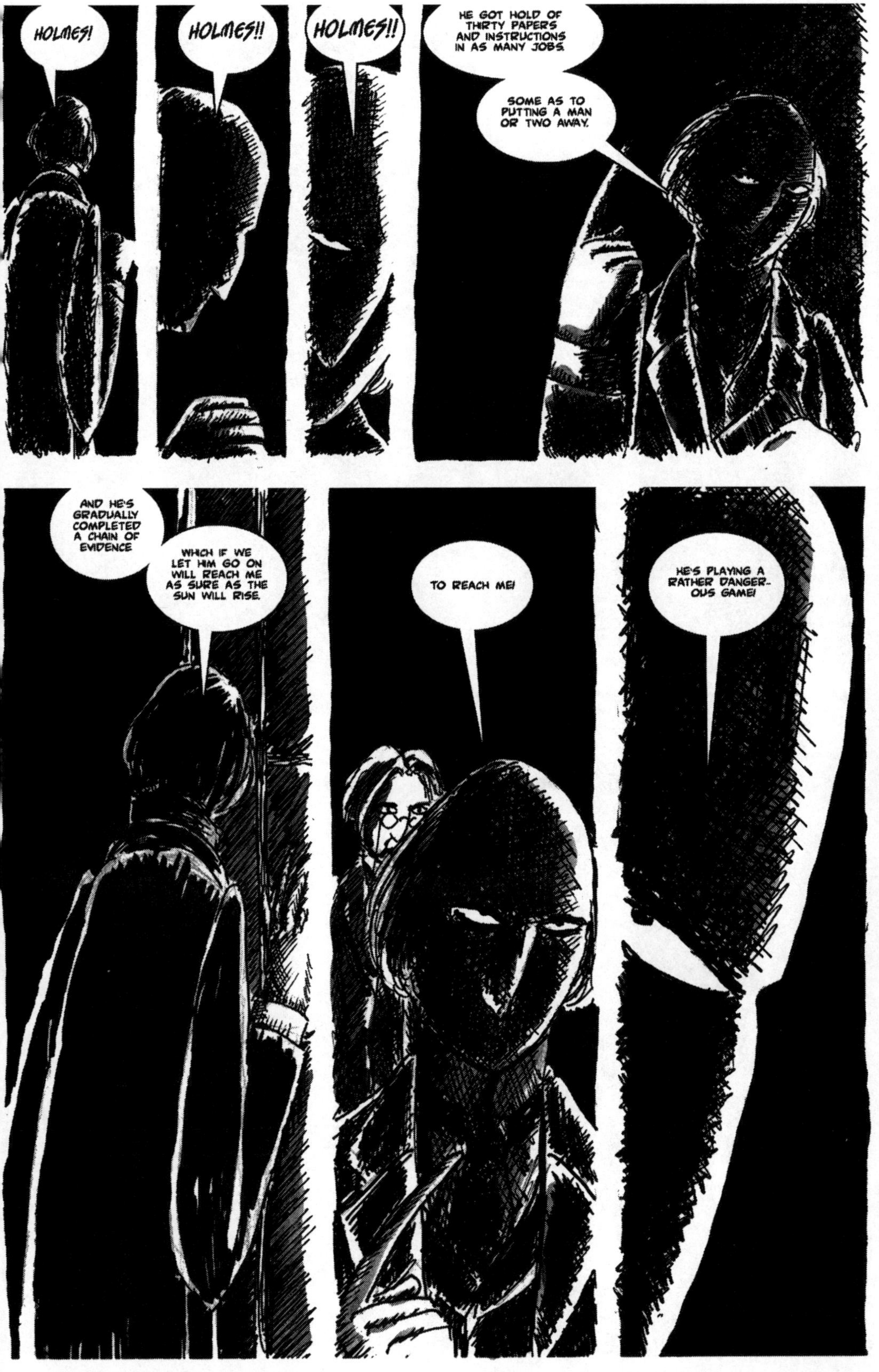
HOLMES!
HOLMES!!
HOLMES!!
HE GOT HOLD OF THIRTY PAPERS AND INSTRUCTIONS IN AS MANY JOBS.
SOME AS TO PUTTING A MAN OR TWO AWAY.
AND HE'S GRADUALLY COMPLETED A CHAIN OF EVIDENCE
WHICH IF WE LET HIM GO ON WILL REACH ME AS SURE AS THE SUN WILL RISE.
TO REACH ME!
HE'S PLAYING A RATHER DANGER-OUS GAME!

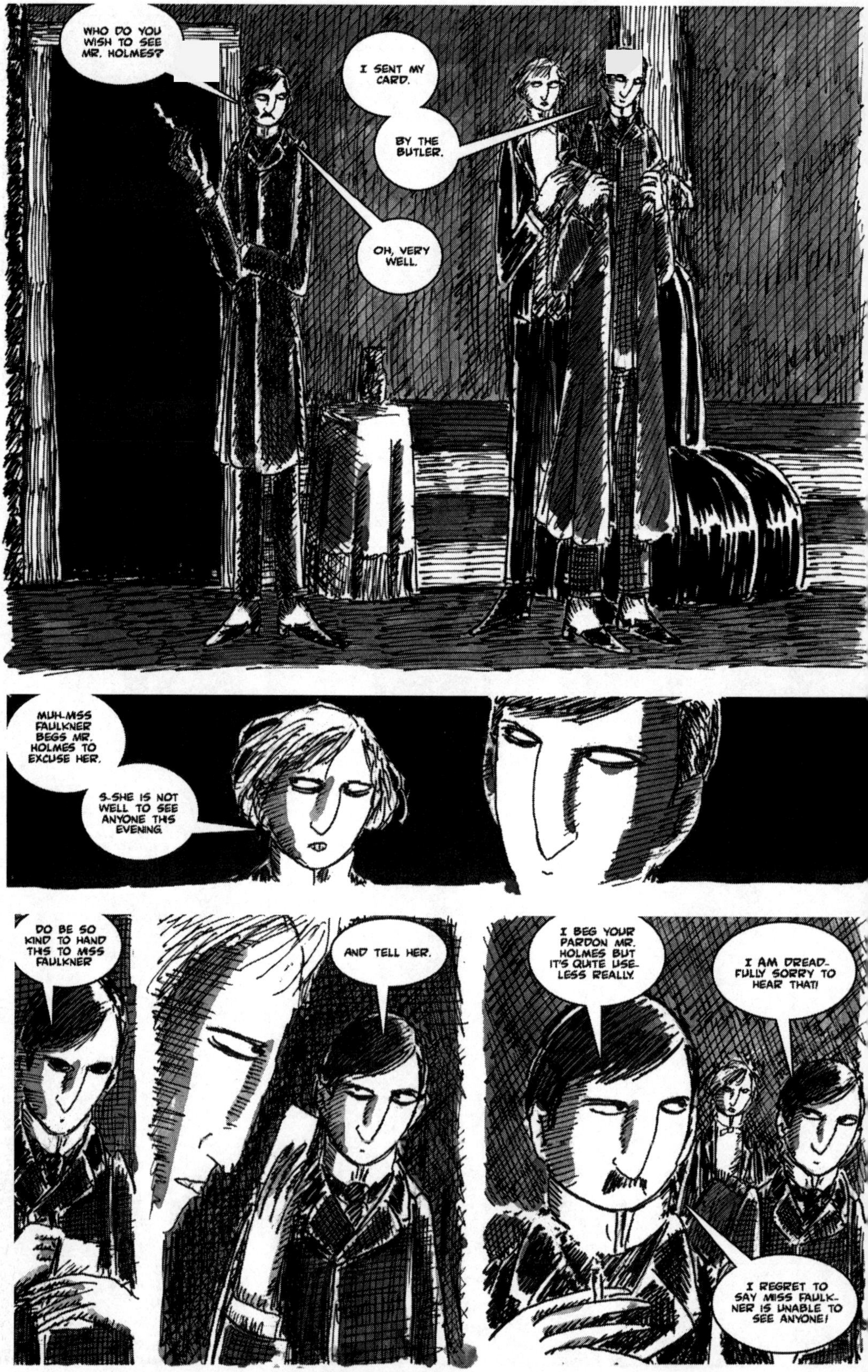
WHO DO YOU WISH TO SEE MR. HOLMES?
I SENT MY CARD.
BY THE BUTLER.
OH, VERY WELL.
MUH-MISS FAULKNER BEGS MR. HOLMES TO EXCUSE HER.
S-SHE IS NOT WELL TO SEE ANYONE THIS EVENING.
DO BE SO KIND TO HAND THIS TO MISS FAULKNER
AND TELL HER.
I BEG YOUR PARDON MR. HOLMES BUT IT'S QUITE USELESS REALLY.
I AM DREADFULLY SORRY TO HEAR THAT!
I REGRET TO SAY MISS FAULKNER IS UNABLE TO SEE ANYONE!

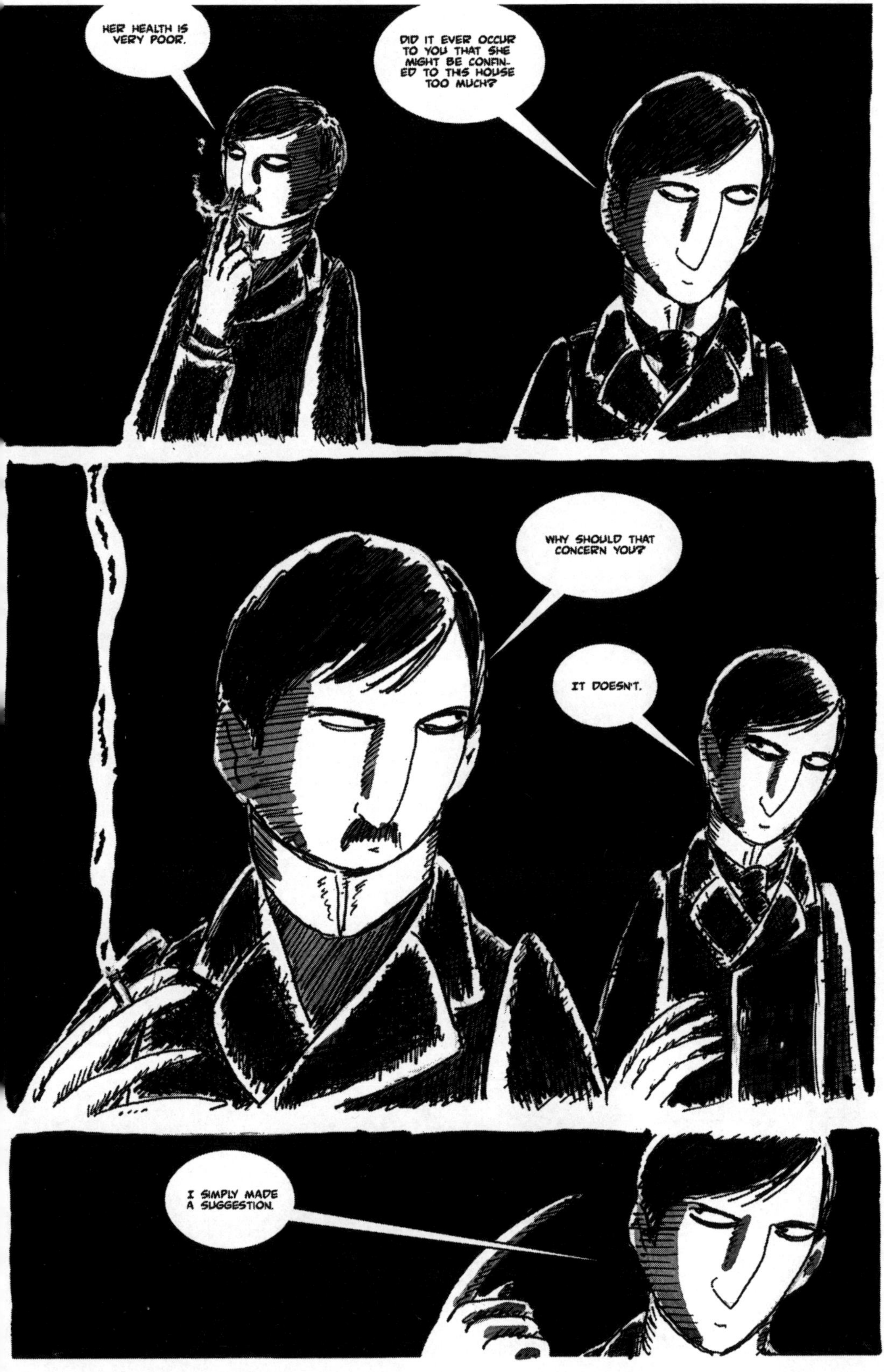
HER HEALTH IS VERY POOR.
DID IT EVER OCCUR TO YOU THAT SHE MIGHT BE CONFIN-ED TO THIS HOUSE TOO MUCH?
WHY SHOULD THAT CONCERN YOU?
IT DOESN'T.
I SIMPLY MADE A SUGGESTION.

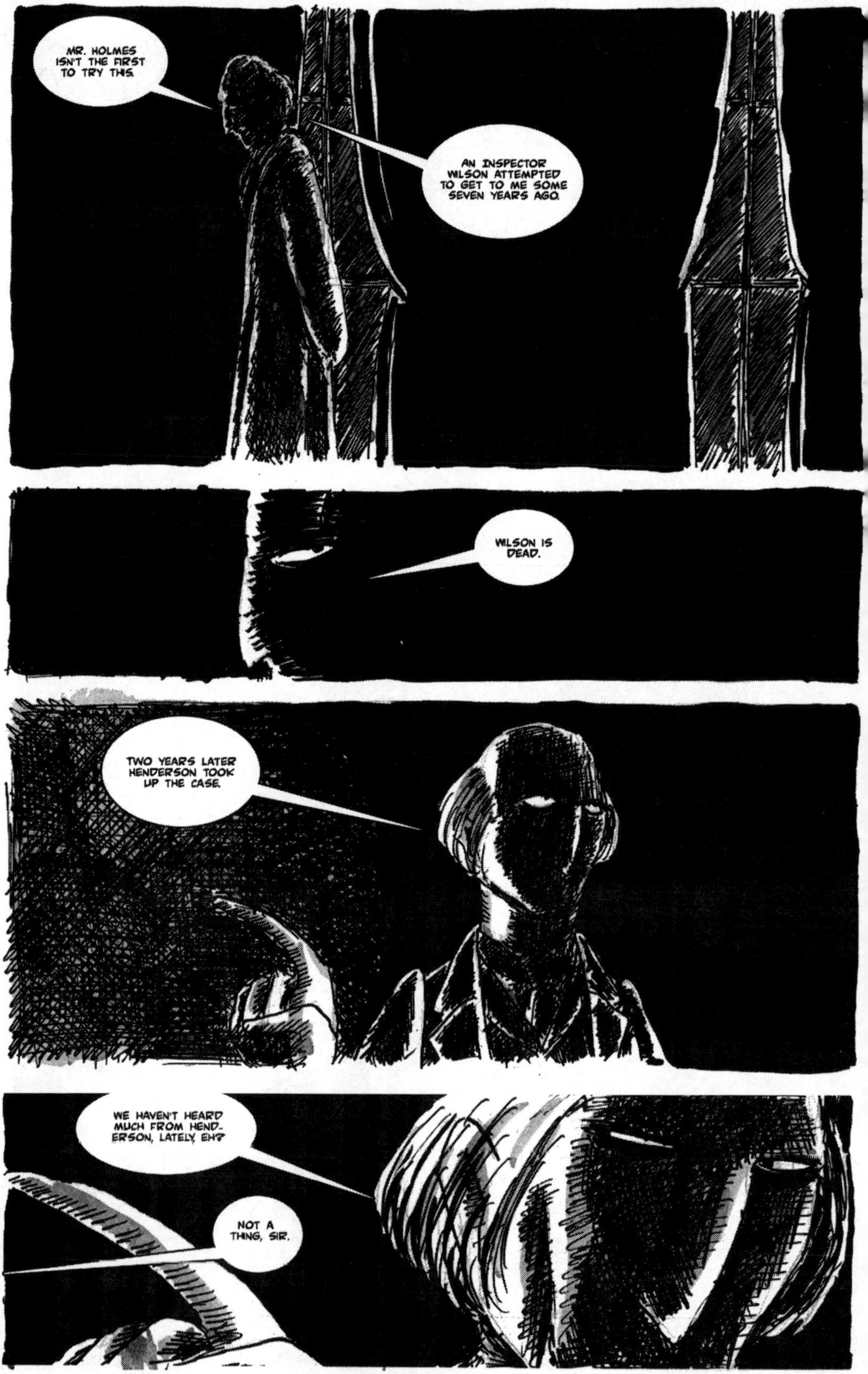
MR. HOLMES ISN'T THE FIRST TO TRY THIS.
AN INSPECTOR WILSON ATTEMPTED TO GET TO ME SOME SEVEN YEARS AGO.
WILSON IS DEAD.
TWO YEARS LATER HENDERSON TOOK UP THE CASE.
WE HAVEN'T HEARD MUCH FROM HEND-ERSON, LATELY, EH?
NOT A THING, SIR.

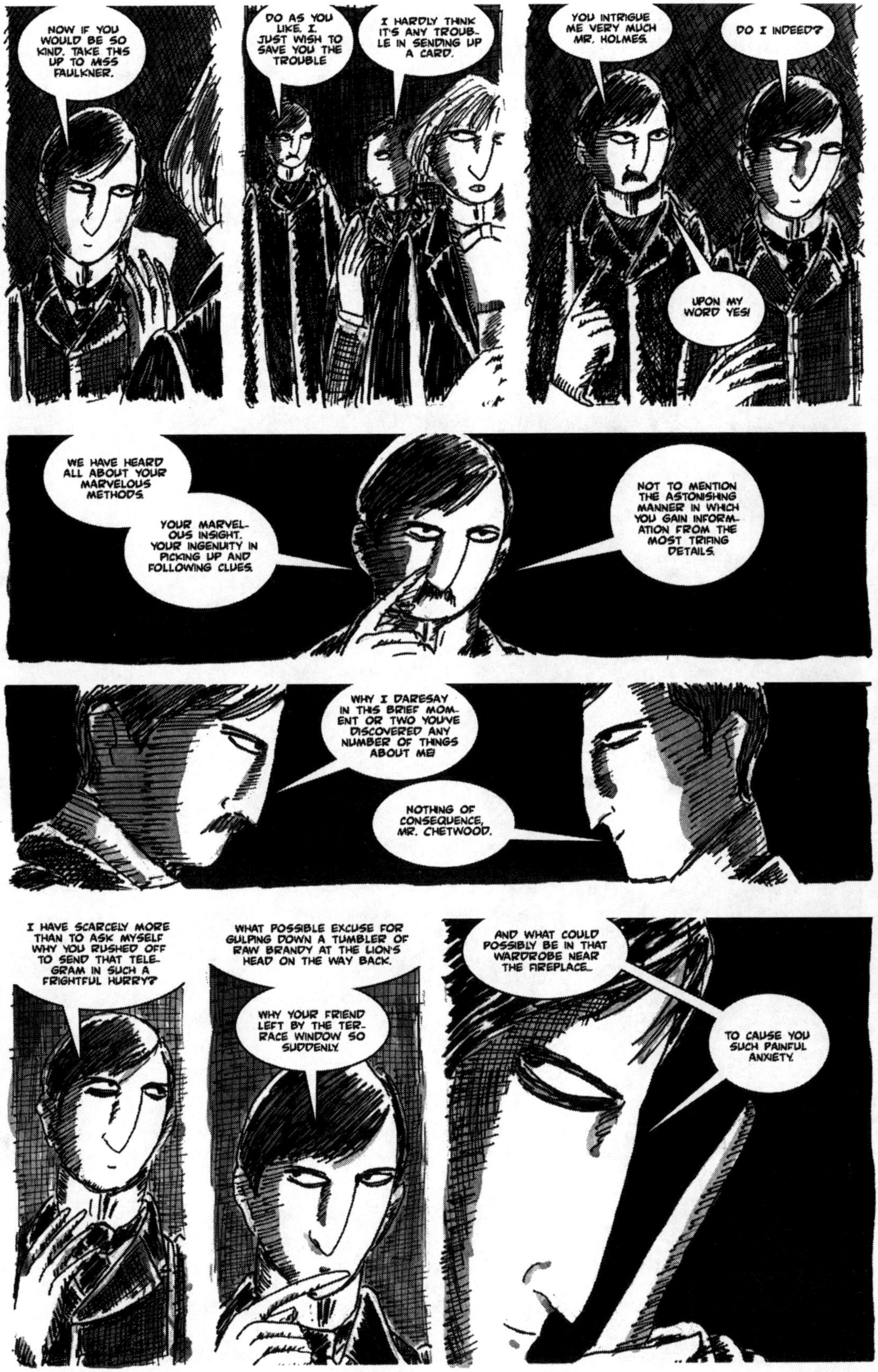
NOW IF YOU WOULD BE SO KIND. TAKE THIS UP TO MISS FAULKNER.
DO AS YOU LIKE, I, JUST WISH TO SAVE YOU THE TROUBLE
I HARDLY THINK IT'S ANY TROUBLE IN SENDING UP A CARD.
YOU INTRIGUE ME VERY MUCH MR. HOLMES.
DO I INDEED?
UPON MY WORD YES!
WE HAVE HEARD ALL ABOUT YOUR MARVELOUS METHODS.
YOUR MARVELOUS INSIGHT. YOUR INGENUITY IN PICKING UP AND FOLLOWING CLUES.
NOT TO MENTION THE ASTONISHING MANNER IN WHICH YOU GAIN INFORMATION FROM THE MOST TRIFING DETAILS.
WHY I DARESAY IN THIS BRIEF MOMENT OR TWO YOU'VE DISCOVERED ANY NUMBER OF THINGS ABOUT ME!
NOTHING OF CONSEQUENCE, MR. CHETWOOD.
I HAVE SCARCELY MORE THAN TO ASK MYSELF WHY YOU RUSHED OFF TO SEND THAT TELEGRAM IN SUCH A FRIGHTFUL HURRY?
WHAT POSSIBLE EXCUSE FOR GULPING DOWN A TUMBLER OF RAW BRANDY AT THE LION'S HEAD ON THE WAY BACK.
WHY YOUR FRIEND LEFT BY THE TERRACE WINDOW SO SUDDENLY.
AND WHAT COULD POSSIBLY BE IN THAT WARDROBE NEAR THE FIREPLACE...
TO CAUSE YOU SUCH PAINFUL ANXIETY.

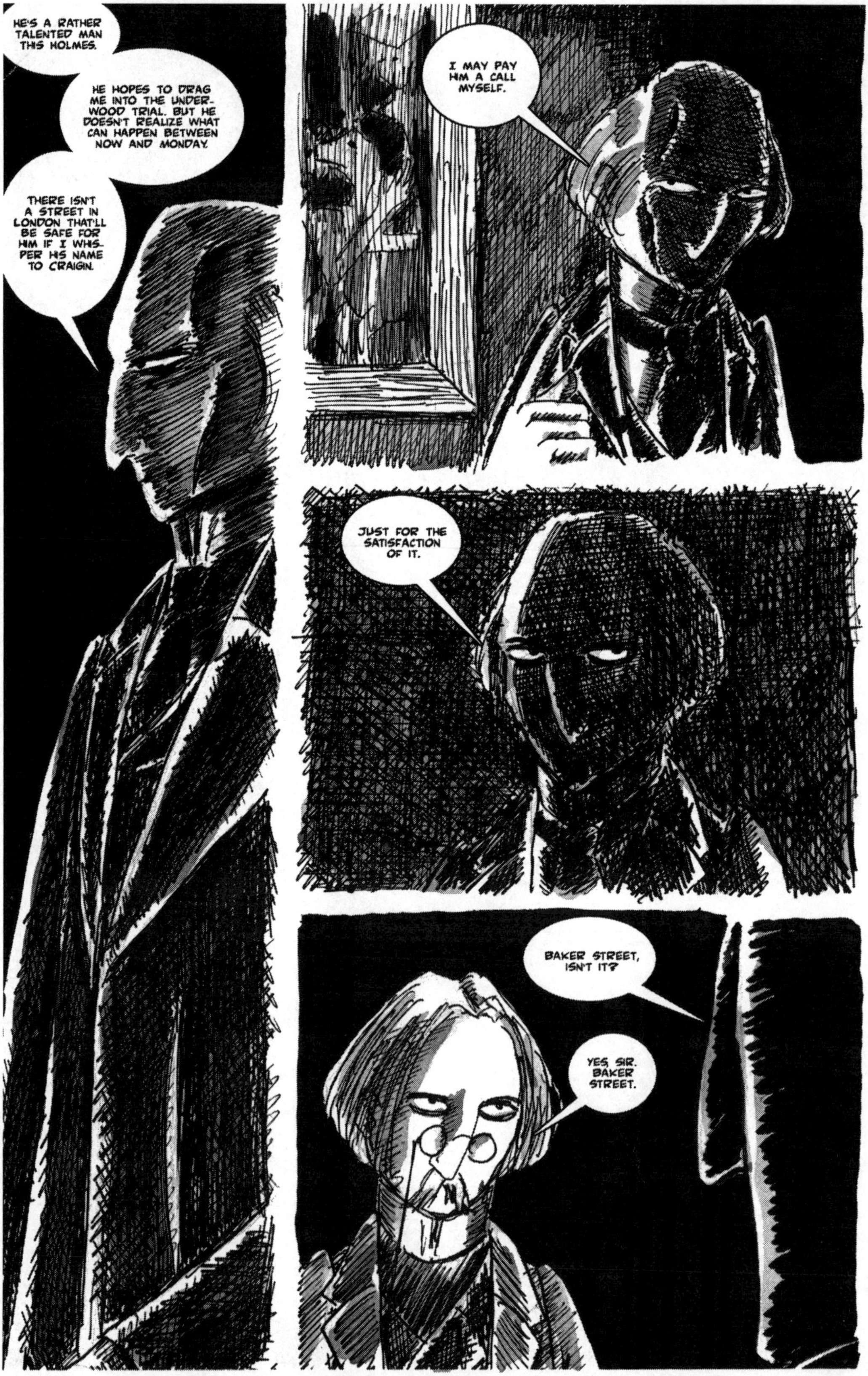
HE'S A RATHER TALENTED MAN THIS HOLMES.
HE HOPES TO DRAG ME INTO THE UNDER-WOOD TRIAL. BUT HE DOESN'T REALIZE WHAT CAN HAPPEN BETWEEN NOW AND MONDAY.
THERE ISN'T A STREET IN LONDON THAT'LL BE SAFE FOR HIM IF I WHIS-PER HIS NAME TO CRAIGIN.
I MAY PAY HIM A CALL MYSELF.
JUST FOR THE SATISFACTION OF IT.
BAKER STREET, ISN'T IT?
YES SIR. BAKER STREET.

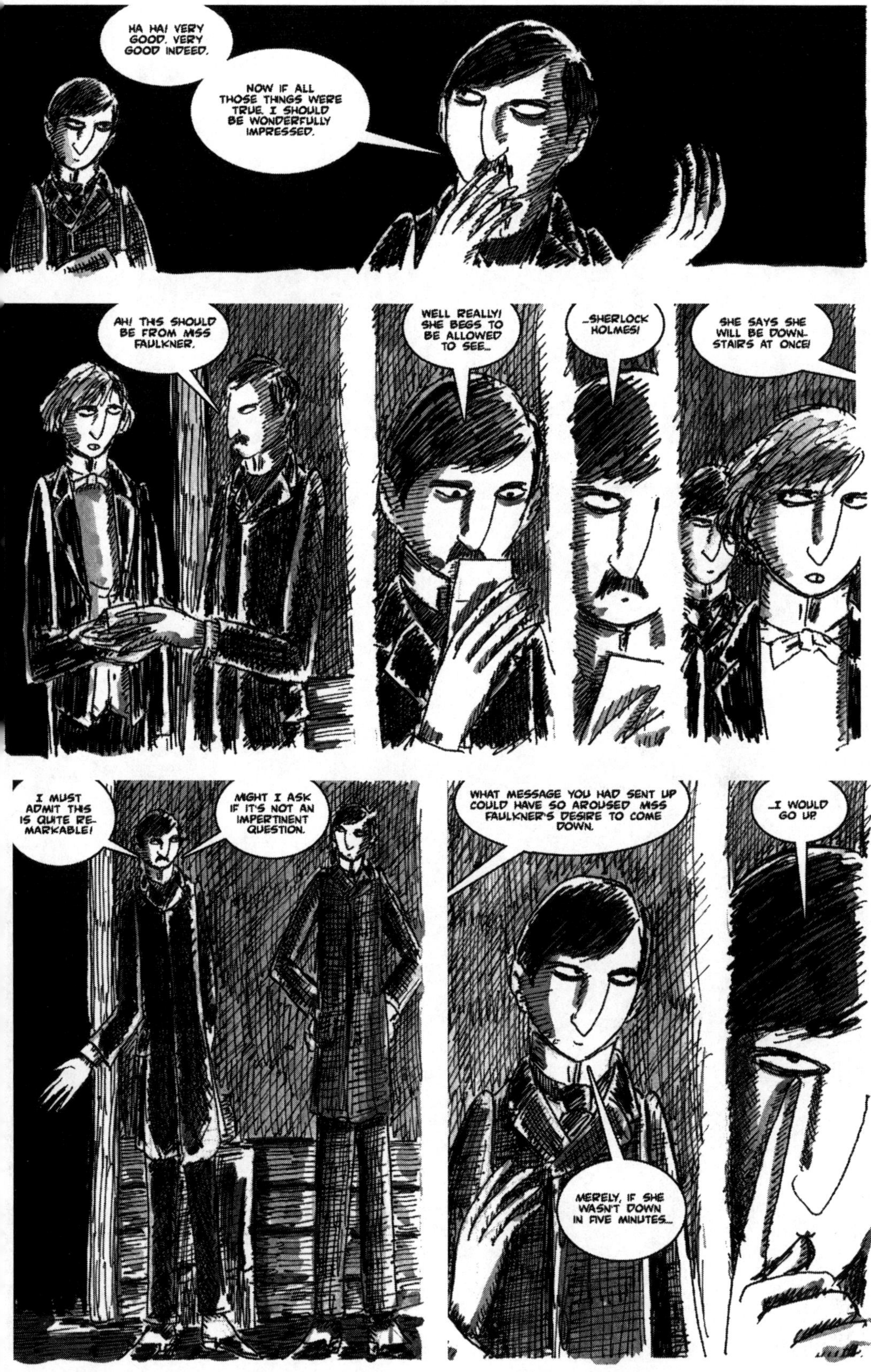
HA HA! VERY GOOD. VERY GOOD INDEED.
NOW IF ALL THOSE THINGS WERE TRUE, I SHOULD BE WONDERFULLY IMPRESSED.
AH! THIS SHOULD BE FROM MISS FAULKNER.
WELL REALLY! SHE BEGS TO BE ALLOWED TO SEE...
...SHERLOCK HOLMES!
SHE SAYS SHE WILL BE DOWN-STAIRS AT ONCE!
I MUST ADMIT THIS IS QUITE RE-MARKABLE!
MIGHT I ASK IF IT'S NOT AN IMPERTINENT QUESTION.
WHAT MESSAGE YOU HAD SENT UP COULD HAVE SO AROUSED MISS FAULKNER'S DESIRE TO COME DOWN.
MERELY, IF SHE WASN'T DOWN IN FIVE MINUTES...
...I WOULD GO UP.

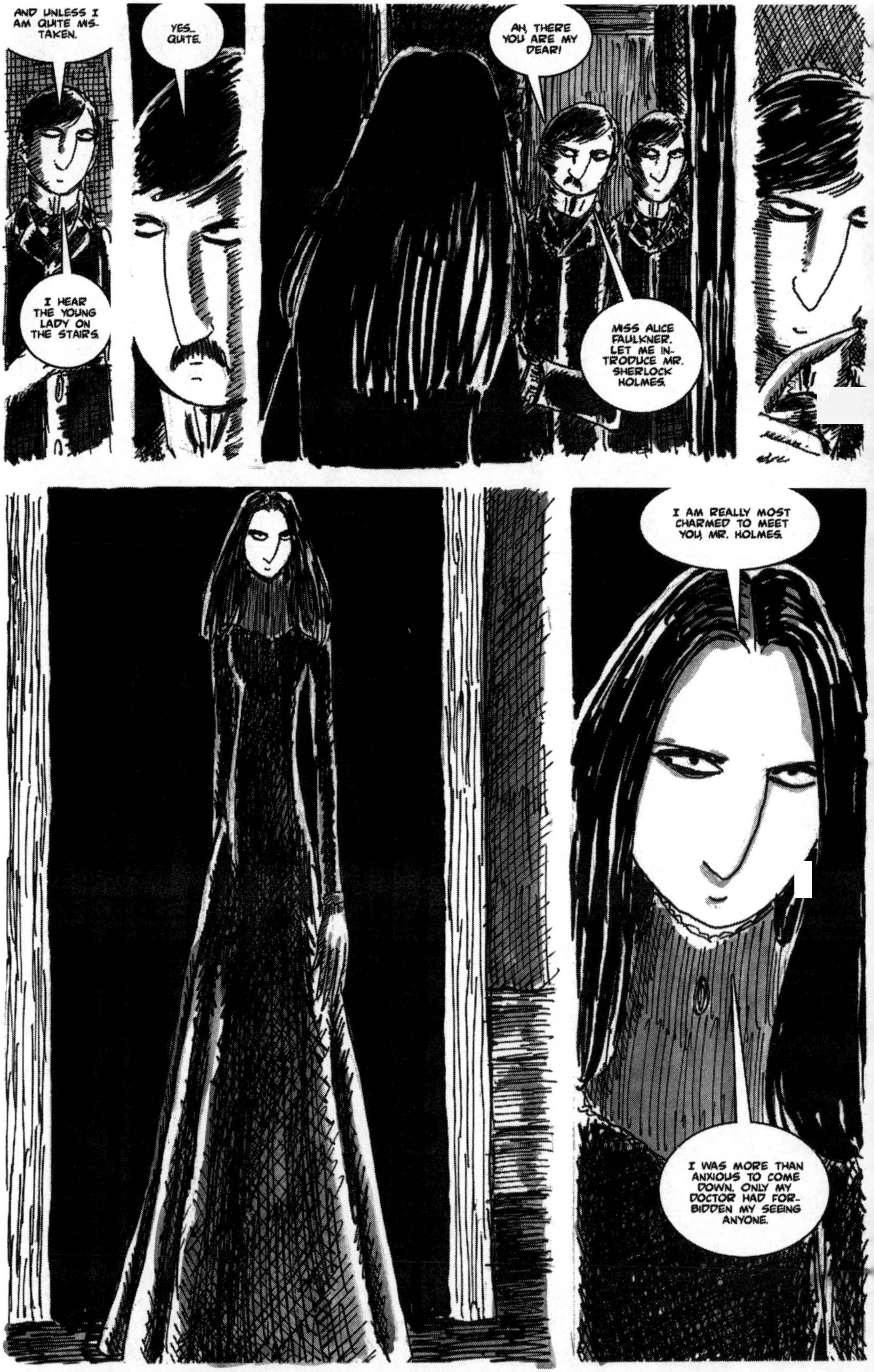
AND UNLESS I AM QUITE MIS-TAKEN.
YES... QUITE.
I HEAR THE YOUNG LADY ON THE STAIRS.
AH, THERE YOU ARE MY DEAR!
MISS ALICE FAULKNER. LET ME IN-TRODUCE MR. SHERLOCK HOLMES.
I AM REALLY MOST CHARMED TO MEET YOU, MR. HOLMES.
I WAS MORE THAN ANXIOUS TO COME DOWN. ONLY MY DOCTOR HAD FOR-BIDDEN MY SEEING ANYONE.

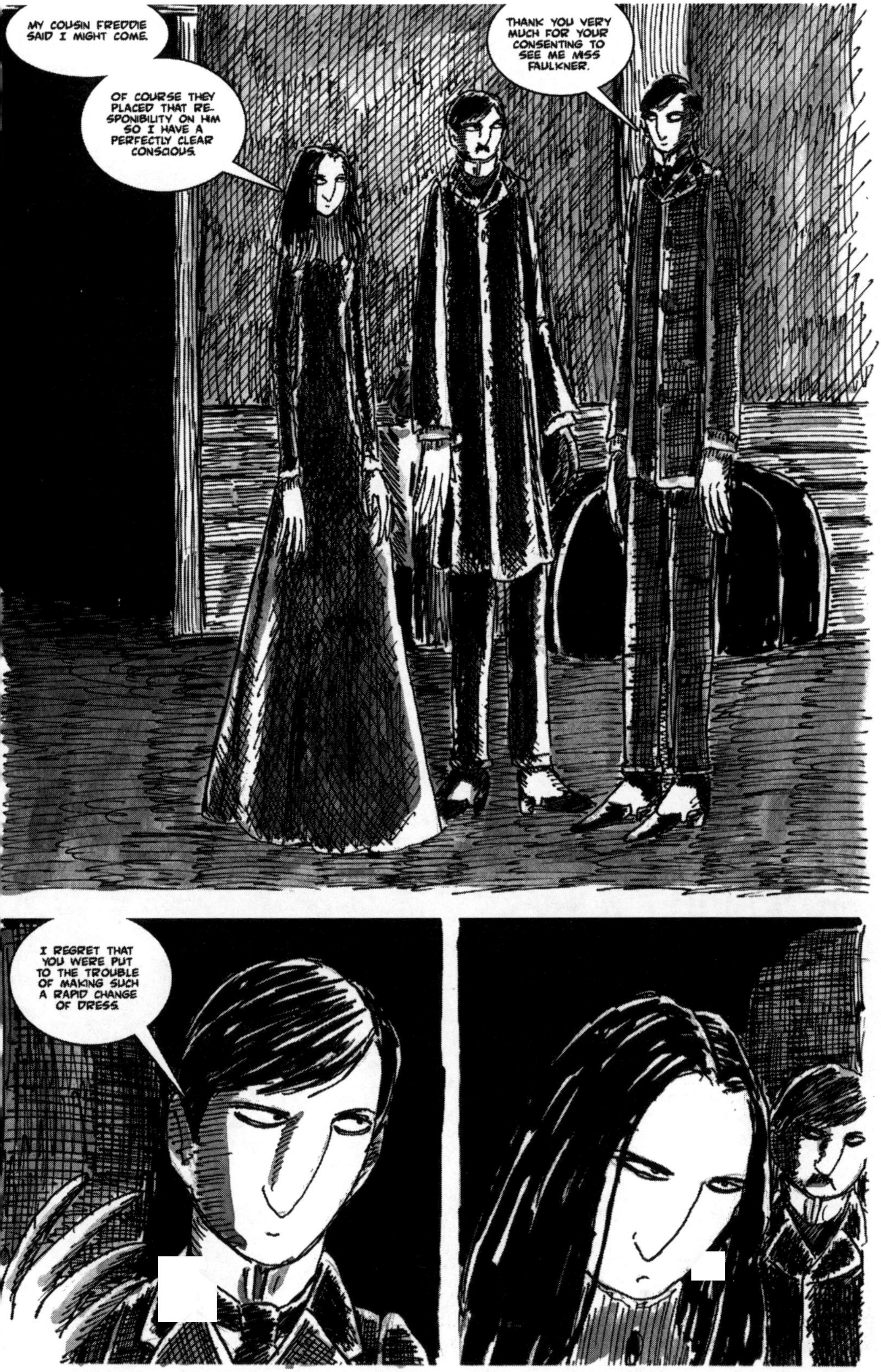
MY COUSIN FREDDIE SAID I MIGHT COME.
OF COURSE THEY PLACED THAT RE-SPONIBILITY ON HIM SO I HAVE A PERFECTLY CLEAR CONSCIOUS.
THANK YOU VERY MUCH FOR YOUR CONSENTING TO SEE ME MISS FAULKNER.
I REGRET THAT YOU WERE PUT TO THE TROUBLE OF MAKING SUCH A RAPID CHANGE OF DRESS.

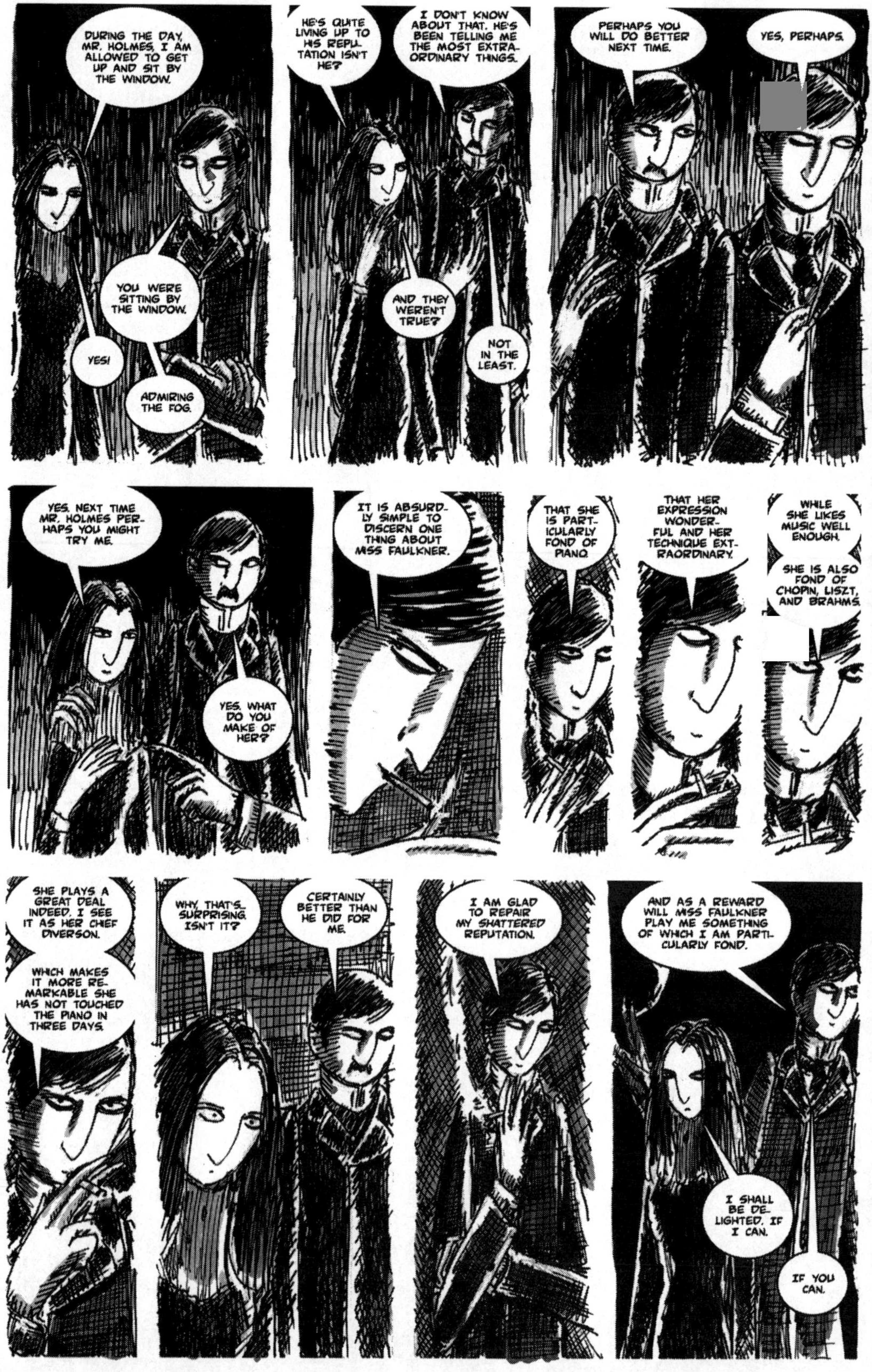
DURING THE DAY, MR. HOLMES, I AM ALLOWED TO GET UP AND SIT BY THE WINDOW.
YOU WERE SITTING BY THE WINDOW.
YES!
ADMIRING THE FOG.
HE'S QUITE LIVING UP TO HIS REPUTATION ISN'T HE?
I DON'T KNOW ABOUT THAT. HE'S BEEN TELLING ME THE MOST EXTRAORDINARY THINGS.
AND THEY WEREN'T TRUE?
NOT IN THE LEAST.
PERHAPS YOU WILL DO BETTER NEXT TIME.
YES, PERHAPS.
YES. NEXT TIME MR. HOLMES PERHAPS YOU MIGHT TRY ME.
YES. WHAT DO YOU MAKE OF HER?
IT IS ABSURDLY SIMPLE TO DISCERN ONE THING ABOUT MISS FAULKNER.
THAT SHE IS PARTICULARLY FOND OF PIANO.
THAT HER EXPRESSION WONDERFUL AND HER TECHNIQUE EXTRAORDINARY.
WHILE SHE LIKES MUSIC WELL ENOUGH.
SHE IS ALSO FOND OF CHOPIN, LISZT, AND BRAHMS.
SHE PLAYS A GREAT DEAL INDEED. I SEE IT AS HER CHIEF DIVERSON.
WHICH MAKES IT MORE REMARKABLE SHE HAS NOT TOUCHED THE PIANO IN THREE DAYS.
WHY, THAT'S... SURPRISING. ISN'T IT?
CERTAINLY BETTER THAN HE DID FOR ME.
I AM GLAD TO REPAIR MY SHATTERED REPUTATION.
AND AS A REWARD WILL MISS FAULKNER PLAY ME SOMETHING OF WHICH I AM PARTICULARLY FOND.
I SHALL BE DELIGHTED. IF I CAN.
IF YOU CAN.

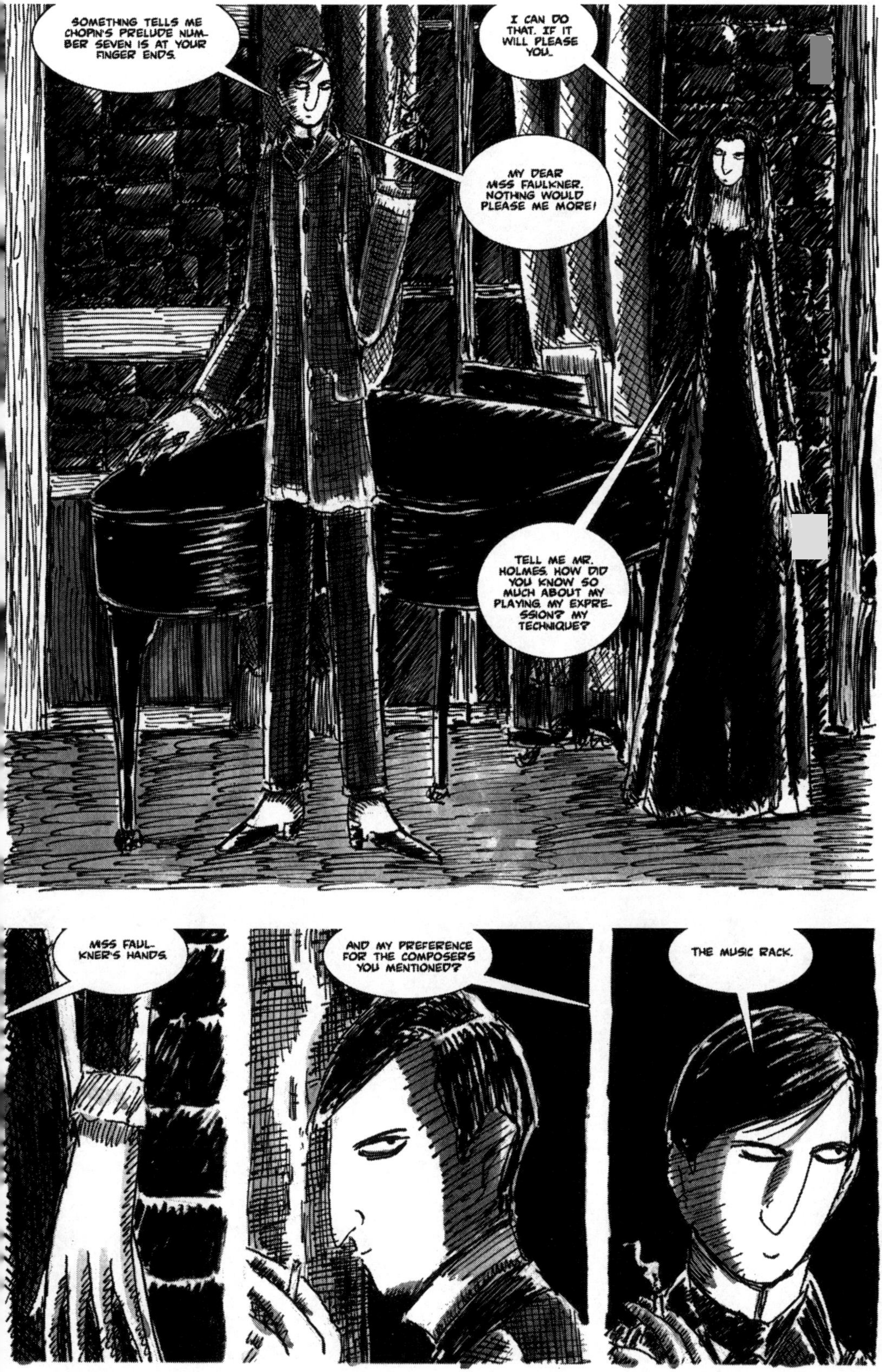
SOMETHING TELLS ME CHOPIN'S PRELUDE NUMBER SEVEN IS AT YOUR FINGER ENDS.
I CAN DO THAT. IF IT WILL PLEASE YOU.
MY DEAR MISS FAULKNER. NOTHING WOULD PLEASE ME MORE!
TELL ME MR. HOLMES. HOW DID YOU KNOW SO MUCH ABOUT MY PLAYING. MY EXPRESSION? MY TECHNIQUE?
MISS FAULKNER'S HANDS.
AND MY PREFERENCE FOR THE COMPOSERS YOU MENTIONED?
THE MUSIC RACK.

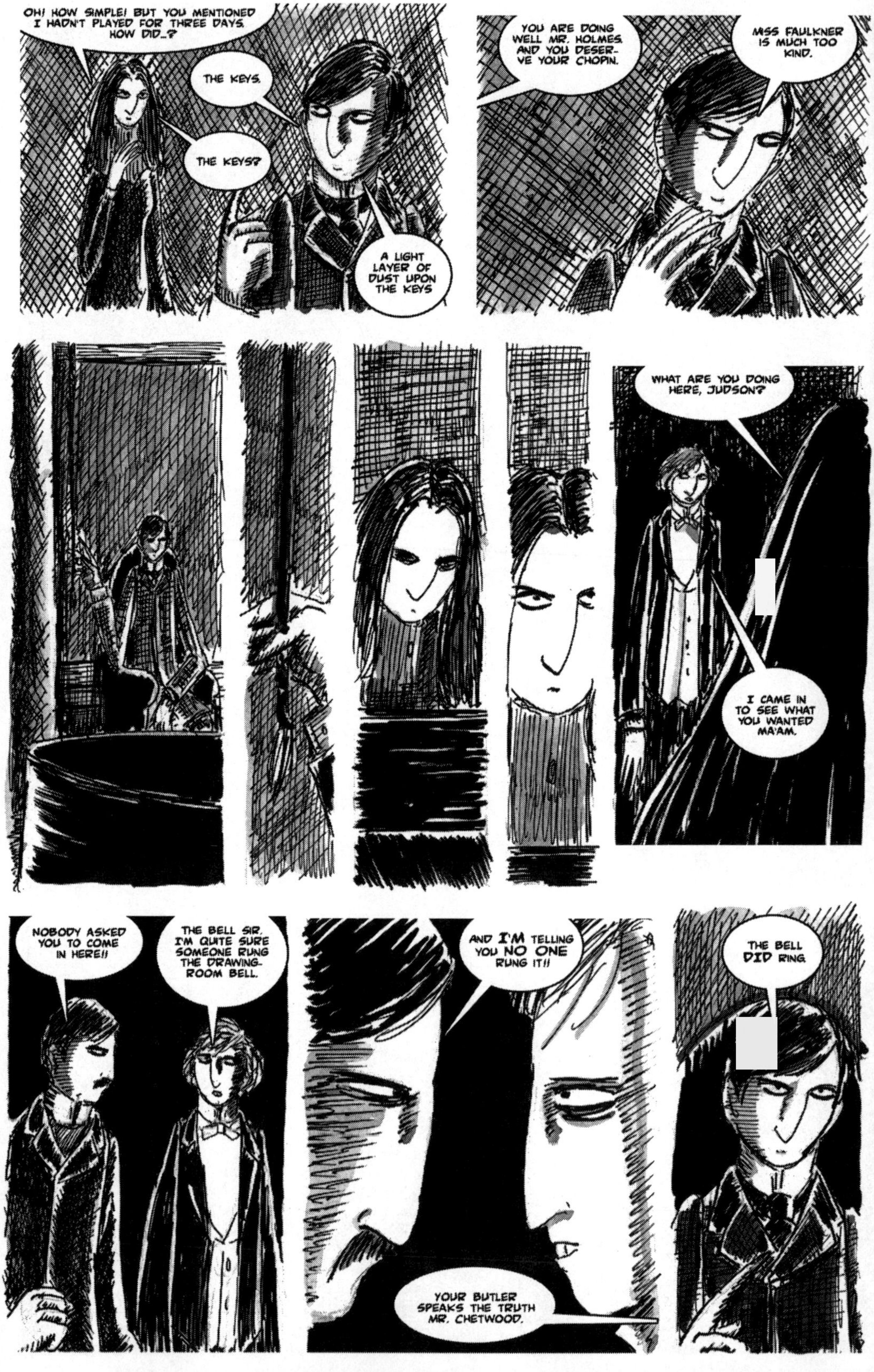
OH! HOW SIMPLE! BUT YOU MENTIONED I HADN'T PLAYED FOR THREE DAYS. HOW DID..?
THE KEYS.
THE KEYS?
A LIGHT LAYER OF DUST UPON THE KEYS
YOU ARE DOING WELL MR. HOLMES. AND YOU DESERVE YOUR CHOPIN.
MISS FAULKNER IS MUCH TOO KIND.
WHAT ARE YOU DOING HERE, JUDSON?
I CAME IN TO SEE WHAT YOU WANTED MA'AM.
NOBODY ASKED YOU TO COME IN HERE!!
THE BELL SIR. I'M QUITE SURE SOMEONE RUNG THE DRAWING-ROOM BELL.
AND I'M TELLING YOU NO ONE RUNG IT!!
YOUR BUTLER SPEAKS THE TRUTH MR. CHETWOOD.
THE BELL DID RING.

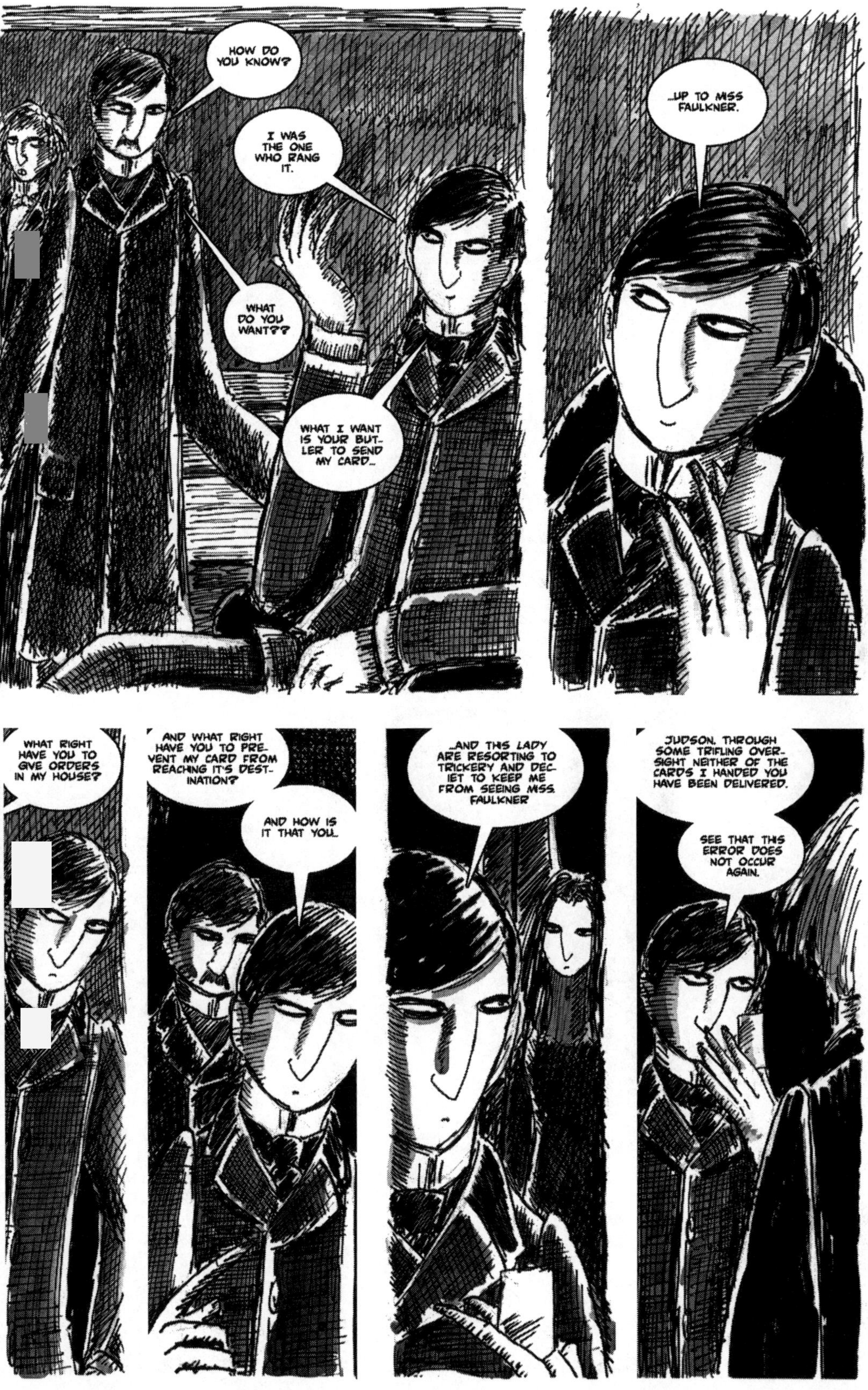
HOW DO YOU KNOW?
I WAS THE ONE WHO RANG IT.
WHAT DO YOU WANT??
WHAT I WANT IS YOUR BUT-LER TO SEND MY CARD...
...UP TO MISS FAULKNER.
WHAT RIGHT HAVE YOU TO GIVE ORDERS IN MY HOUSE?
AND WHAT RIGHT HAVE YOU TO PRE-VENT MY CARD FROM REACHING IT'S DEST-INATION?
AND HOW IS IT THAT YOU...
...AND THIS LADY ARE RESORTING TO TRICKERY AND DEC-IET TO KEEP ME FROM SEEING MISS FAULKNER
JUDSON, THROUGH SOME TRIFLING OVER-SIGHT NEITHER OF THE CARDS I HANDED YOU HAVE BEEN DELIVERED.
SEE THAT THIS ERROR DOES NOT OCCUR AGAIN.

M-MY ORDERS...
OH YOU HAVE ORDERS?
I... I CAN'T SAY SIR.
YOU WERE TOLD NOT TO DELIVER MY CARD WEREN'T YOU?
AND WHAT BUSINESS IS THAT OF YOURS? I'D LIKE TO KNOW?
ALL IN GOOD TIME MR. CHETWOOD. I SHALL SATISFY YOUR CURIOSITY.
IT IS NOT SAFE TO MEDDLE WITH ME.
I WOULD HAVE NO TROUBLE IN THROWIN YOU OUT.
I THINK YOU WOULD FIND TROUBLE WOULD SWIFTLY FOLLOW SUCH AN EXPERIMENT ON YOUR PART.
I SHALL CALL THE POLICE. AND WHAT'S MORE I SHALL DO IT NOW!!
HA! YOU SHALL DO NOTHING OF THE SORT.
YOU WILL REMAIN WHERE YOU ARE UNTIL THE YOUNG LADY HAS ENTERED THE ROOM.
WHAT MAKES YOU SO DAMN SURE OF THAT??
BECAUSE YOU WILL INFINITELY PREFER TO AVOID AN INVESTIGATION OF YOUR VERY SUSPICIOUS CONDUCT...
MR. JAMES LARRABEE.
WHICH SHALL CERTAINLY TAKE PLACE IF YOU OR YOUR WIFE PRESUME FURTHER TO INTERFERE WITH MY BUSINESS.

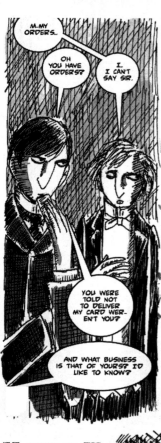

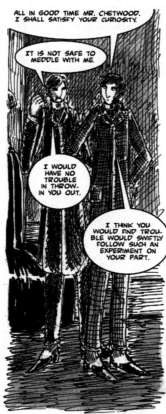

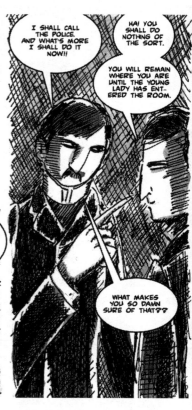

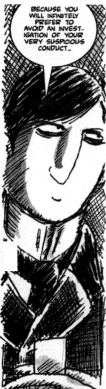

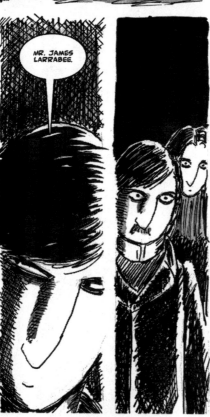

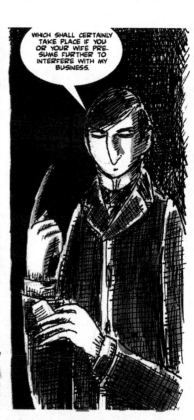

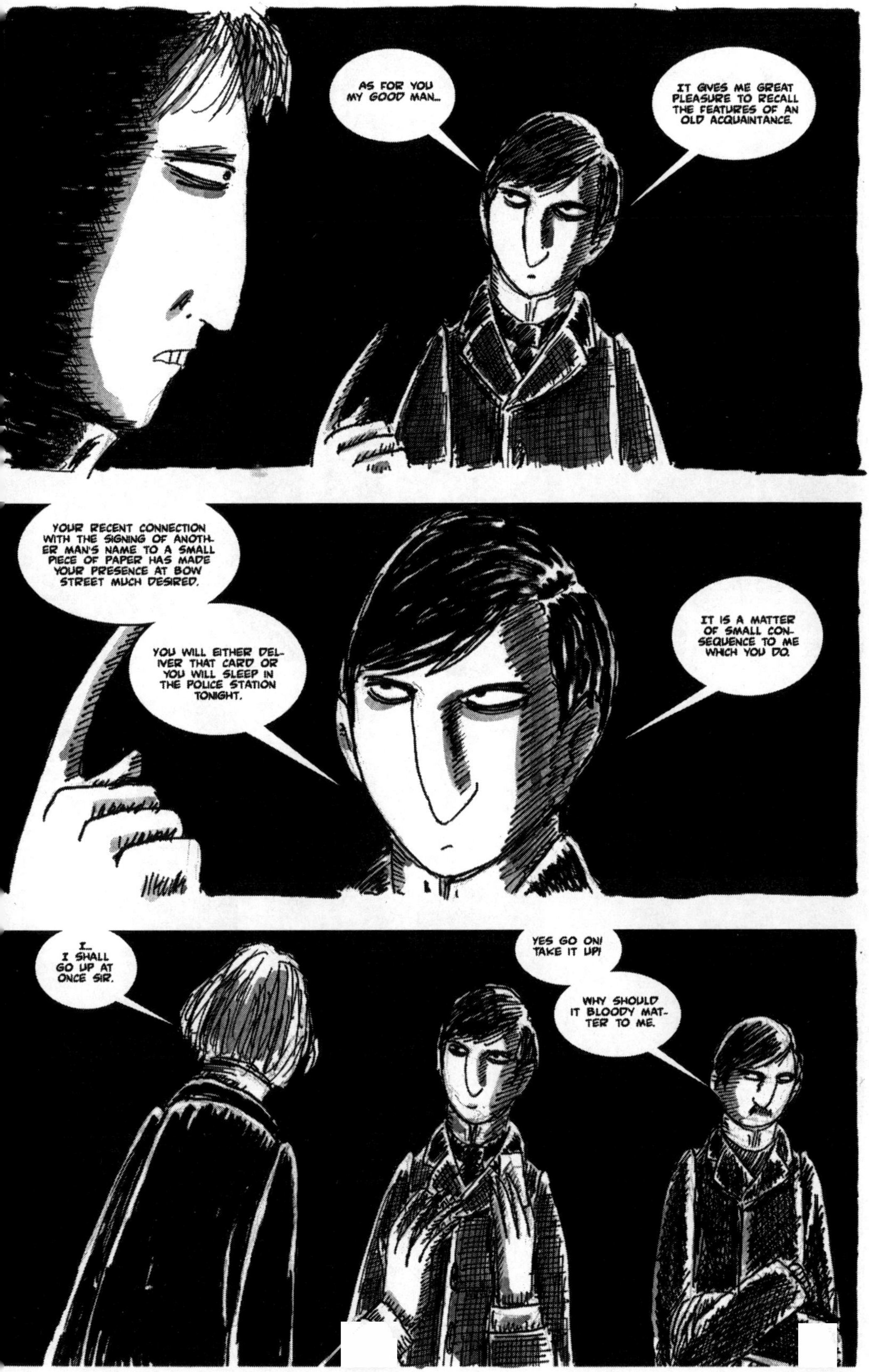
AS FOR YOU MY GOOD MAN...
IT GIVES ME GREAT PLEASURE TO RECALL THE FEATURES OF AN OLD ACQUAINTANCE.
YOUR RECENT CONNECTION WITH THE SIGNING OF ANOTHER MAN'S NAME TO A SMALL PIECE OF PAPER HAS MADE YOUR PRESENCE AT BOW STREET MUCH DESIRED.
YOU WILL EITHER DELIVER THAT CARD OR YOU WILL SLEEP IN THE POLICE STATION TONIGHT.
IT IS A MATTER OF SMALL CONSEQUENCE TO ME WHICH YOU DO.
I... I SHALL GO UP AT ONCE SIR.
YES GO ON! TAKE IT UP!
WHY SHOULD IT BLOODY MATTER TO ME.

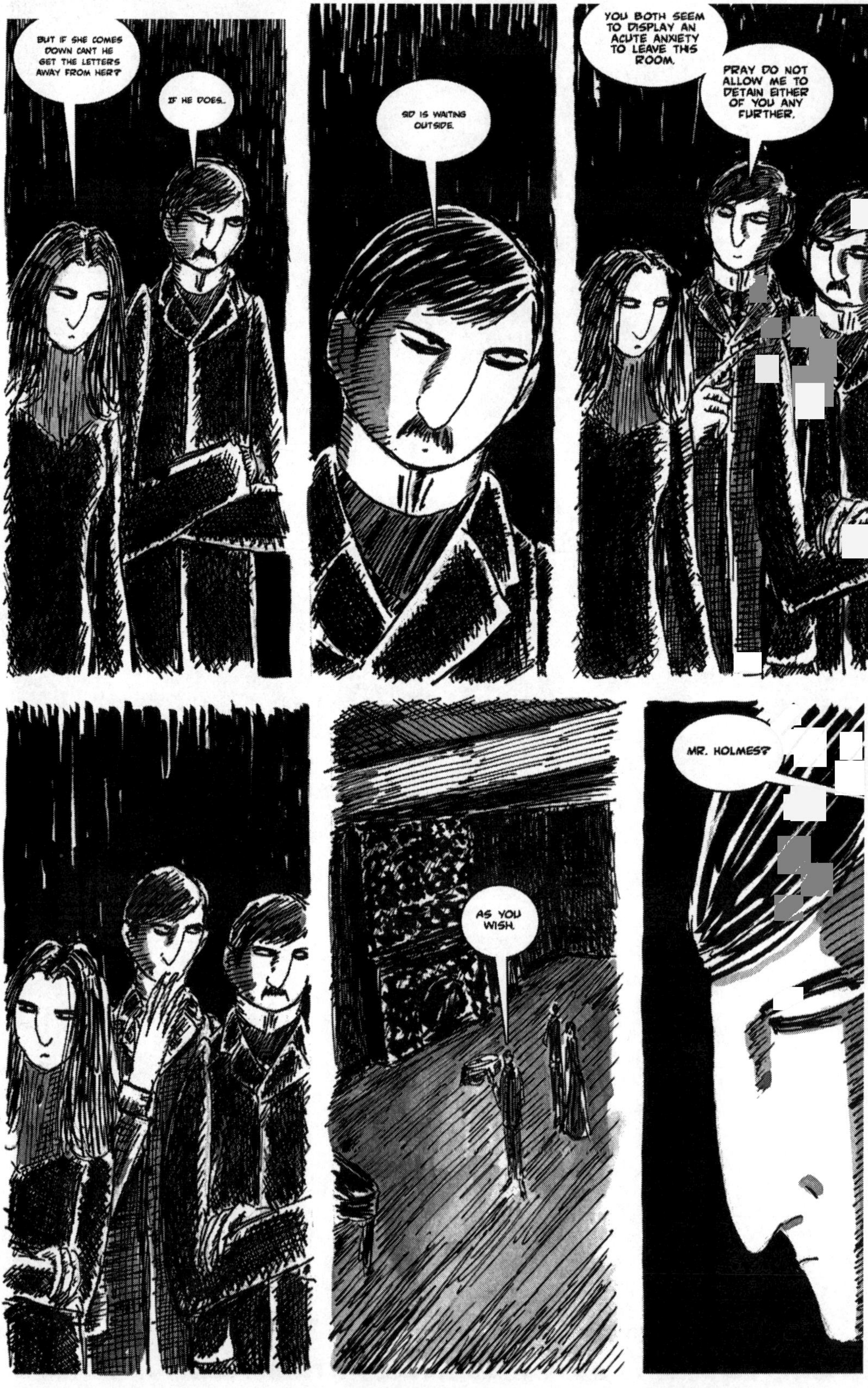
BUT IF SHE COMES DOWN CAN'T HE GET THE LETTERS AWAY FROM HER?
IF HE DOES...
SID IS WAITING OUTSIDE.
YOU BOTH SEEM TO DISPLAY AN ACUTE ANXIETY TO LEAVE THIS ROOM.
PRAY DO NOT ALLOW ME TO DETAIN EITHER OF YOU ANY FURTHER.
AS YOU WISH.
MR. HOLMES?

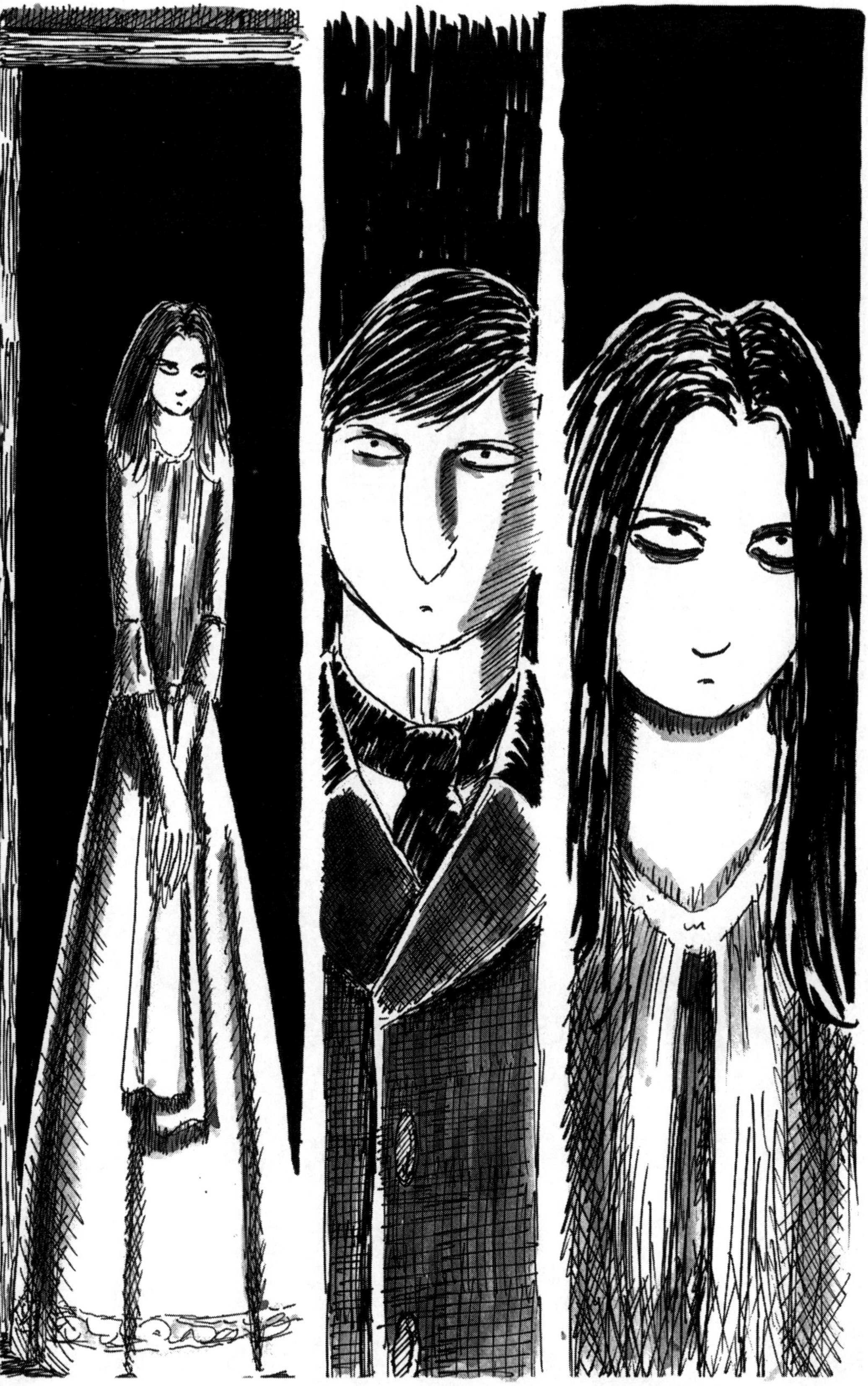

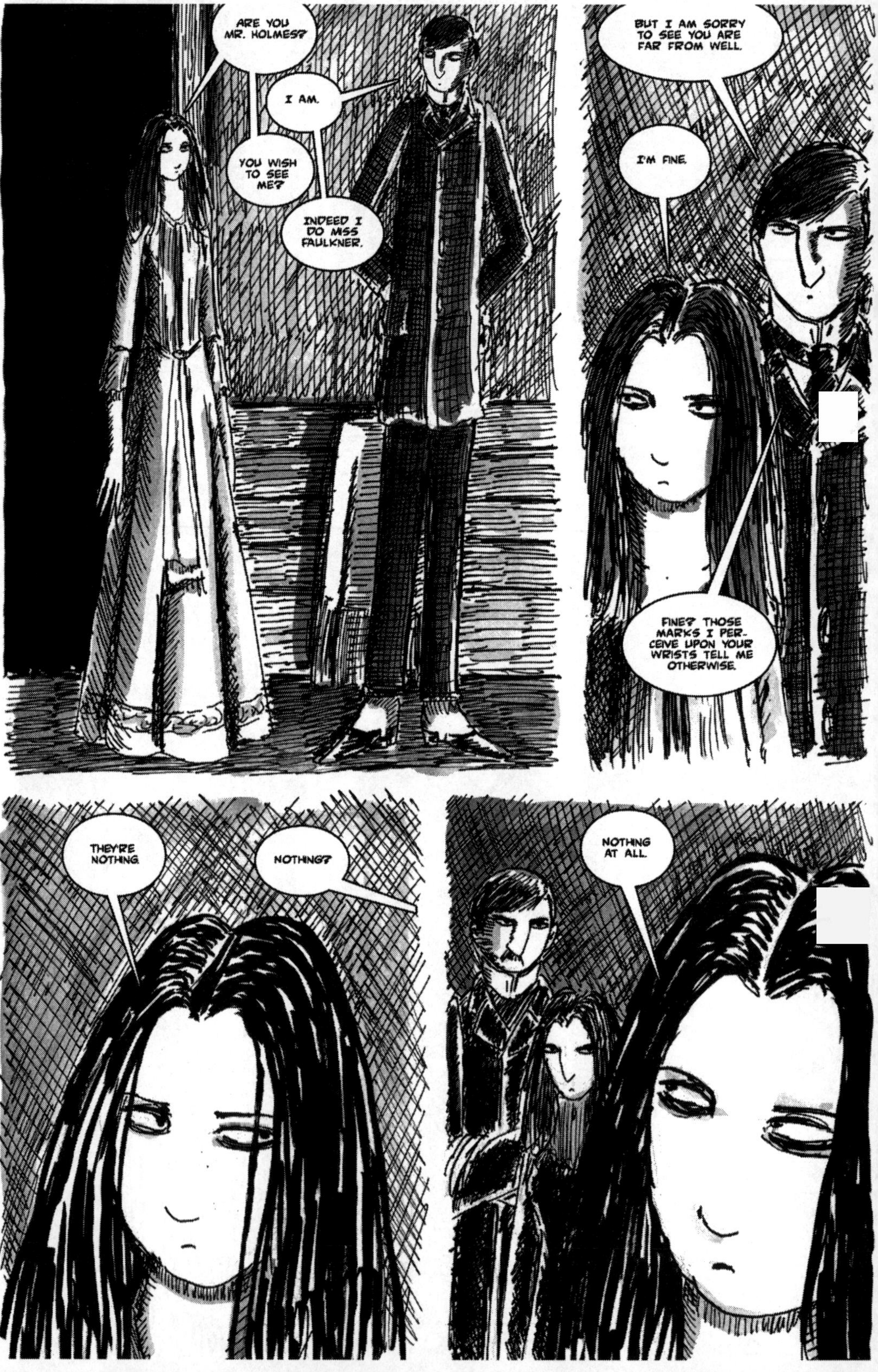
ARE YOU MR. HOLMES?
I AM.
YOU WISH TO SEE ME?
INDEED I DO MISS FAULKNER.
BUT I AM SORRY TO SEE YOU ARE FAR FROM WELL.
I'M FINE.
FINE? THOSE MARKS I PERCEIVE UPON YOUR WRISTS TELL ME OTHERWISE.
THEY'RE NOTHING.
NOTHING?
NOTHING AT ALL.

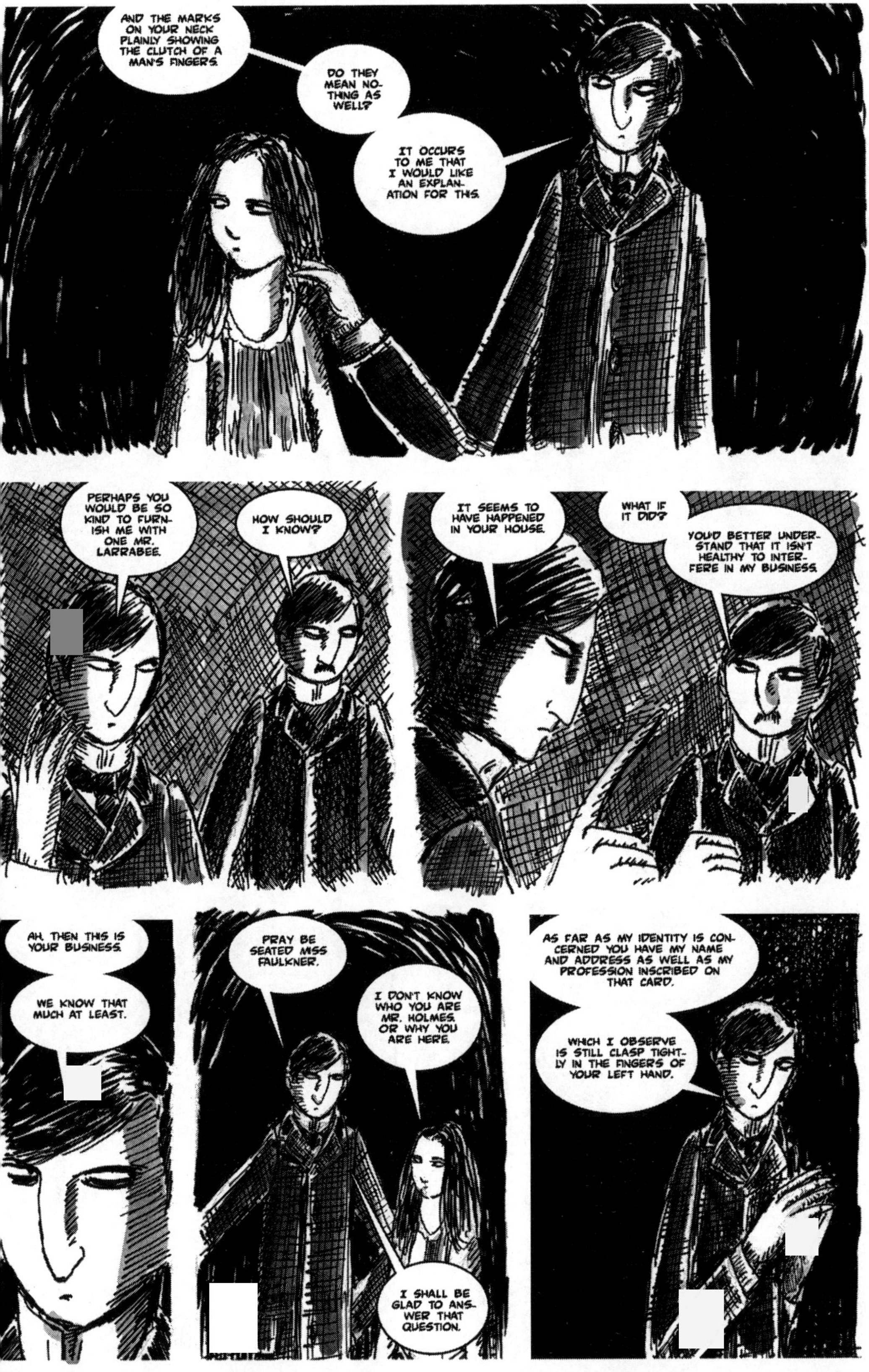
AND THE MARKS ON YOUR NECK PLAINLY SHOWING THE CLUTCH OF A MAN'S FINGERS.
DO THEY MEAN NO-THING AS WELL?
IT OCCURS TO ME THAT I WOULD LIKE AN EXPLAN-ATION FOR THIS.
PERHAPS YOU WOULD BE SO KIND TO FURN-ISH ME WITH ONE MR. LARRABEE.
HOW SHOULD I KNOW?
IT SEEMS TO HAVE HAPPENED IN YOUR HOUSE.
WHAT IF IT DID?
YOU'D BETTER UNDER-STAND THAT IT ISN'T HEALTHY TO INTER-FERE IN MY BUSINESS.
AH, THEN THIS IS YOUR BUSINESS.
WE KNOW THAT MUCH AT LEAST.
PRAY BE SEATED MISS FAULKNER.
I DON'T KNOW WHO YOU ARE MR. HOLMES, OR WHY YOU ARE HERE.
I SHALL BE GLAD TO ANS-WER THAT QUESTION.
AS FAR AS MY IDENTITY IS CON-CERNED YOU HAVE MY NAME AND ADDRESS AS WELL AS MY PROFESSION INSCRIBED ON THAT CARD.
WHICH I OBSERVE IS STILL CLASP TIGHT-LY IN THE FINGERS OF YOUR LEFT HAND.

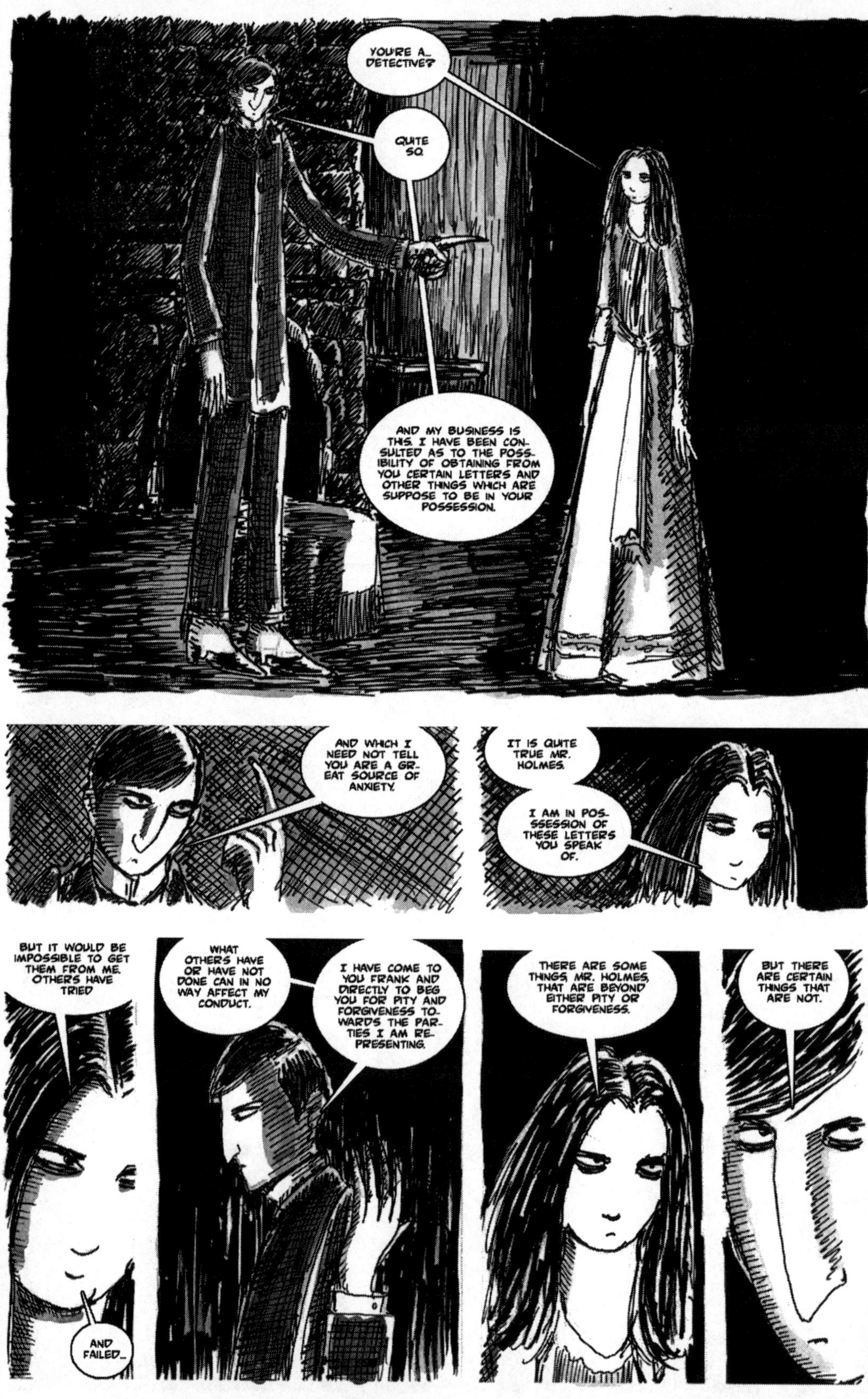
YOU'RE A... DETECTIVE?
QUITE SO.
AND MY BUSINESS IS THIS. I HAVE BEEN CON-SULTED AS TO THE POSS-IBILITY OF OBTAINING FROM YOU CERTAIN LETTERS AND OTHER THINGS WHICH ARE SUPPOSE TO BE IN YOUR POSSESSION.
AND WHICH I NEED NOT TELL YOU ARE A GR-EAT SOURCE OF ANXIETY.
IT IS QUITE TRUE MR. HOLMES.
I AM IN POS-SSESSION OF THESE LETTERS YOU SPEAK OF.
BUT IT WOULD BE IMPOSSIBLE TO GET THEM FROM ME. OTHERS HAVE TRIED
AND FAILED...
WHAT OTHERS HAVE OR HAVE NOT DONE CAN IN NO WAY AFFECT MY CONDUCT.
I HAVE COME TO YOU FRANK AND DIRECTLY TO BEG YOU FOR PITY AND FORGIVENESS TO-WARDS THE PAR-TIES I AM RE-PRESENTING.
THERE ARE SOME THINGS, MR. HOLMES, THAT ARE BEYOND EITHER PITY OR FORGIVENESS.
BUT THERE ARE CERTAIN THINGS THAT ARE NOT.

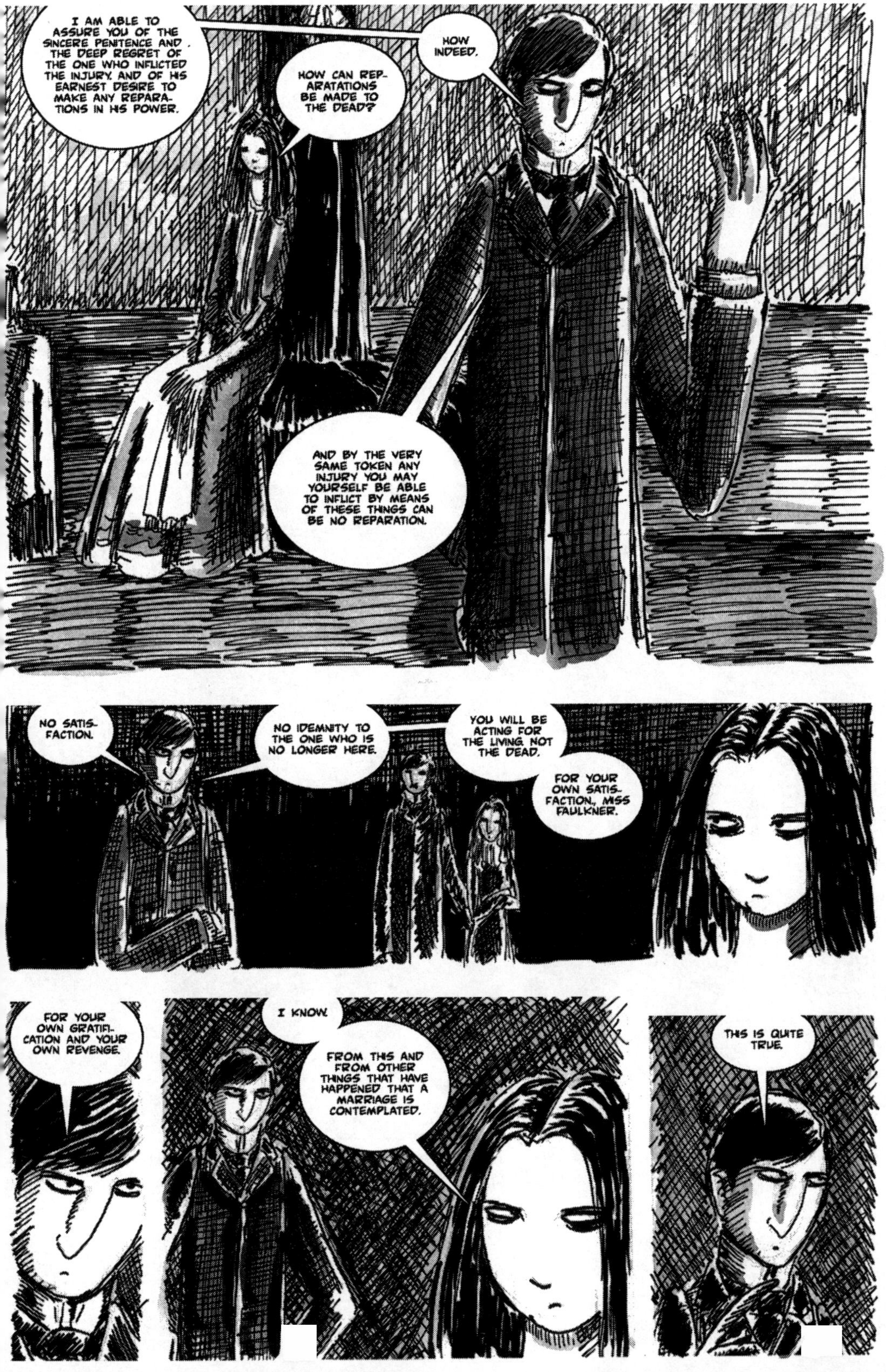
I AM ABLE TO ASSURE YOU OF THE SINCERE PENITENCE AND THE DEEP REGRET OF THE ONE WHO INFLICTED THE INJURY, AND OF HIS EARNEST DESIRE TO MAKE ANY REPARATIONS IN HIS POWER.
HOW CAN REPARATATIONS BE MADE TO THE DEAD?
HOW INDEED.
AND BY THE VERY SAME TOKEN ANY INJURY YOU MAY YOURSELF BE ABLE TO INFLICT BY MEANS OF THESE THINGS CAN BE NO REPARATION.
NO SATISFACTION.
NO IDEMNITY TO THE ONE WHO IS NO LONGER HERE.
YOU WILL BE ACTING FOR THE LIVING, NOT THE DEAD.
FOR YOUR OWN SATISFACTION, MISS FAULKNER.
FOR YOUR OWN GRATIFICATION AND YOUR OWN REVENGE.
I KNOW.
FROM THIS AND FROM OTHER THINGS THAT HAVE HAPPENED THAT A MARRIAGE IS CONTEMPLATED.
THIS IS QUITE TRUE.

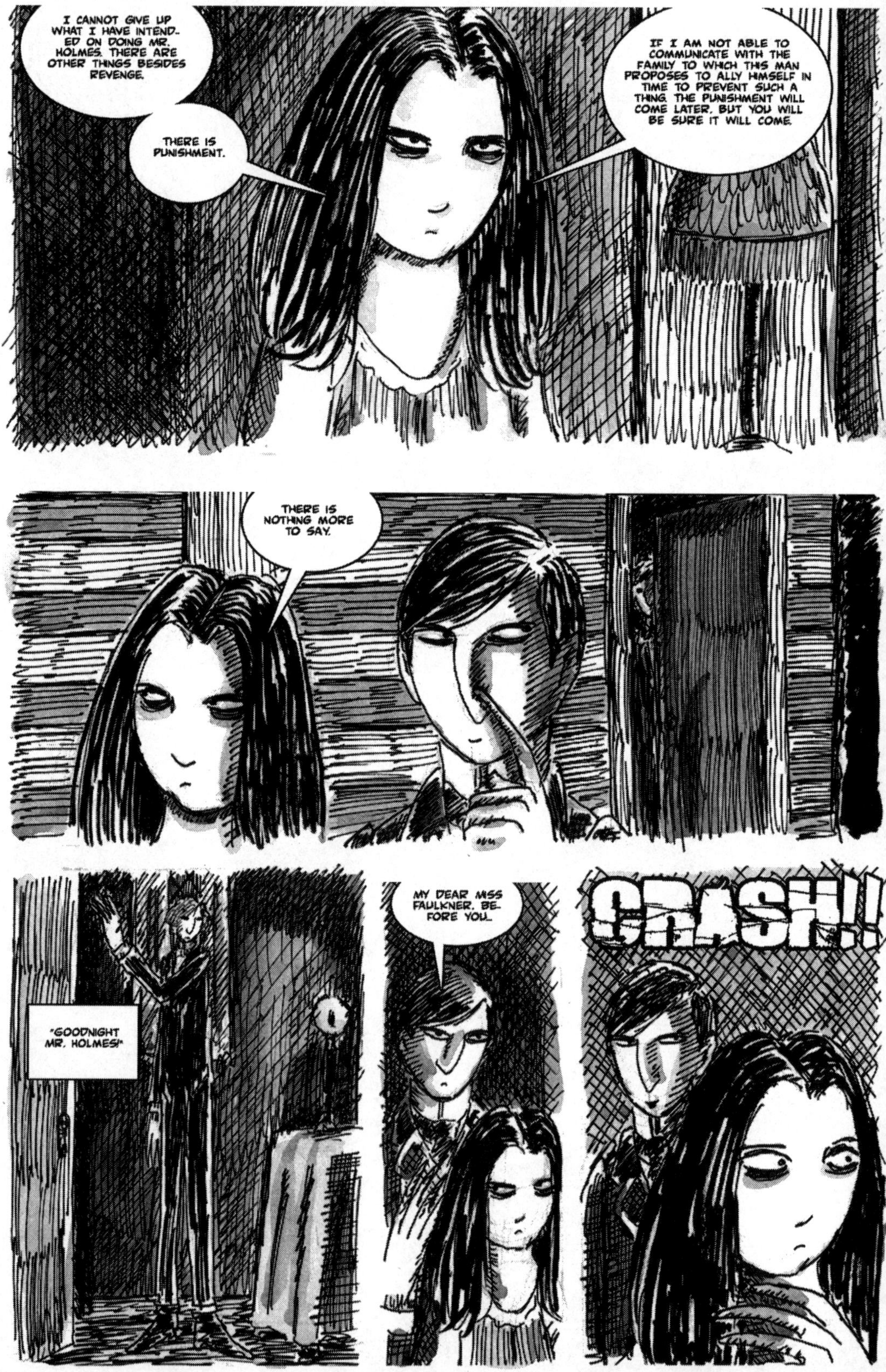
I CANNOT GIVE UP WHAT I HAVE INTEND-ED ON DOING MR. HOLMES. THERE ARE OTHER THINGS BESIDES REVENGE.
THERE IS PUNISHMENT.
IF I AM NOT ABLE TO COMMUNICATE WITH THE FAMILY TO WHICH THIS MAN PROPOSES TO ALLY HIMSELF IN TIME TO PREVENT SUCH A THING THE PUNISHMENT WILL COME LATER. BUT YOU WILL BE SURE IT WILL COME.
THERE IS NOTHING MORE TO SAY.
"GOODNIGHT MR. HOLMES!"
MY DEAR MISS FAULKNER. BE-FORE YOU..
CRASH!!

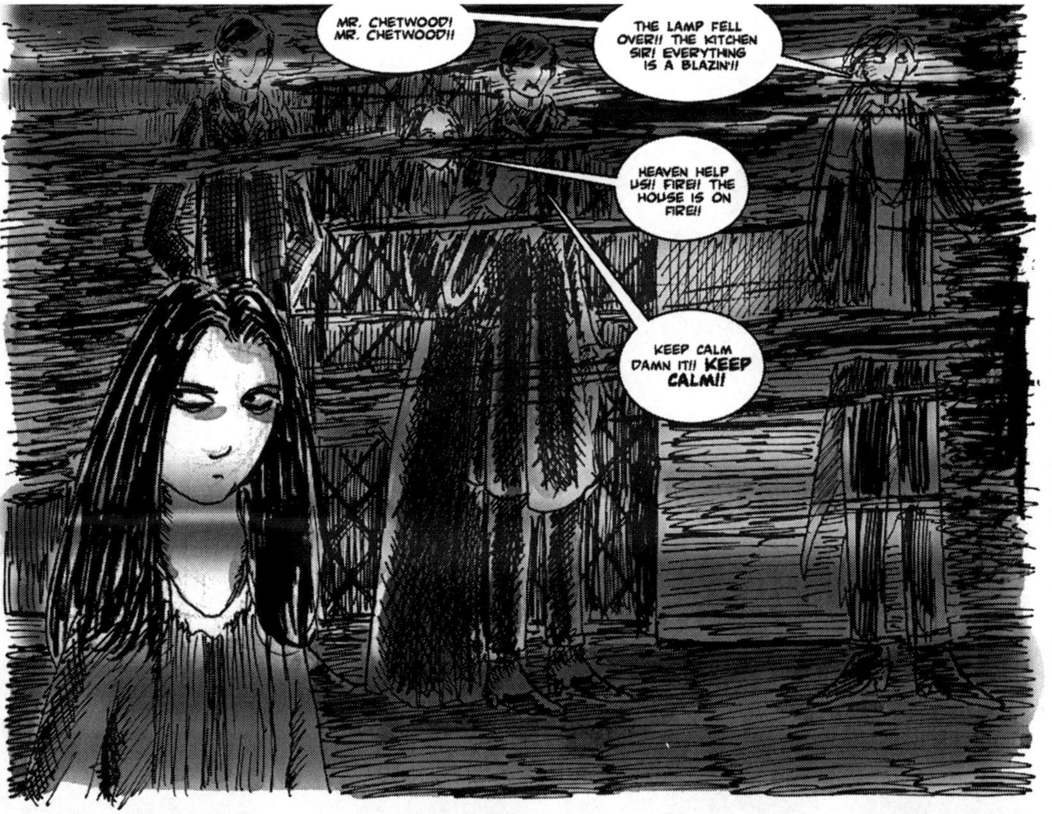
MR. CHETWOOD! MR. CHETWOOD!!
THE LAMP FELL OVER!! THE KITCHEN SIR! EVERYTHING IS A BLAZIN'!!
HEAVEN HELP US!! FIRE!! THE HOUSE IS ON FIRE!!
KEEP CALM DAMN IT!! KEEP CALM!!

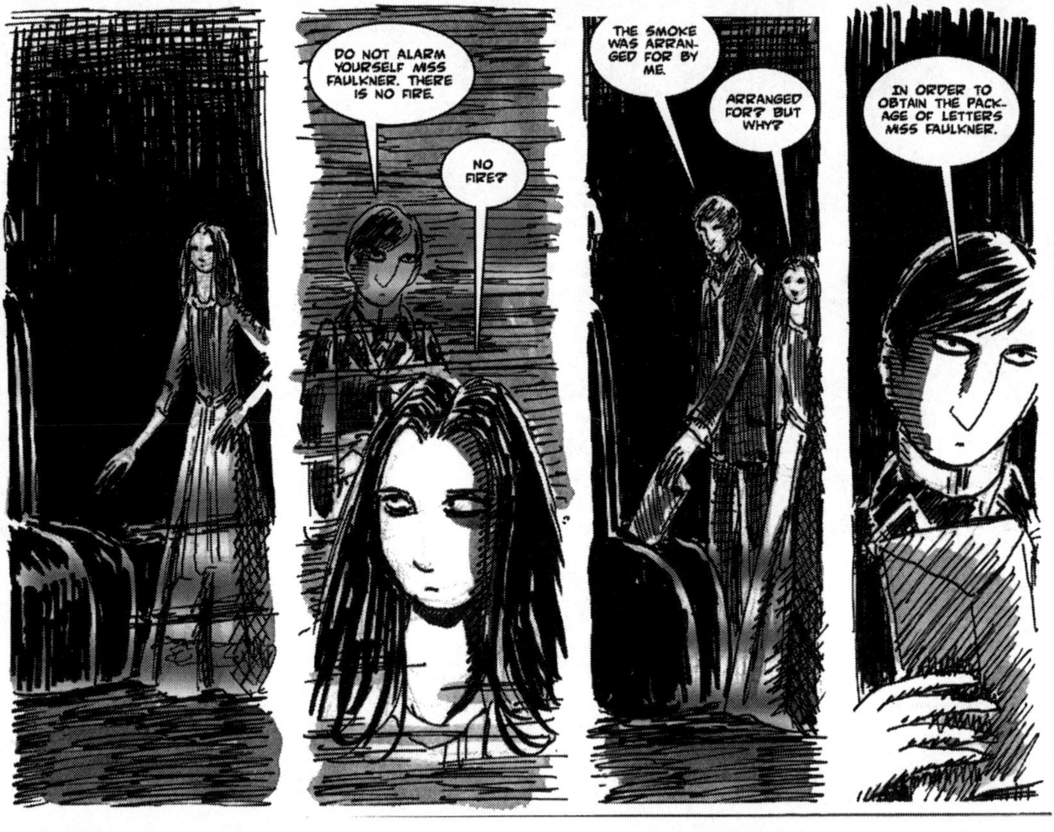
DO NOT ALARM YOURSELF MISS FAULKNER. THERE IS NO FIRE.
NO FIRE?
THE SMOKE WAS ARRANGED FOR BY ME.
ARRANGED FOR? BUT WHY?
IN ORDER TO OBTAIN THE PACKAGE OF LETTERS MISS FAULKNER.

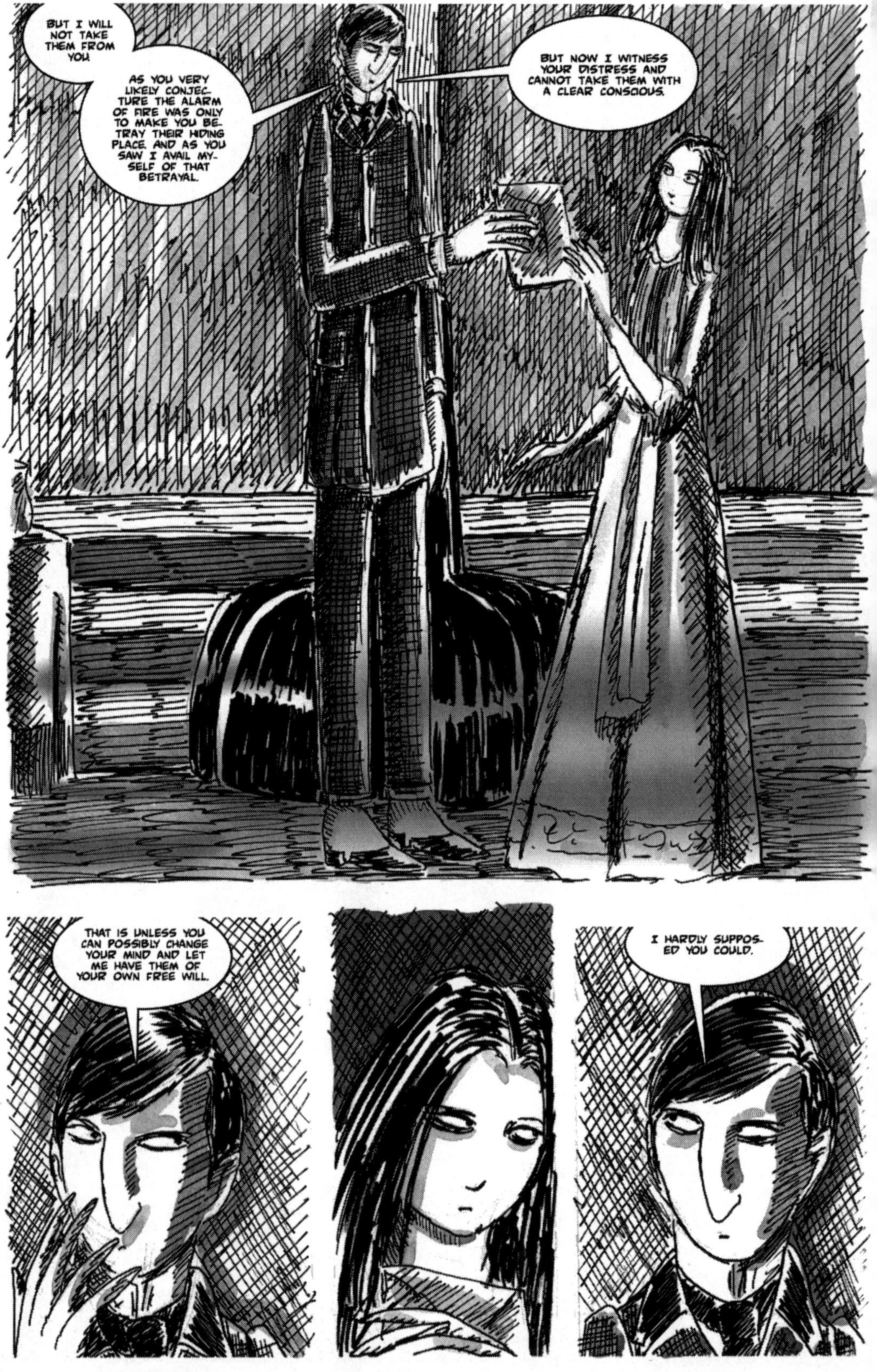
BUT I WILL NOT TAKE THEM FROM YOU.
AS YOU VERY LIKELY CONJECTURE THE ALARM OF FIRE WAS ONLY TO MAKE YOU BETRAY THEIR HIDING PLACE. AND AS YOU SAW I AVAIL MYSELF OF THAT BETRAYAL.
BUT NOW I WITNESS YOUR DISTRESS AND CANNOT TAKE THEM WITH A CLEAR CONSCIOUS.
THAT IS UNLESS YOU CAN POSSIBLY CHANGE YOUR MIND AND LET ME HAVE THEM OF YOUR OWN FREE WILL.
I HARDLY SUPPOSED YOU COULD.

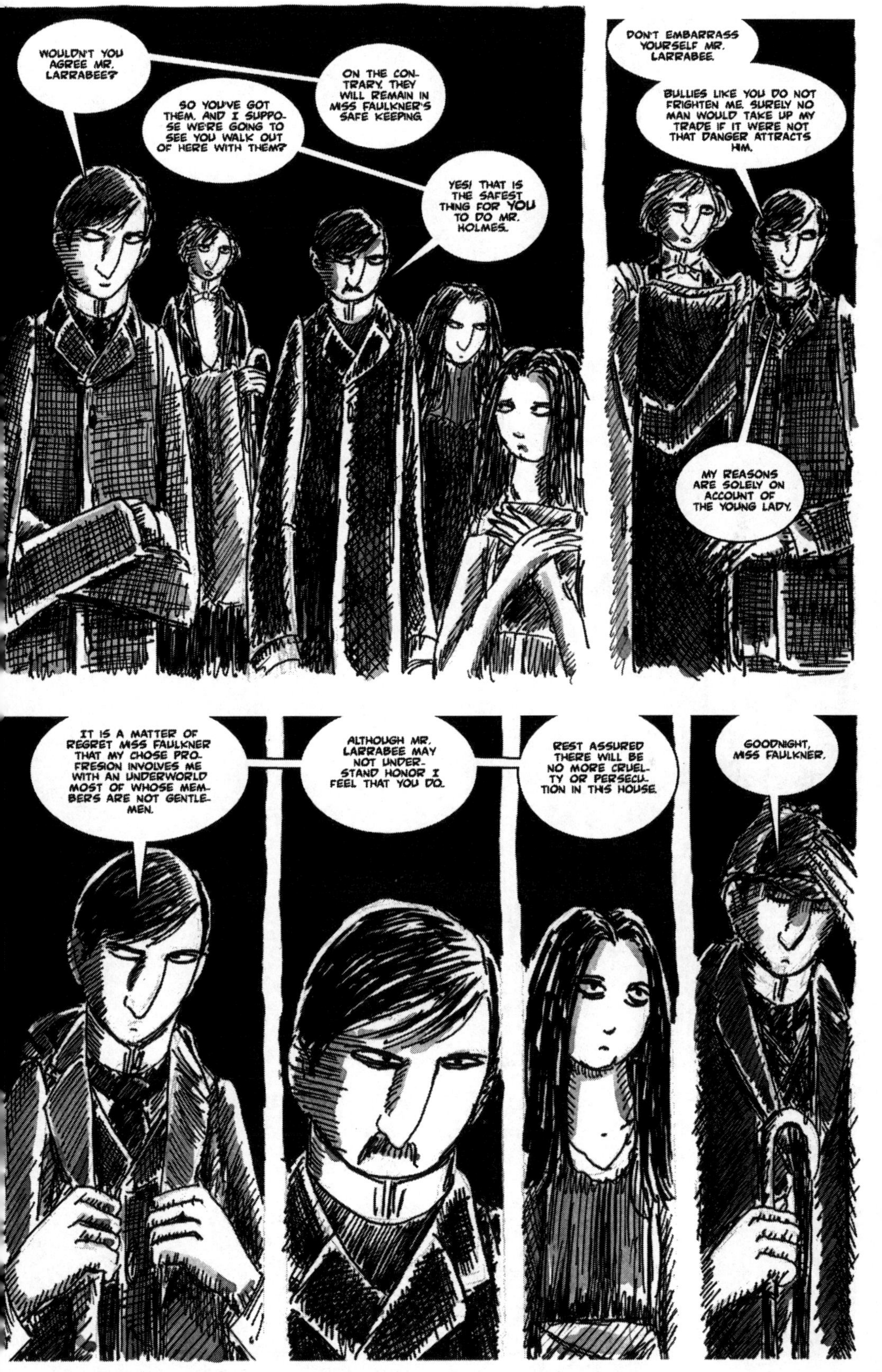

WOULDN'T YOU AGREE MR. LARRABEE?
SO YOU'VE GOT THEM. AND I SUPPOSE SEE WE'RE GOING TO SEE YOU WALK OUT OF HERE WITH THEM?
ON THE CONTRARY. THEY WILL REMAIN IN MISS FAULKNER'S SAFE KEEPING.
YES! THAT IS THE SAFEST THING FOR YOU TO DO MR. HOLMES.
DON'T EMBARRASS YOURSELF MR. LARRABEE.
BULLIES LIKE YOU DO NOT FRIGHTEN ME. SURELY NO MAN WOULD TAKE UP MY TRADE IF IT WERE NOT THAT DANGER ATTRACTS HIM.
MY REASONS ARE SOLELY ON ACCOUNT OF THE YOUNG LADY.
IT IS A MATTER OF REGRET MISS FAULKNER THAT MY CHOSE PROFRESION INVOLVES ME WITH AN UNDERWORLD MOST OF WHOSE MEMBERS ARE NOT GENTLEMEN.
ALTHOUGH MR. LARRABEE MAY NOT UNDERSTAND HONOR I FEEL THAT YOU DO.
REST ASSURED THERE WILL BE NO MORE CRUELTY OR PERSECUTION IN THIS HOUSE.
GOODNIGHT, MISS FAULKNER.

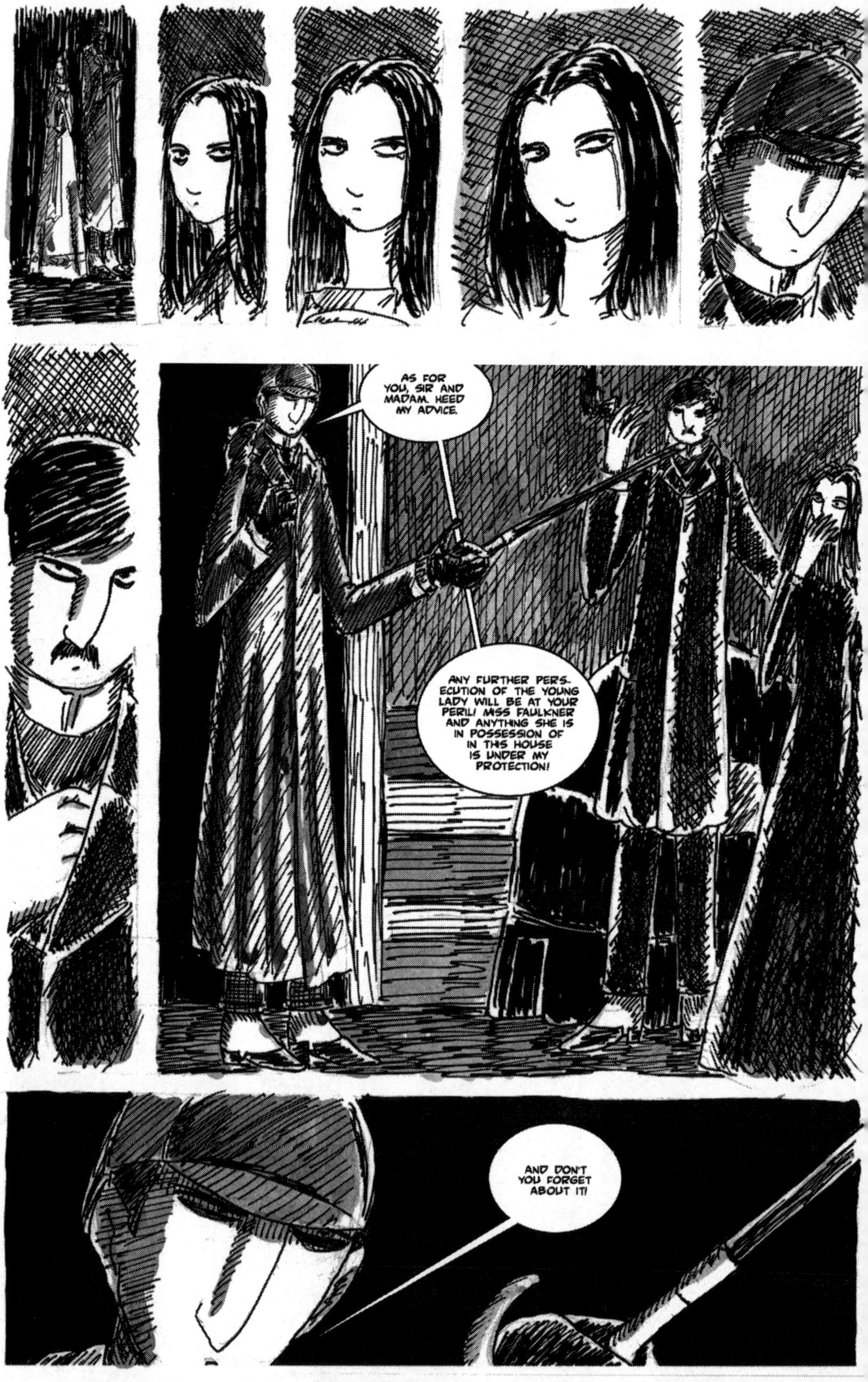
AS FOR YOU, SIR AND MADAM, HEED MY ADVICE.
ANY FURTHER PERSECUTION OF THE YOUNG LADY WILL BE AT YOUR PERIL! MISS FAULKNER AND ANYTHING SHE IS IN POSSESSION OF IN THIS HOUSE IS UNDER MY PROTECTION!
AND DON'T YOU FORGET ABOUT IT!

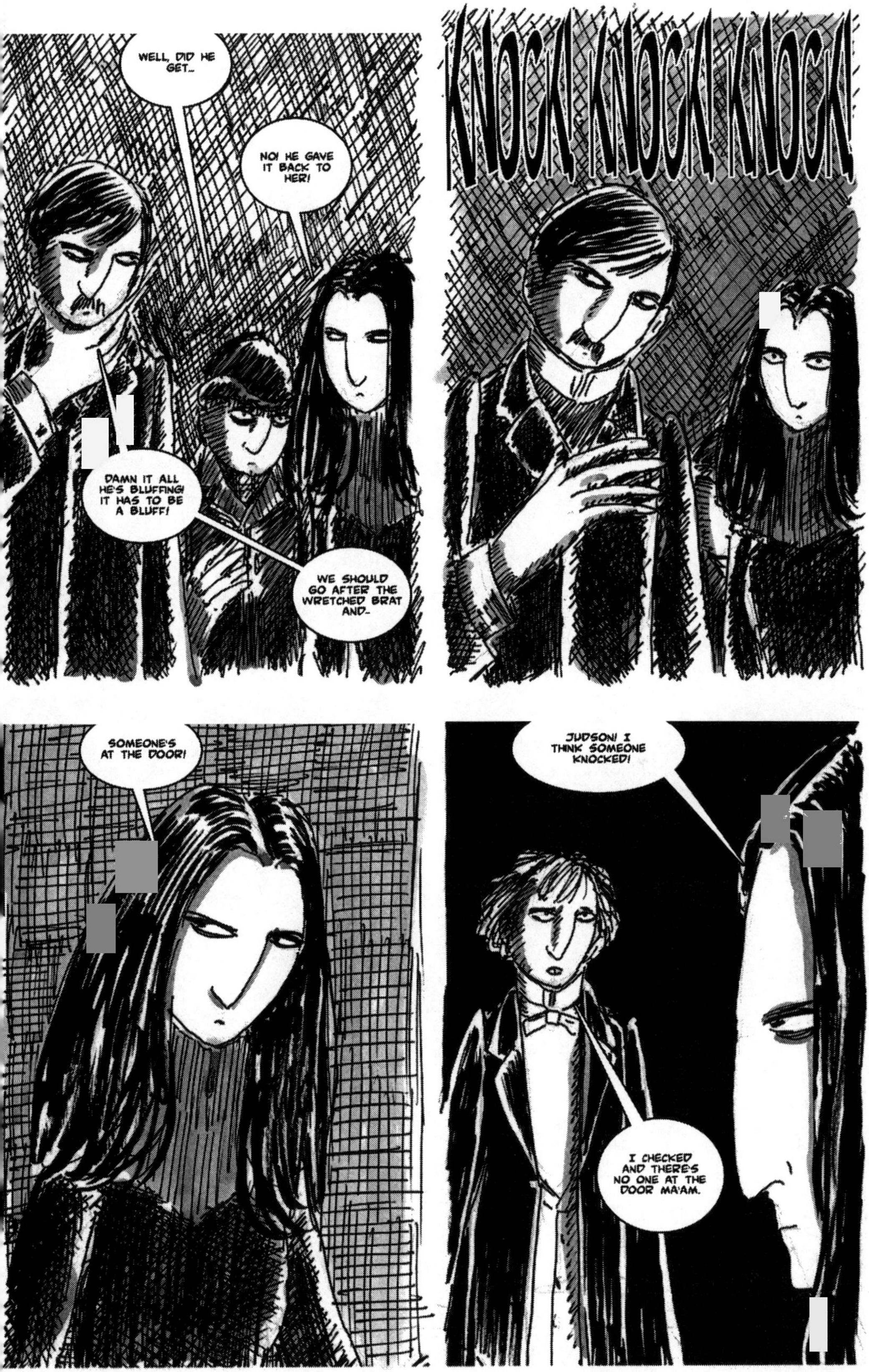

WELL, DID HE GET...
NO! HE GAVE IT BACK TO HER!
DAMN IT ALL HE'S BLUFFING! IT HAS TO BE A BLUFF!
WE SHOULD GO AFTER THE WRETCHED BRAT AND...
KNOCK! KNOCK! KNOCK!
SOMEONE'S AT THE DOOR!
JUDSON! I THINK SOMEONE KNOCKED!
I CHECKED AND THERE'S NO ONE AT THE DOOR MA'AM.

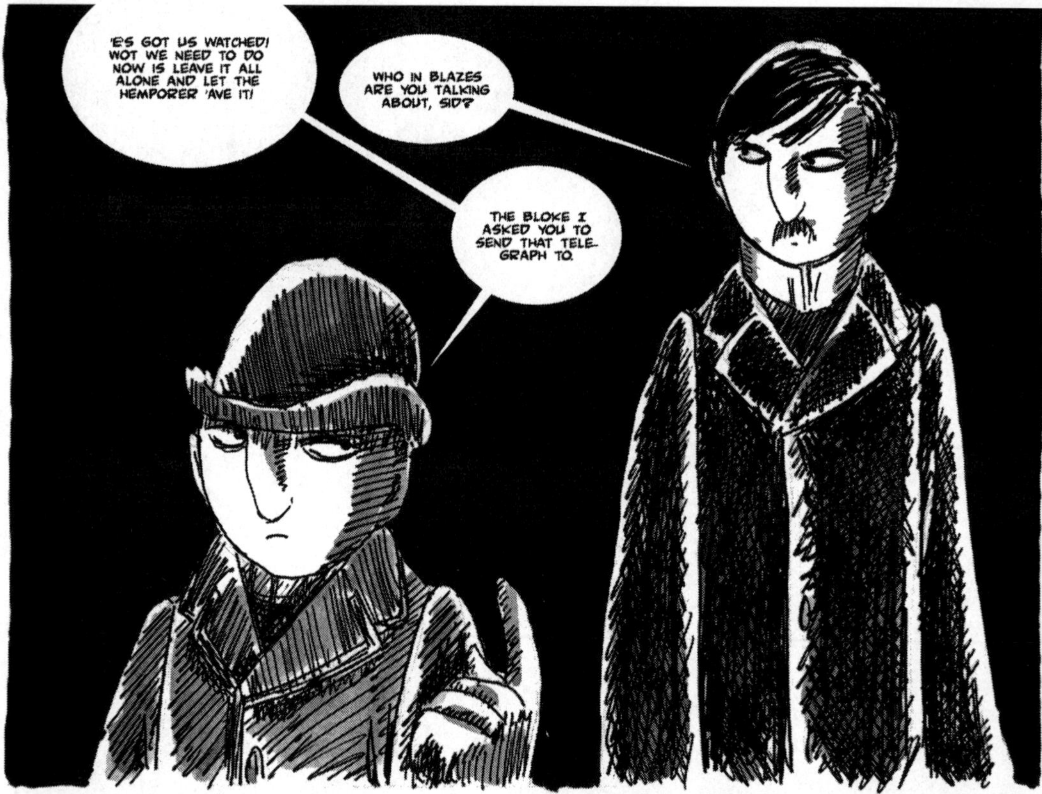
'E'S GOT US WATCHED! WOT WE NEED TO DO NOW IS LEAVE IT ALL ALONE AND LET THE HEMPORER 'AVE IT!
WHO IN BLAZES ARE YOU TALKING ABOUT, SID?
THE BLOKE I ASKED YOU TO SEND THAT TELE-GRAPH TO.

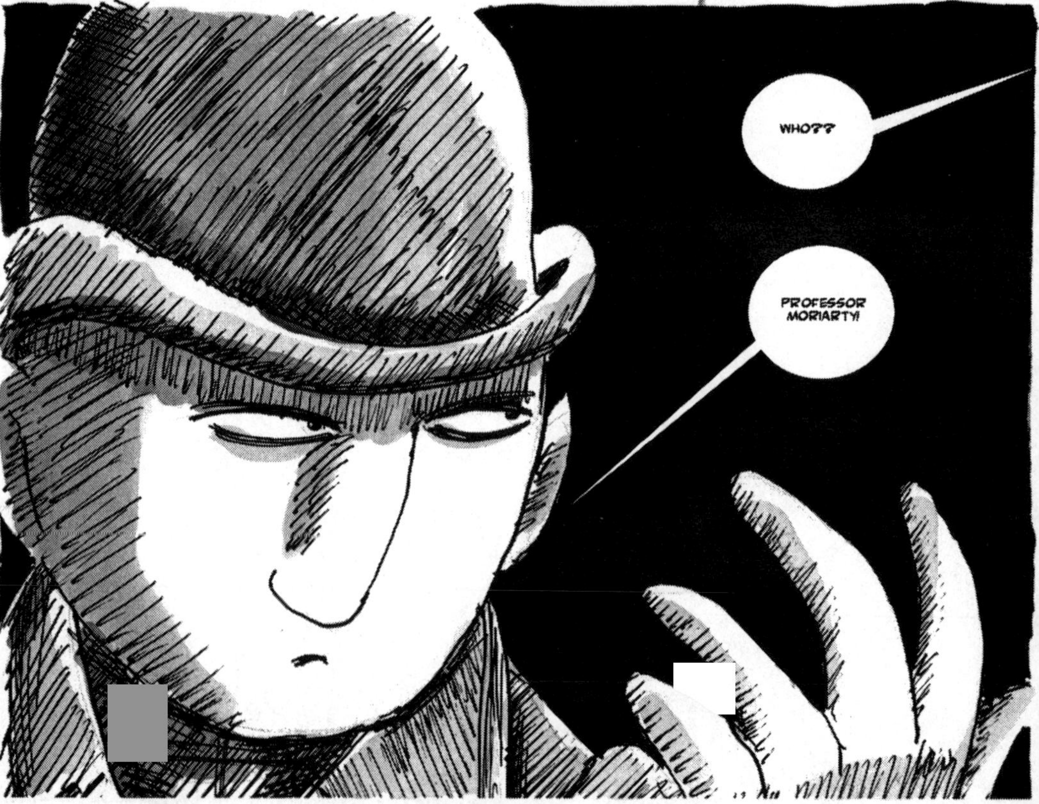
WHO??
PROFESSOR MORIARTY!

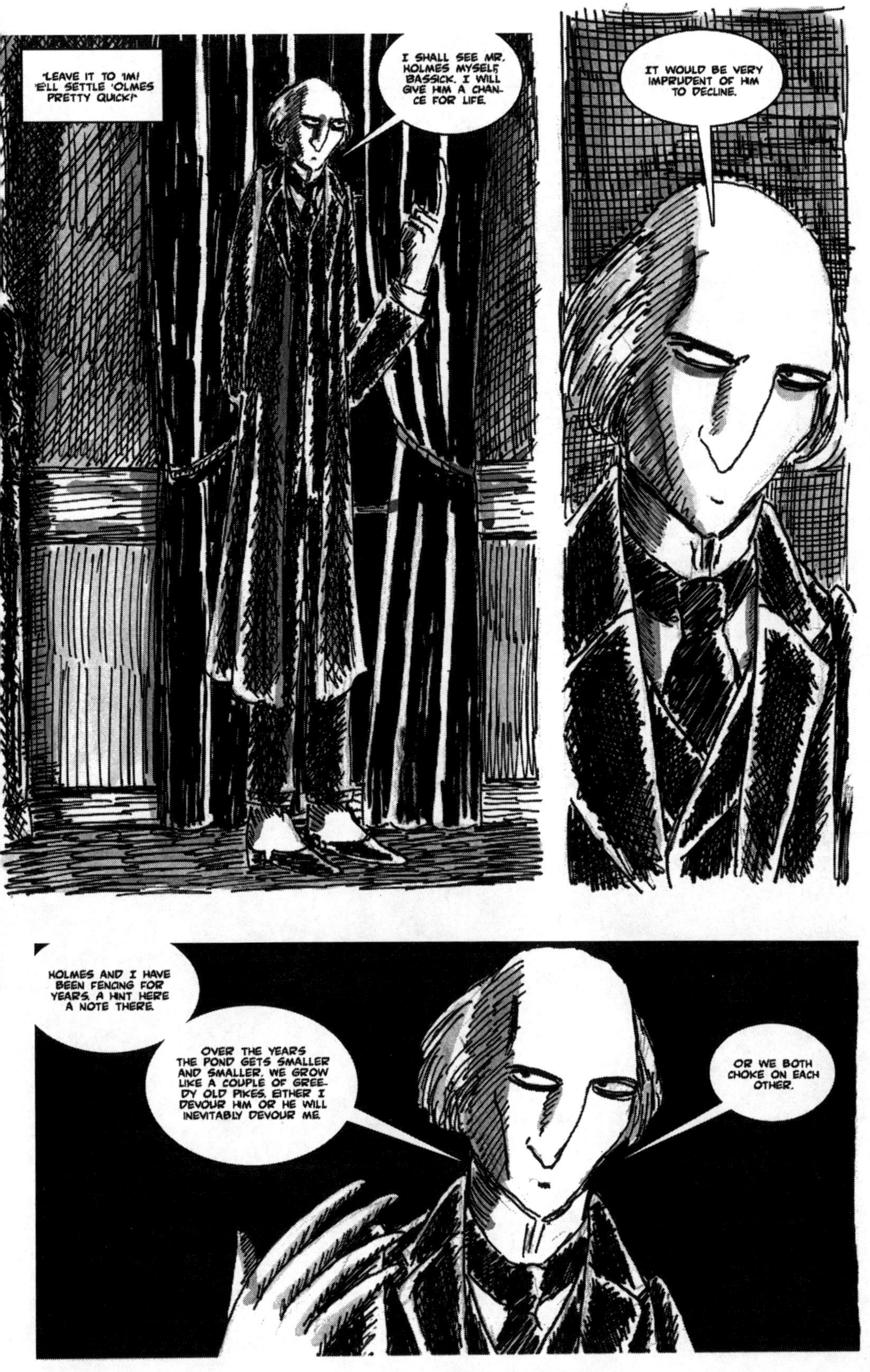
"LEAVE IT TO 'IM! 'E'LL SETTLE 'OLMES PRETTY QUICK!"
I SHALL SEE MR. HOLMES MYSELF BASSICK. I WILL GIVE HIM A CHANCE FOR LIFE.
IT WOULD BE VERY IMPRUDENT OF HIM TO DECLINE.
HOLMES AND I HAVE BEEN FENCING FOR YEARS. A HINT HERE A NOTE THERE.
OVER THE YEARS THE POND GETS SMALLER AND SMALLER. WE GROW LIKE A COUPLE OF GREEDY OLD PIKES. EITHER I DEVOUR HIM OR HE WILL INEVITABLY DEVOUR ME.
OR WE BOTH CHOKE ON EACH OTHER.

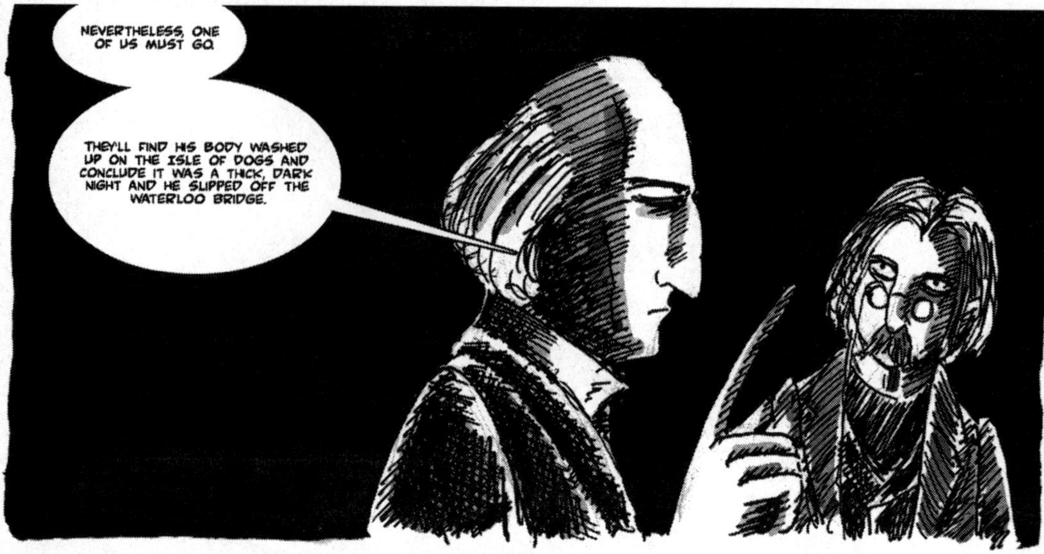
NEVERTHELESS, ONE OF US MUST GO.
THEY'LL FIND HIS BODY WASHED UP ON THE ISLE OF DOGS AND CONCLUDE IT WAS A THICK, DARK NIGHT AND HE SLIPPED OFF THE WATERLOO BRIDGE.

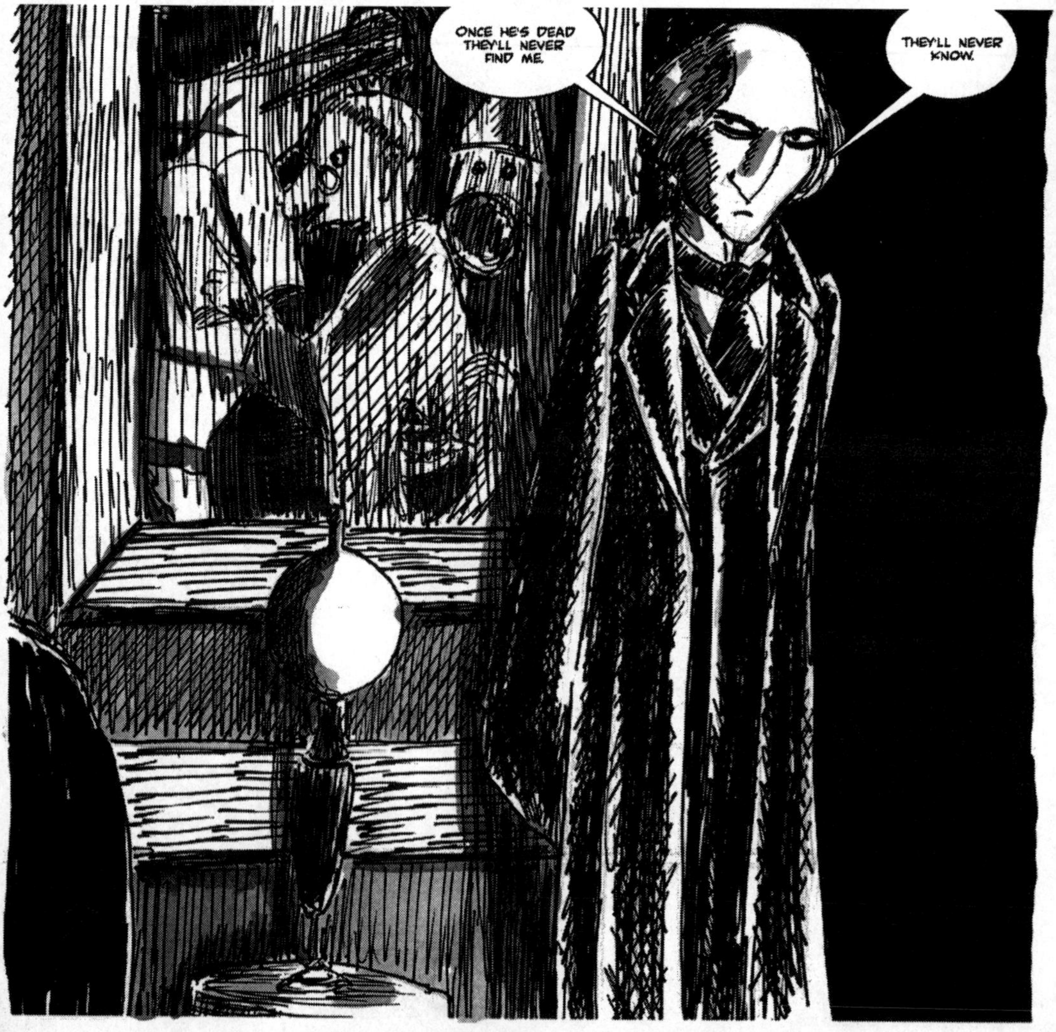
ONCE HE'S DEAD THEY'LL NEVER FIND ME.
THEY'LL NEVER KNOW.

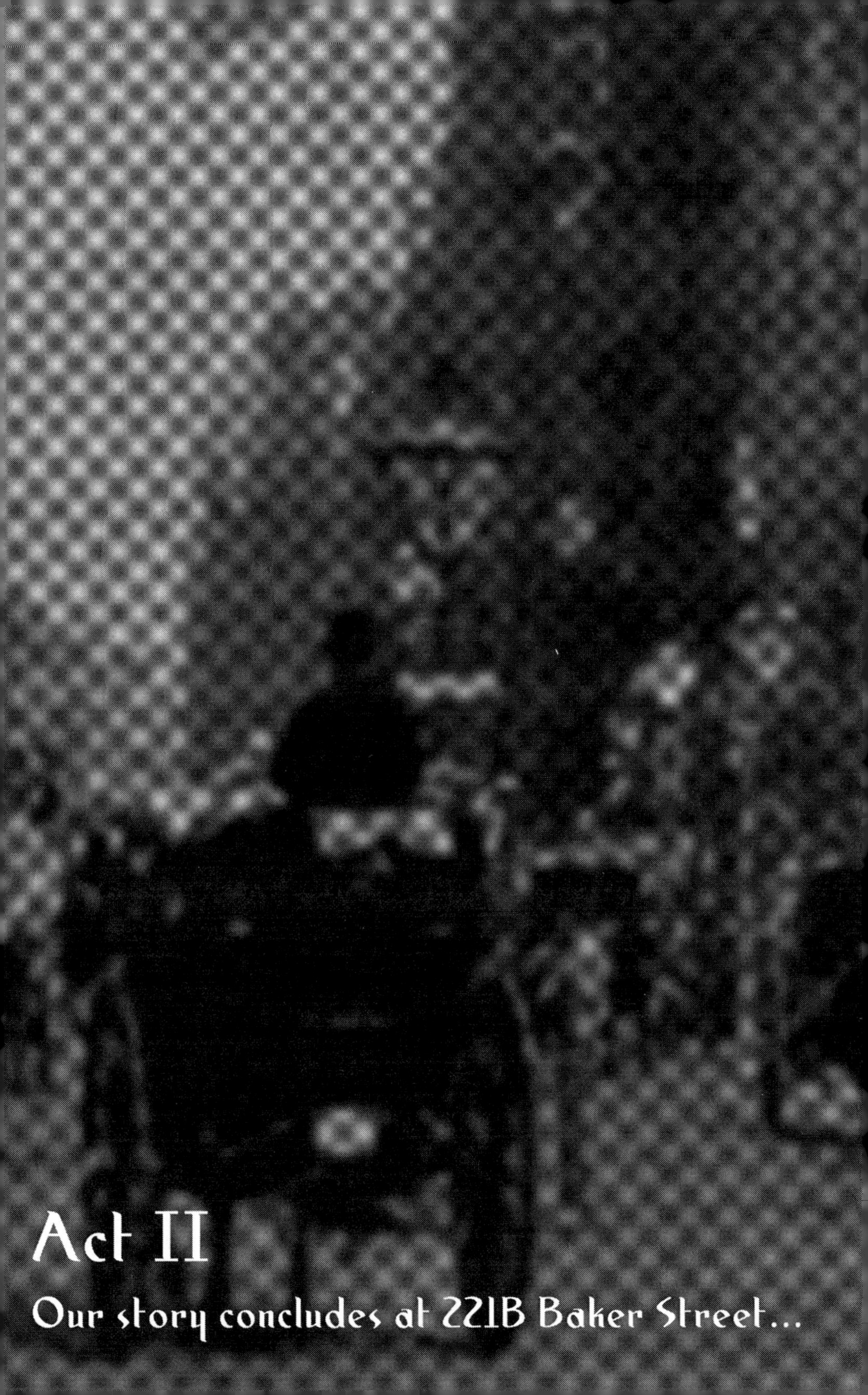

Act II

Our story concludes at 221B Baker Street...

It would not be until April of 1891 that I would see my good friend and colleague Sherlock Holmes again..

My marriage had drifted us away from each other. From time to time I would hear vague accounts of his doings.

Beyond these signs of activity, however, which I merely shared with all the readers of the daily press, I knew little of my former friend and companion.

221B

One morning in late April I was returning from a journey to a patient, when my way was led to Baker Street..

As I passed the well remembered door I was seized with a keen desire to see Holmes again.

Even as I looked up I could see his tall, sparse figure pass twice in a dark silhouette against the blinds.

He was pacing the room swiftly, eagerly, with his head sunk upon his chest and his hands clasp behind him.

To me, who knew his every mood and habit, his attitude and matter told their own story.

He was at work again.

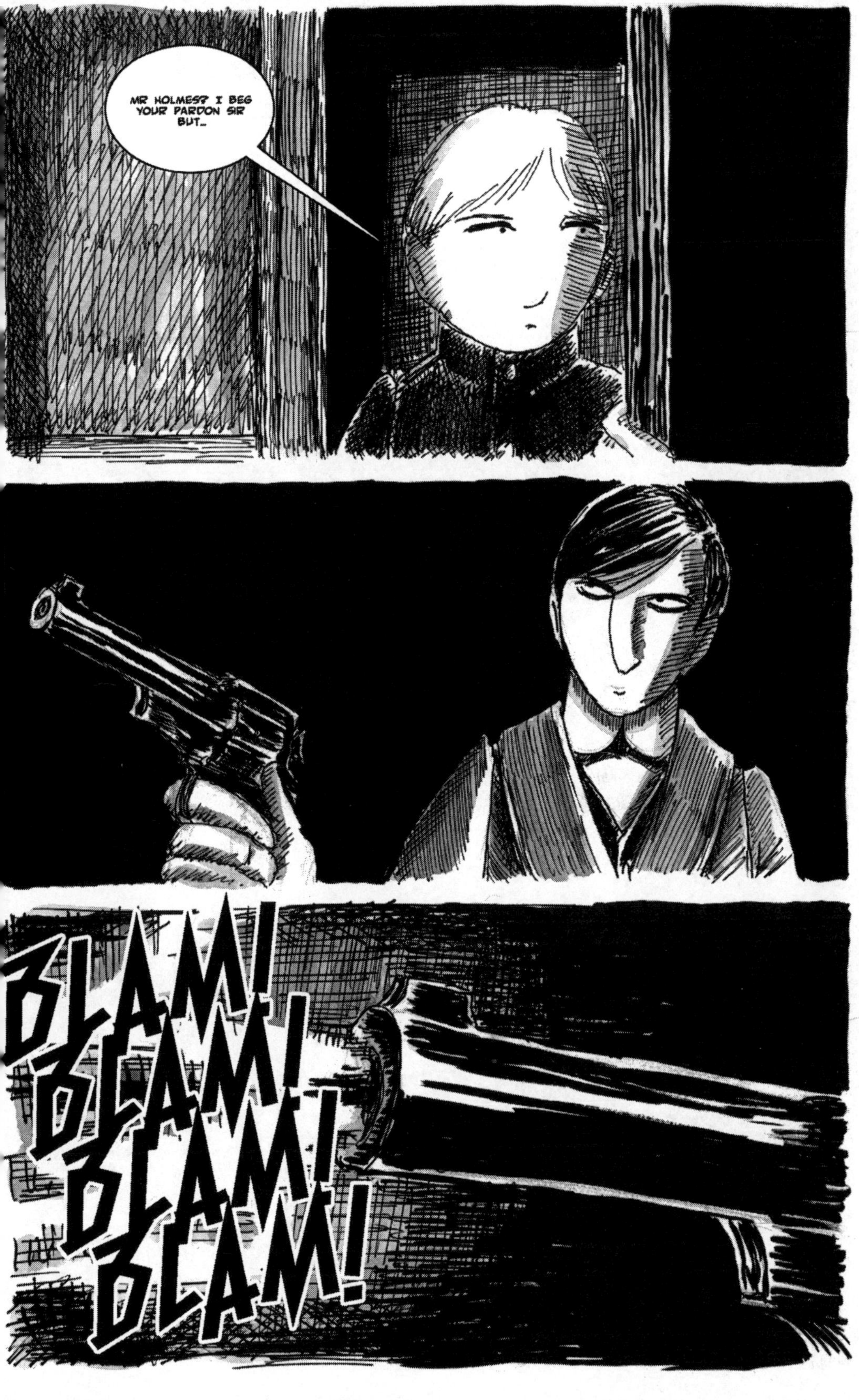
MR HOLMES? I BEG YOUR PARDON SIR BUT...
BLAM! BLAM! BLAM! BLAM!

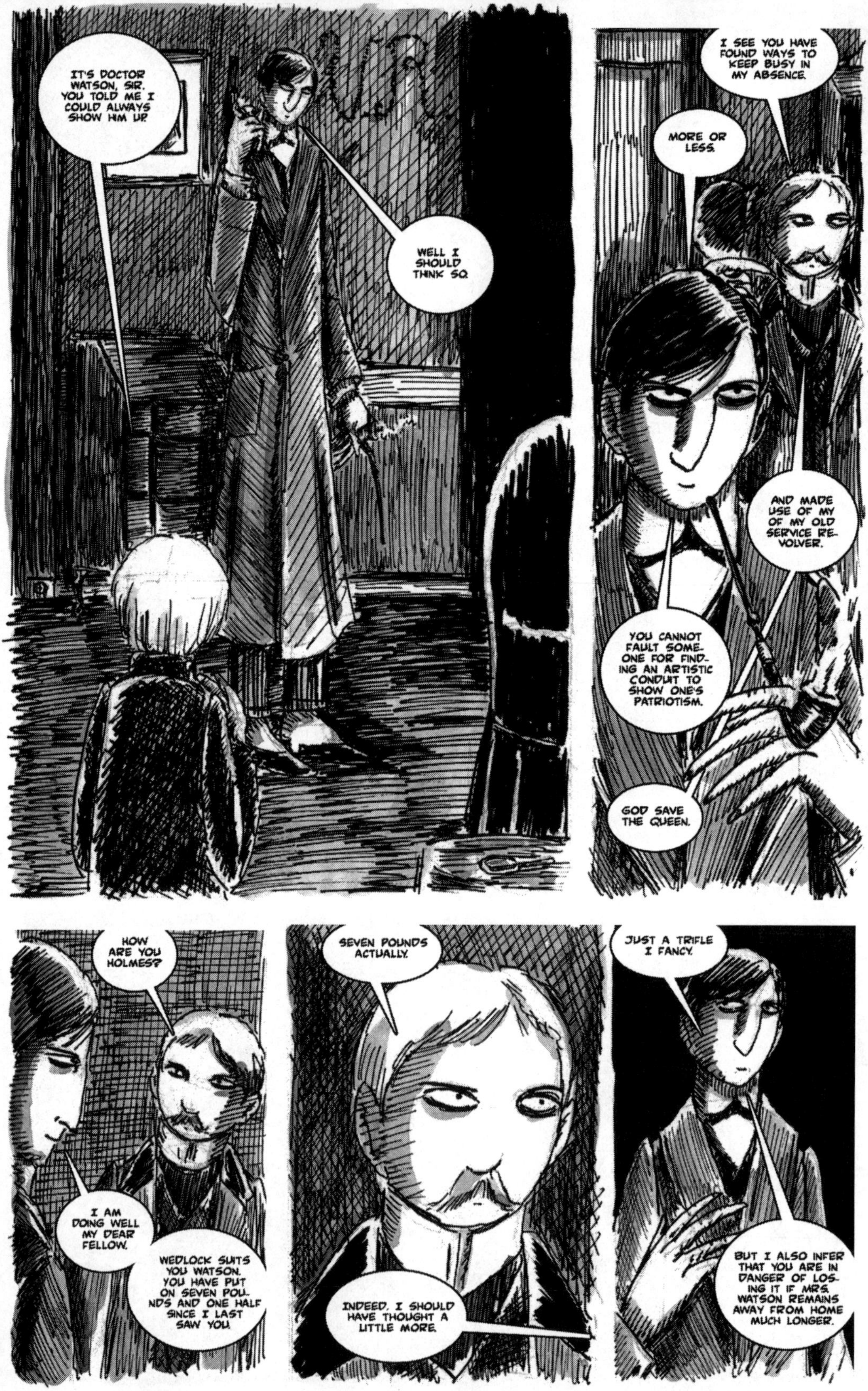
IT'S DOCTOR WATSON, SIR. YOU TOLD ME I COULD ALWAYS SHOW HIM UP.
WELL I SHOULD THINK SO.
I SEE YOU HAVE FOUND WAYS TO KEEP BUSY IN MY ABSENCE.
MORE OR LESS.
AND MADE USE OF MY OF MY OLD SERVICE RE-VOLVER.
YOU CANNOT FAULT SOME-ONE FOR FIND-ING AN ARTISTIC CONDUIT TO SHOW ONE'S PATRIOTISM.
GOD SAVE THE QUEEN.
HOW ARE YOU HOLMES?
I AM DOING WELL MY DEAR FELLOW.
WEDLOCK SUITS YOU WATSON. YOU HAVE PUT ON SEVEN POU-NDS AND ONE HALF SINCE I LAST SAW YOU.
SEVEN POUNDS ACTUALLY.
INDEED. I SHOULD HAVE THOUGHT A LITTLE MORE.
JUST A TRIFLE I FANCY.
BUT I ALSO INFER THAT YOU ARE IN DANGER OF LOS-ING IT IF MRS. WATSON REMAINS AWAY FROM HOME MUCH LONGER.

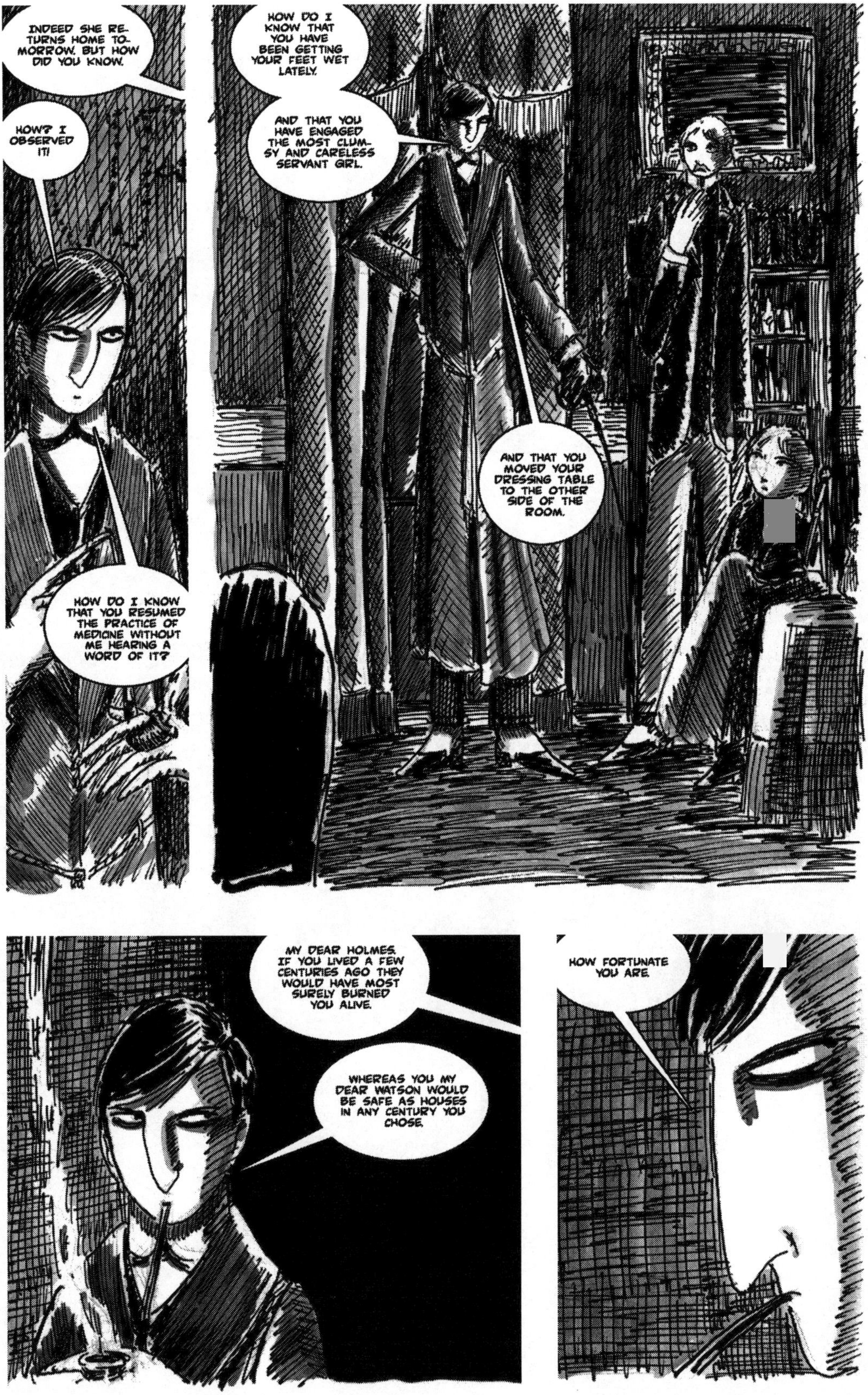
INDEED SHE RETURNS HOME TOMORROW. BUT HOW DID YOU KNOW.
HOW? I OBSERVED IT!
HOW DO I KNOW THAT YOU RESUMED THE PRACTICE OF MEDICINE WITHOUT ME HEARING A WORD OF IT?
HOW DO I KNOW THAT YOU HAVE BEEN GETTING YOUR FEET WET LATELY.
AND THAT YOU HAVE ENGAGED THE MOST CLUMSY AND CARELESS SERVANT GIRL.
AND THAT YOU MOVED YOUR DRESSING TABLE TO THE OTHER SIDE OF THE ROOM.
MY DEAR HOLMES. IF YOU LIVED A FEW CENTURIES AGO THEY WOULD HAVE MOST SURELY BURNED YOU ALIVE.
WHEREAS YOU MY DEAR WATSON WOULD BE SAFE AS HOUSES IN ANY CENTURY YOU CHOSE.
HOW FORTUNATE YOU ARE.

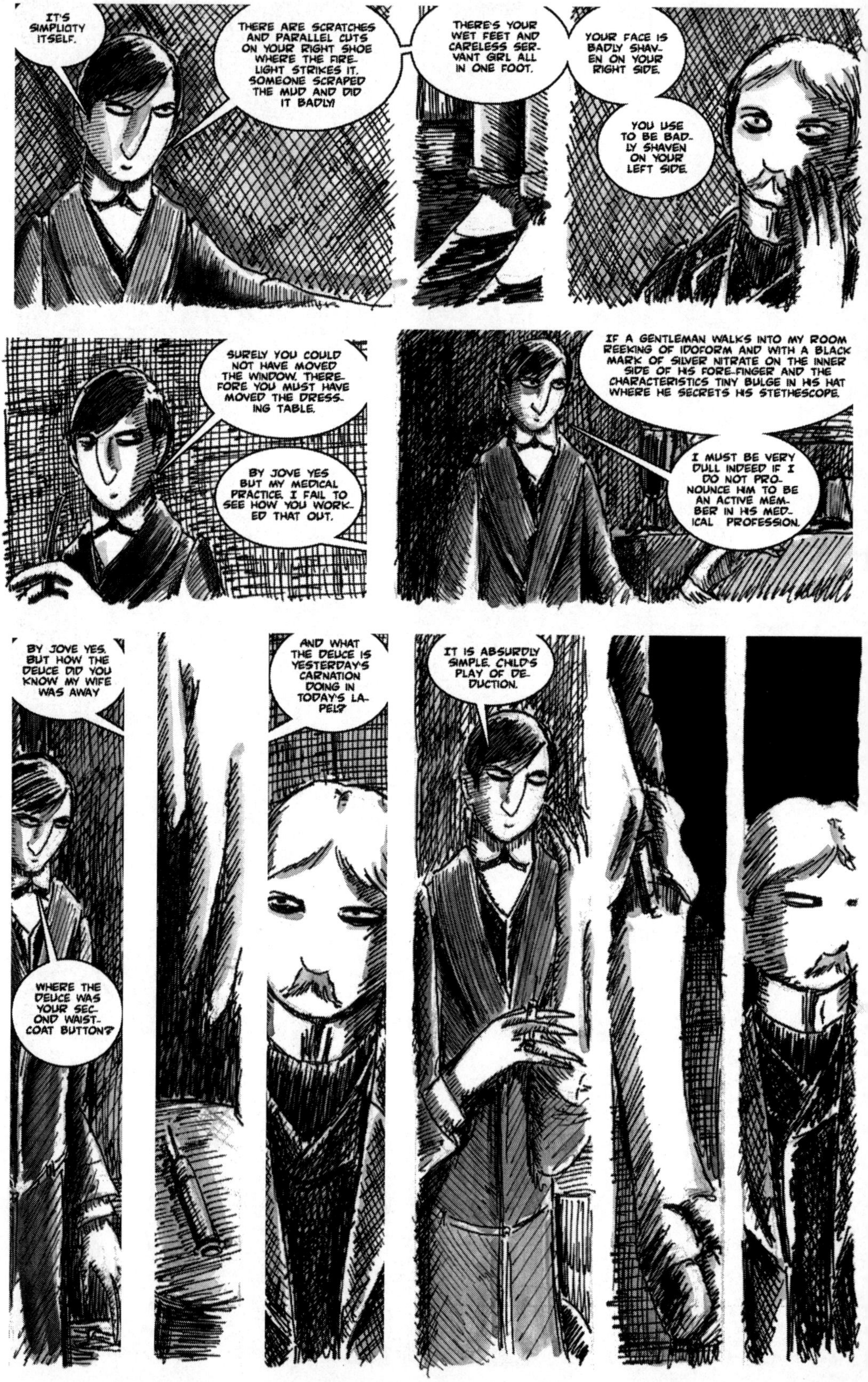
IT'S SIMPLICITY ITSELF.
THERE ARE SCRATCHES AND PARALLEL CUTS ON YOUR RIGHT SHOE WHERE THE FIRE-LIGHT STRIKES IT. SOMEONE SCRAPED THE MUD AND DID IT BADLY!
THERE'S YOUR WET FEET AND CARELESS SERVANT GIRL ALL IN ONE FOOT.
YOUR FACE IS BADLY SHAVEN ON YOUR RIGHT SIDE.
YOU USE TO BE BADLY SHAVEN ON YOUR LEFT SIDE.
SURELY YOU COULD NOT HAVE MOVED THE WINDOW. THEREFORE YOU MUST HAVE MOVED THE DRESSING TABLE.
BY JOVE YES BUT MY MEDICAL PRACTICE. I FAIL TO SEE HOW YOU WORKED THAT OUT.
IF A GENTLEMAN WALKS INTO MY ROOM REEKING OF IDOFORM AND WITH A BLACK MARK OF SILVER NITRATE ON THE INNER SIDE OF HIS FORE-FINGER AND THE CHARACTERISTICS TINY BULGE IN HIS HAT WHERE HE SECRETS HIS STETHESCOPE.
I MUST BE VERY DULL INDEED IF I DO NOT PRONOUNCE HIM TO BE AN ACTIVE MEMBER IN HIS MEDICAL PROFESSION.
BY JOVE YES, BUT HOW THE DEUCE DID YOU KNOW MY WIFE WAS AWAY
WHERE THE DEUCE WAS YOUR SECOND WAIST-COAT BUTTON?
AND WHAT THE DEUCE IS YESTERDAY'S CARNATION DOING IN TODAY'S LAPEL?
IT IS ABSURDLY SIMPLE. CHILD'S PLAY OF DEDUCTION.

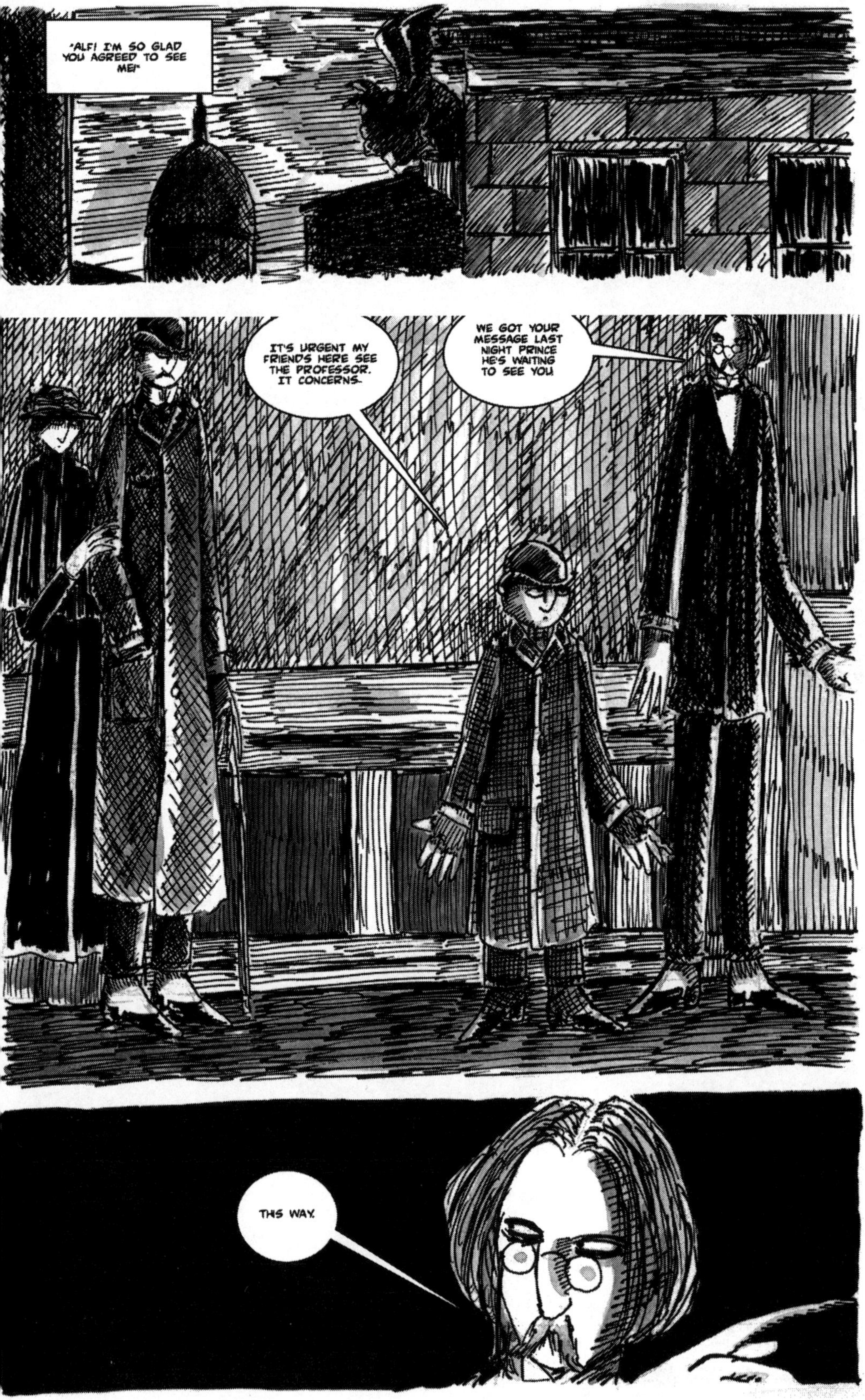
"ALF! I'M SO GLAD YOU AGREED TO SEE ME!"
IT'S URGENT MY FRIENDS HERE SEE THE PROFESSOR. IT CONCERNS-
WE GOT YOUR MESSAGE LAST NIGHT PRINCE HE'S WAITING TO SEE YOU.
THIS WAY.

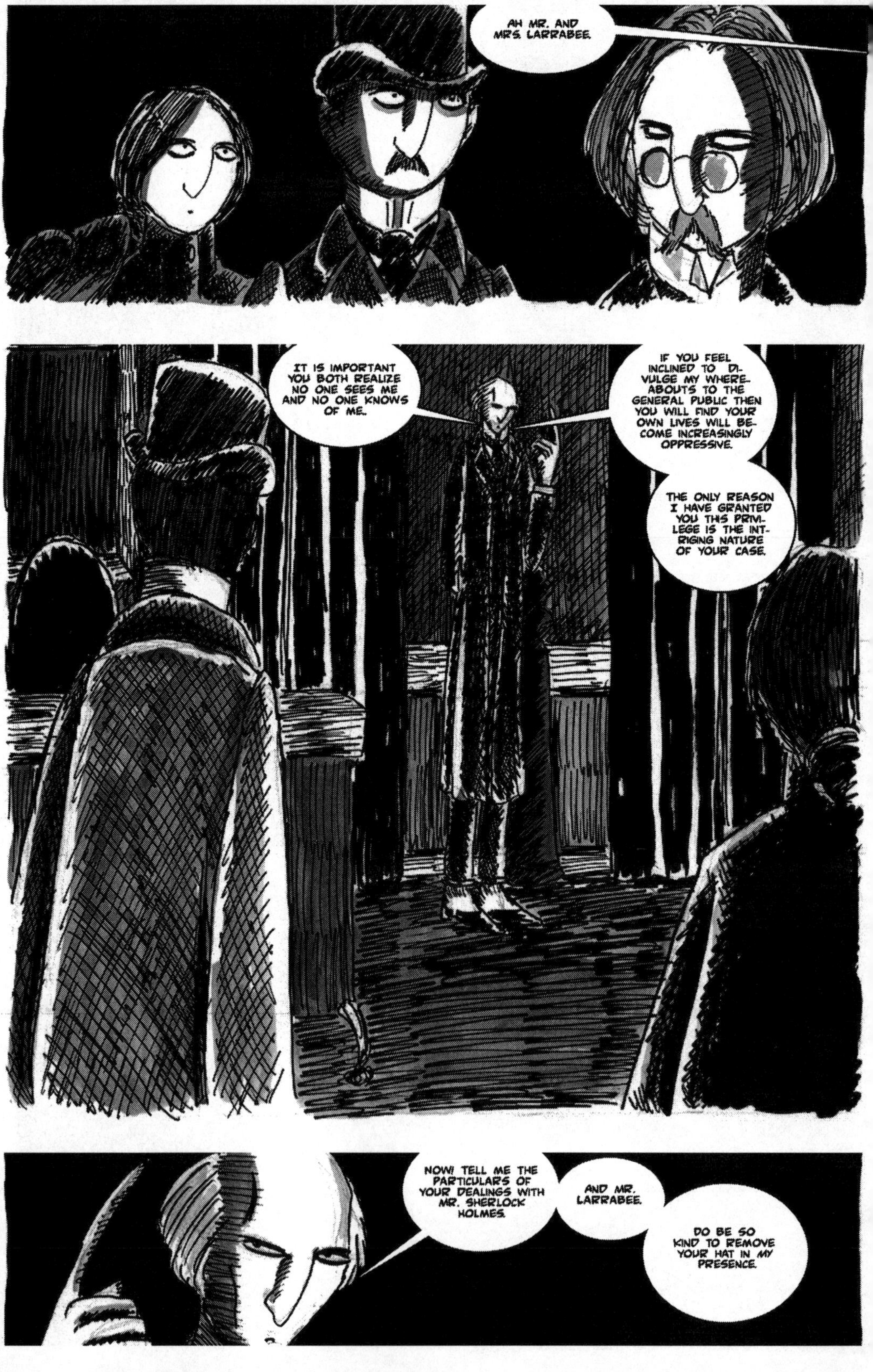
AH MR. AND MRS. LARRABEE.
IT IS IMPORTANT YOU BOTH REALIZE NO ONE SEES ME AND NO ONE KNOWS OF ME.
IF YOU FEEL INCLINED TO DI- VULGE MY WHERE- ABOUTS TO THE GENERAL PUBLIC THEN YOU WILL FIND YOUR OWN LIVES WILL BE- COME INCREASINGLY OPPRESSIVE.
THE ONLY REASON I HAVE GRANTED YOU THIS PRIVI- LEGE IS THE INT- RIGING NATURE OF YOUR CASE.
NOW! TELL ME THE PARTICULARS OF YOUR DEALINGS WITH MR. SHERLOCK HOLMES.
AND MR. LARRABEE.
DO BE SO KIND TO REMOVE YOUR HAT IN MY PRESENCE.

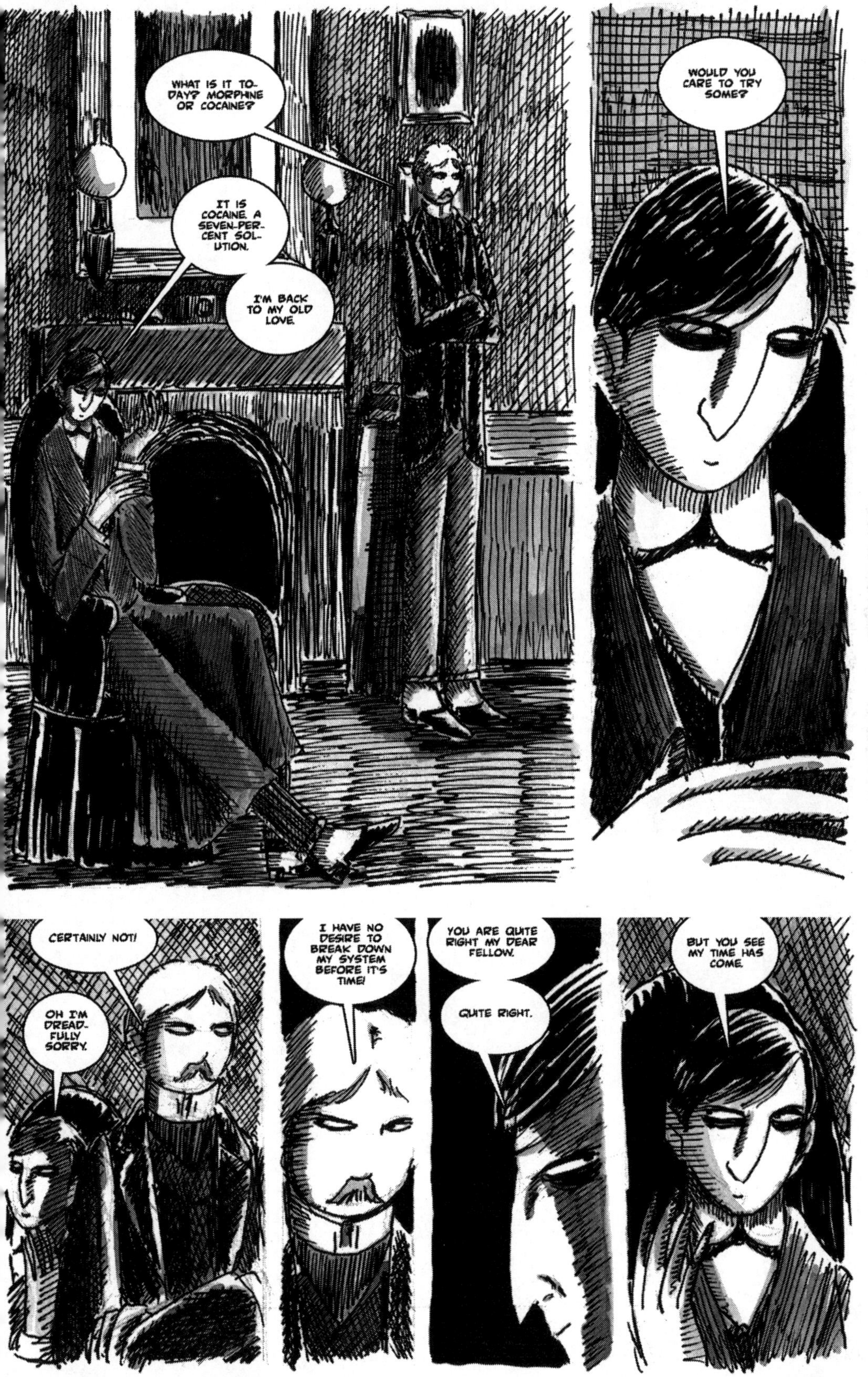
WHAT IS IT TO-DAY? MORPHINE OR COCAINE?
IT IS COCAINE. A SEVEN-PER-CENT SOL-UTION.
I'M BACK TO MY OLD LOVE.
WOULD YOU CARE TO TRY SOME?
CERTAINLY NOT!
OH I'M DREAD-FULLY SORRY.
I HAVE NO DESIRE TO BREAK DOWN MY SYSTEM BEFORE IT'S TIME!
YOU ARE QUITE RIGHT MY DEAR FELLOW.
QUITE RIGHT.
BUT YOU SEE MY TIME HAS COME.

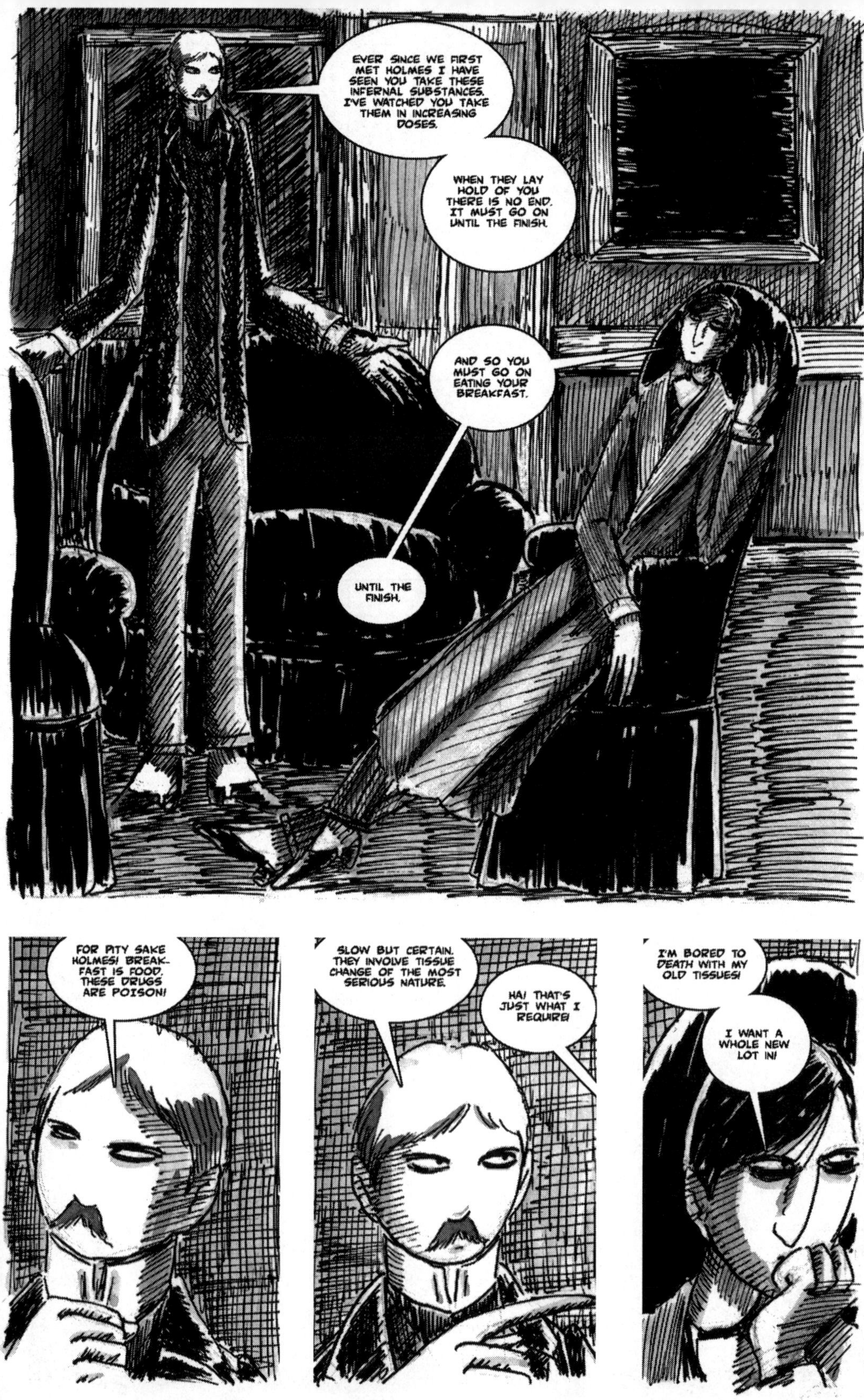
EVER SINCE WE FIRST MET HOLMES I HAVE SEEN YOU TAKE THESE INFERNAL SUBSTANCES. I'VE WATCHED YOU TAKE THEM IN INCREASING DOSES.
WHEN THEY LAY HOLD OF YOU THERE IS NO END. IT MUST GO ON UNTIL THE FINISH.
AND SO YOU MUST GO ON EATING YOUR BREAKFAST.
UNTIL THE FINISH.
FOR PITY SAKE HOLMES! BREAK-FAST IS FOOD. THESE DRUGS ARE POISON!
SLOW BUT CERTAIN. THEY INVOLVE TISSUE CHANGE OF THE MOST SERIOUS NATURE.
HA! THAT'S JUST WHAT I REQUIRE!
I'M BORED TO DEATH WITH MY OLD TISSUES!
I WANT A WHOLE NEW LOT IN!

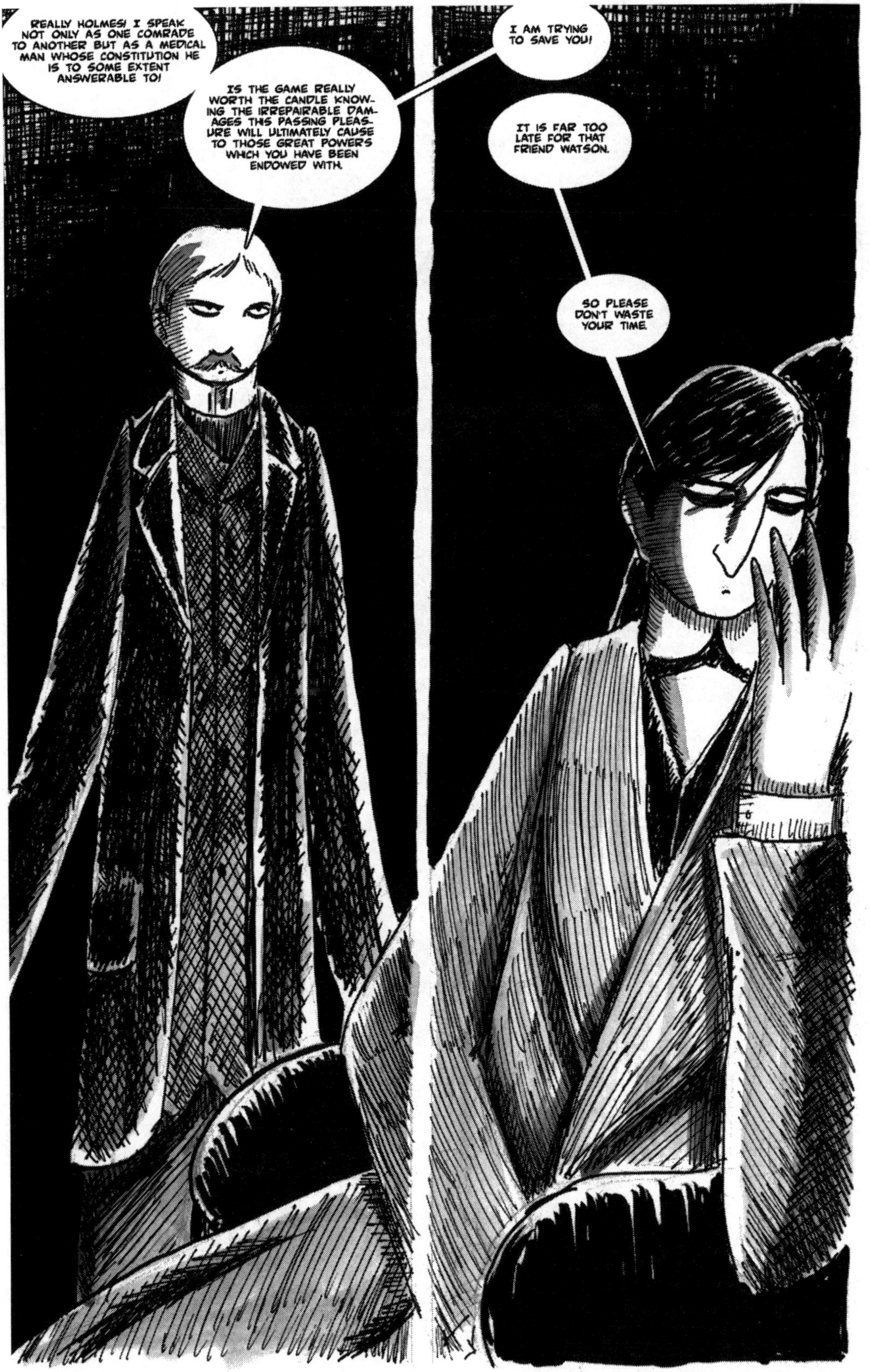
REALLY HOLMES! I SPEAK NOT ONLY AS ONE COMRADE TO ANOTHER BUT AS A MEDICAL MAN WHOSE CONSTITUTION HE IS TO SOME EXTENT ANSWERABLE TO!
IS THE GAME REALLY WORTH THE CANDLE KNOWING THE IRREPAIRABLE DAMAGES THIS PASSING PLEASURE WILL ULTIMATELY CAUSE TO THOSE GREAT POWERS WHICH YOU HAVE BEEN ENDOWED WITH.
I AM TRYING TO SAVE YOU!
IT IS FAR TOO LATE FOR THAT FRIEND WATSON.
SO PLEASE DON'T WASTE YOUR TIME.

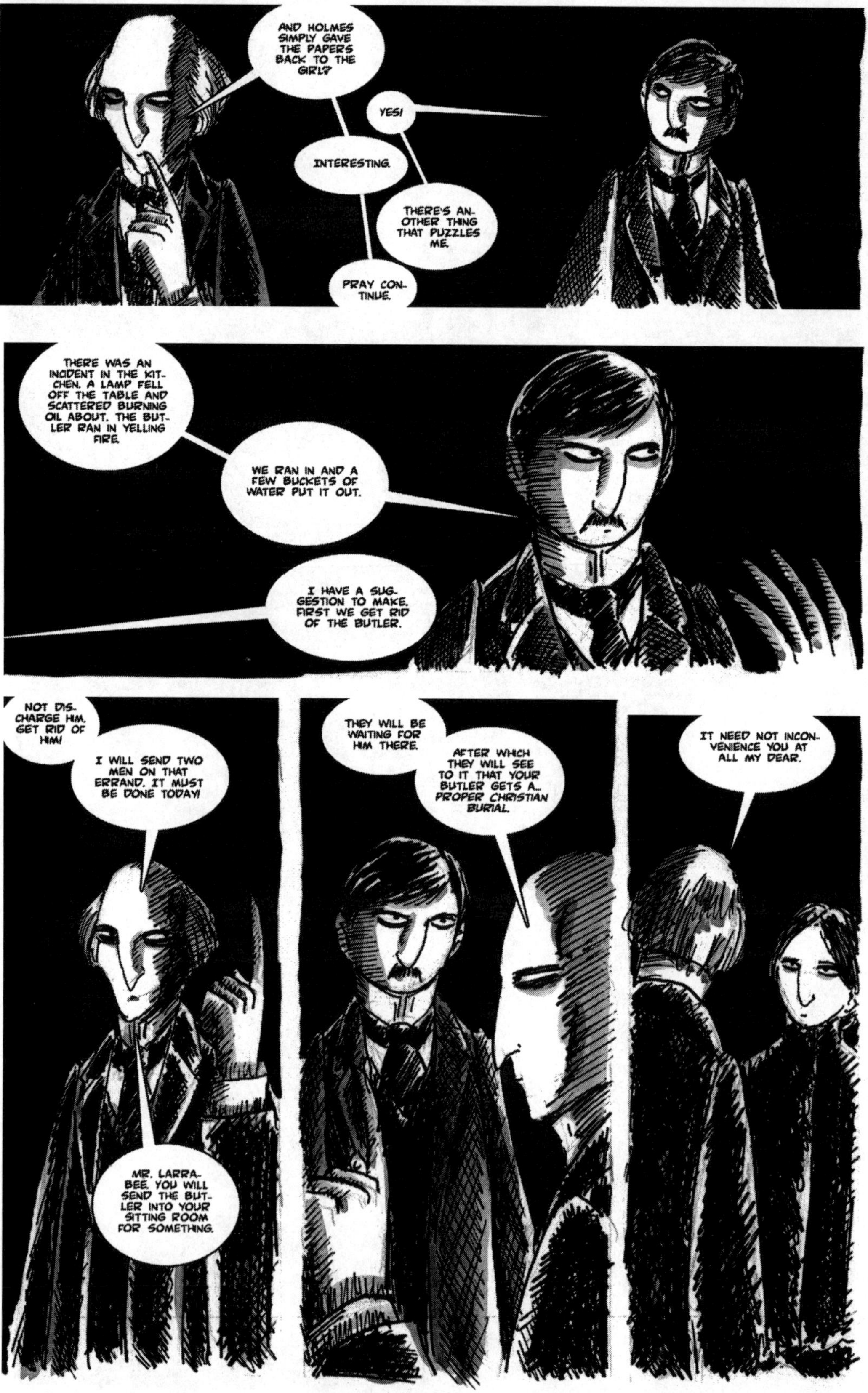
AND HOLMES SIMPLY GAVE THE PAPERS BACK TO THE GIRL?
YES!
INTERESTING.
THERE'S ANOTHER THING THAT PUZZLES ME.
PRAY CONTINUE.
THERE WAS AN INCIDENT IN THE KITCHEN. A LAMP FELL OFF THE TABLE AND SCATTERED BURNING OIL ABOUT. THE BUTLER RAN IN YELLING FIRE.
WE RAN IN AND A FEW BUCKETS OF WATER PUT IT OUT.
I HAVE A SUGGESTION TO MAKE. FIRST WE GET RID OF THE BUTLER.
NOT DISCHARGE HIM. GET RID OF HIM!
I WILL SEND TWO MEN ON THAT ERRAND. IT MUST BE DONE TODAY!
MR. LARRABEE. YOU WILL SEND THE BUTLER INTO YOUR SITTING ROOM FOR SOMETHING.
THEY WILL BE WAITING FOR HIM THERE.
AFTER WHICH THEY WILL SEE TO IT THAT YOUR BUTLER GETS A... PROPER CHRISTIAN BURIAL.
IT NEED NOT INCONVENIENCE YOU AT ALL MY DEAR.

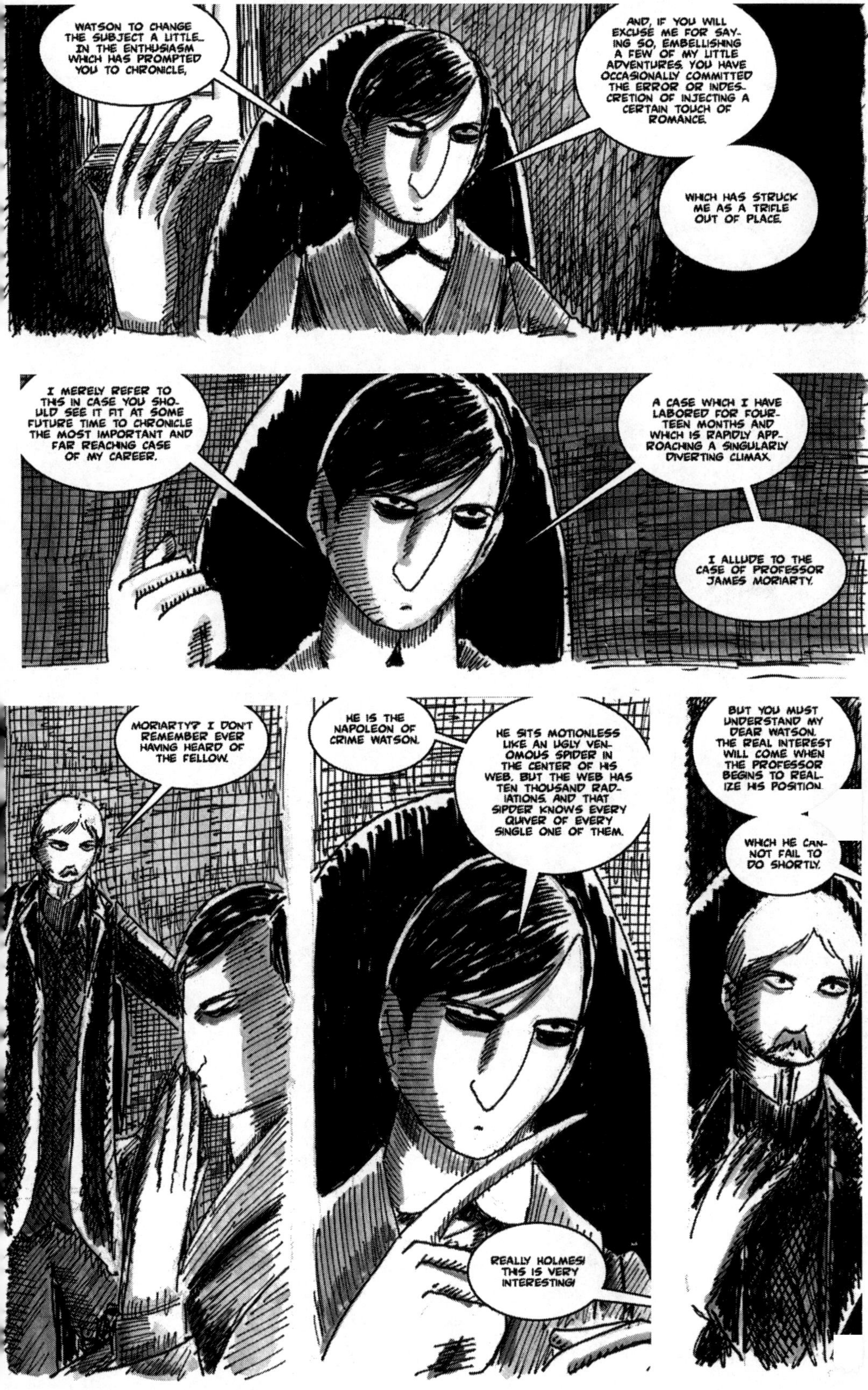
WATSON TO CHANGE THE SUBJECT A LITTLE.. IN THE ENTHUSIASM WHICH HAS PROMPTED YOU TO CHRONICLE,
AND, IF YOU WILL EXCUSE ME FOR SAYING SO, EMBELLISHING A FEW OF MY LITTLE ADVENTURES. YOU HAVE OCCASIONALLY COMMITTED THE ERROR OR INDESCRETION OF INJECTING A CERTAIN TOUCH OF ROMANCE.
WHICH HAS STRUCK ME AS A TRIFLE OUT OF PLACE.
I MERELY REFER TO THIS IN CASE YOU SHOULD SEE IT FIT AT SOME FUTURE TIME TO CHRONICLE THE MOST IMPORTANT AND FAR REACHING CASE OF MY CAREER.
A CASE WHICH I HAVE LABORED FOR FOURTEEN MONTHS AND WHICH IS RAPIDLY APPROACHING A SINGULARLY DIVERTING CLIMAX.
I ALLUDE TO THE CASE OF PROFESSOR JAMES MORIARTY.
MORIARTY? I DON'T REMEMBER EVER HAVING HEARD OF THE FELLOW.
HE IS THE NAPOLEON OF CRIME WATSON.
HE SITS MOTIONLESS LIKE AN UGLY VENOMOUS SPIDER IN THE CENTER OF HIS WEB. BUT THE WEB HAS TEN THOUSAND RADIATIONS. AND THAT SIPDER KNOWS EVERY QUIVER OF EVERY SINGLE ONE OF THEM.
REALLY HOLMES! THIS IS VERY INTERESTING!
BUT YOU MUST UNDERSTAND MY DEAR WATSON. THE REAL INTEREST WILL COME WHEN THE PROFESSOR BEGINS TO REALIZE HIS POSITION.
WHICH HE CANNOT FAIL TO DO SHORTLY.

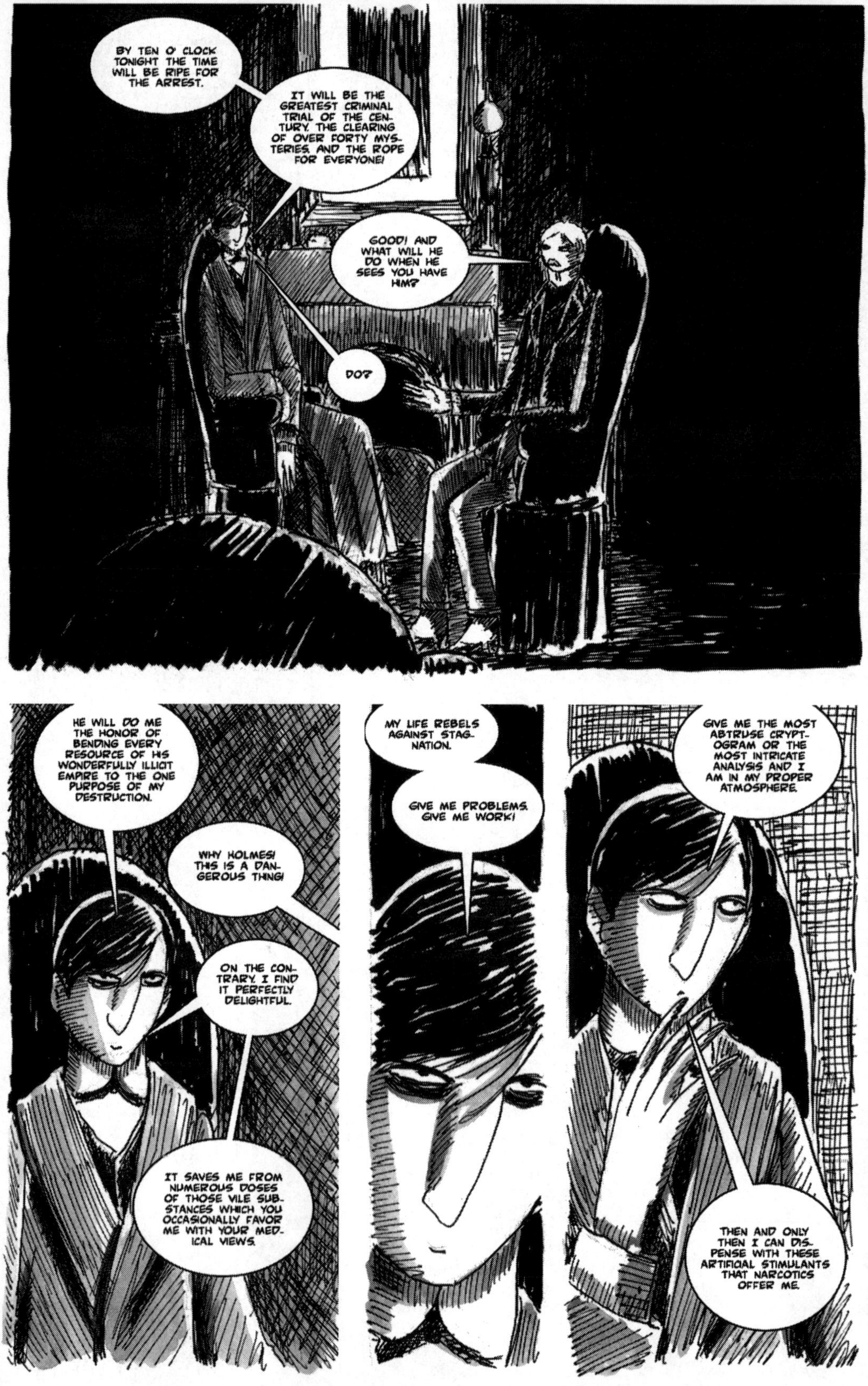
BY TEN O' CLOCK TONIGHT THE TIME WILL BE RIPE FOR THE ARREST.
IT WILL BE THE GREATEST CRIMINAL TRIAL OF THE CENTURY. THE CLEARING OF OVER FORTY MYSTERIES, AND THE ROPE FOR EVERYONE!
GOOD! AND WHAT WILL HE DO WHEN HE SEES YOU HAVE HIM?
DO?
HE WILL DO ME THE HONOR OF BENDING EVERY RESOURCE OF HIS WONDERFULLY ILLICIT EMPIRE TO THE ONE PURPOSE OF MY DESTRUCTION.
WHY HOLMES! THIS IS A DANGEROUS THING!
ON THE CONTRARY, I FIND IT PERFECTLY DELIGHTFUL.
IT SAVES ME FROM NUMEROUS DOSES OF THOSE VILE SUBSTANCES WHICH YOU OCCASIONALLY FAVOR ME WITH YOUR MEDICAL VIEWS.
MY LIFE REBELS AGAINST STAGNATION.
GIVE ME PROBLEMS. GIVE ME WORK!
GIVE ME THE MOST ABTRUSE CRYPTOGRAM OR THE MOST INTRICATE ANALYSIS AND I AM IN MY PROPER ATMOSPHERE.
THEN AND ONLY THEN I CAN DISPENSE WITH THESE ARTIFICIAL STIMULANTS THAT NARCOTICS OFFER ME.

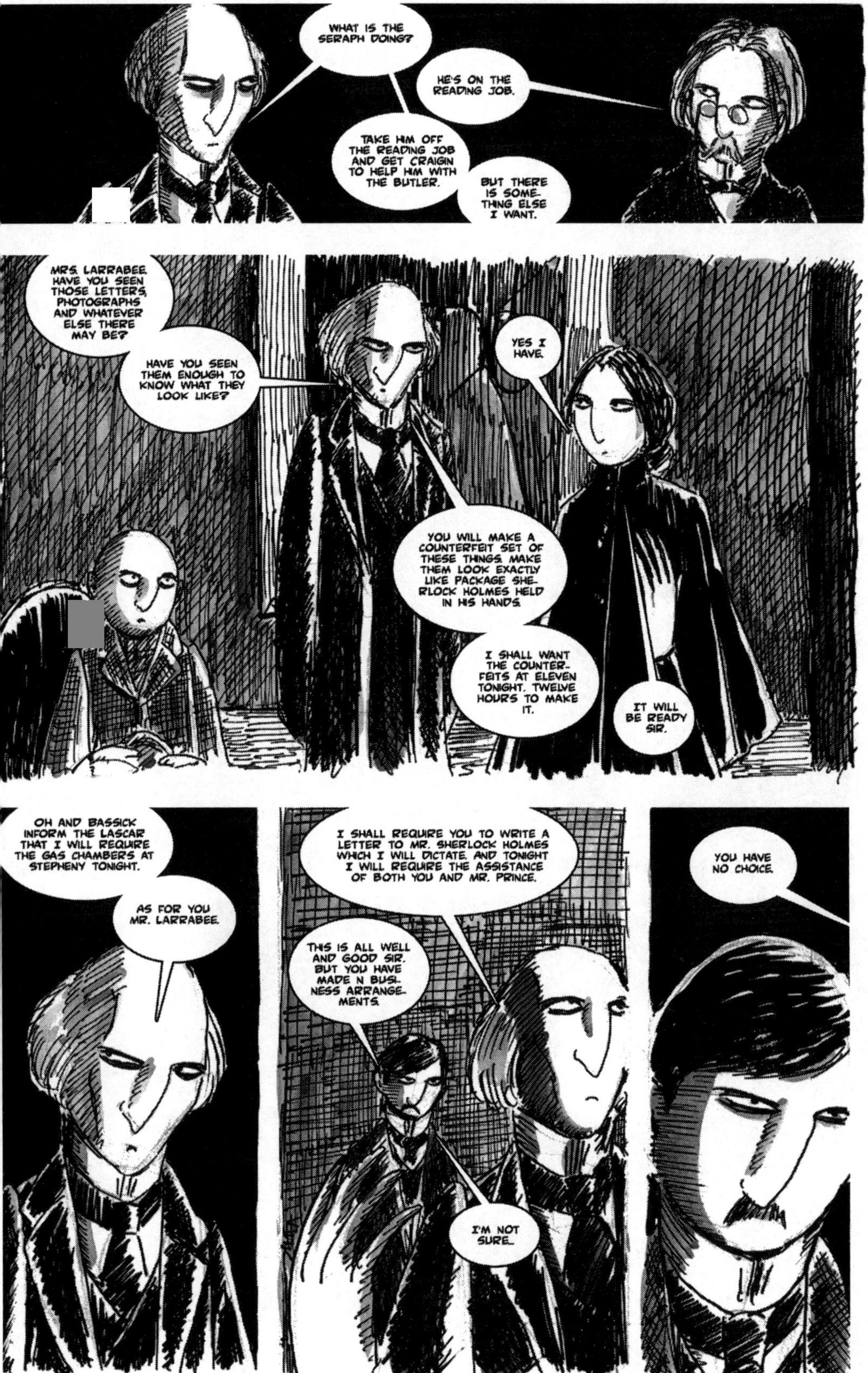
WHAT IS THE SERAPH DOING?
HE'S ON THE READING JOB.
TAKE HIM OFF THE READING JOB AND GET CRAIGIN TO HELP HIM WITH THE BUTLER.
BUT THERE IS SOME-THING ELSE I WANT.
MRS. LARRABEE. HAVE YOU SEEN THOSE LETTERS, PHOTOGRAPHS AND WHATEVER ELSE THERE MAY BE?
HAVE YOU SEEN THEM ENOUGH TO KNOW WHAT THEY LOOK LIKE?
YES I HAVE.
YOU WILL MAKE A COUNTERFEIT SET OF THESE THINGS. MAKE THEM LOOK EXACTLY LIKE PACKAGE SHE-RLOCK HOLMES HELD IN HIS HANDS.
I SHALL WANT THE COUNTER-FEITS AT ELEVEN TONIGHT. TWELVE HOURS TO MAKE IT.
IT WILL BE READY SIR.
OH AND BASSICK INFORM THE LASCAR THAT I WILL REQUIRE THE GAS CHAMBERS AT STEPHENY TONIGHT.
AS FOR YOU MR. LARRABEE.
I SHALL REQUIRE YOU TO WRITE A LETTER TO MR. SHERLOCK HOLMES WHICH I WILL DICTATE. AND TONIGHT I WILL REQUIRE THE ASSISTANCE OF BOTH YOU AND MR. PRINCE.
THIS IS ALL WELL AND GOOD SIR. BUT YOU HAVE MADE N BUSI-NESS ARRANGE-MENTS.
I'M NOT SURE.
YOU HAVE NO CHOICE.

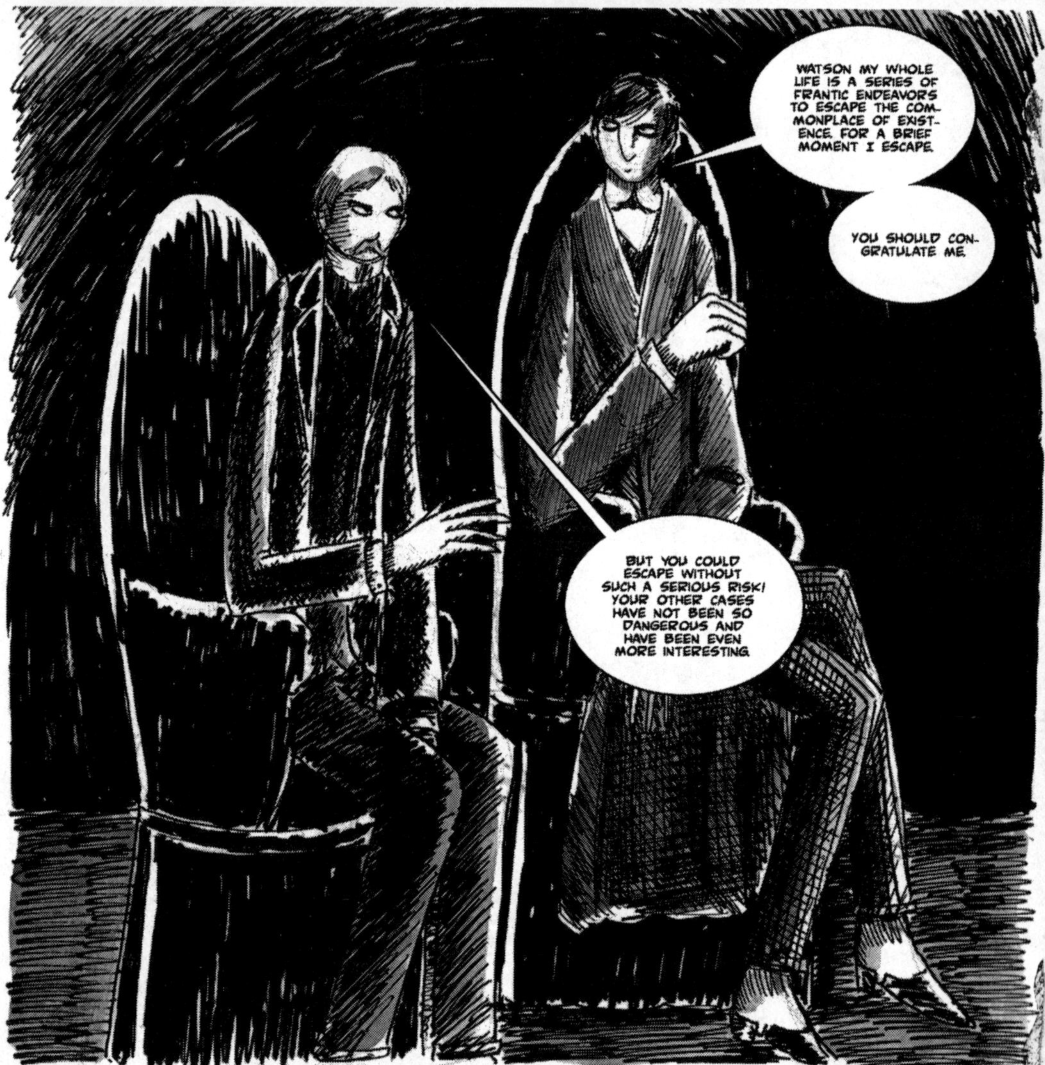
WATSON MY WHOLE LIFE IS A SERIES OF FRANTIC ENDEAVORS TO ESCAPE THE COMMONPLACE OF EXISTENCE. FOR A BRIEF MOMENT I ESCAPE.
YOU SHOULD CONGRATULATE ME.
BUT YOU COULD ESCAPE WITHOUT SUCH A SERIOUS RISK! YOUR OTHER CASES HAVE NOT BEEN SO DANGEROUS AND HAVE BEEN EVEN MORE INTERESTING.

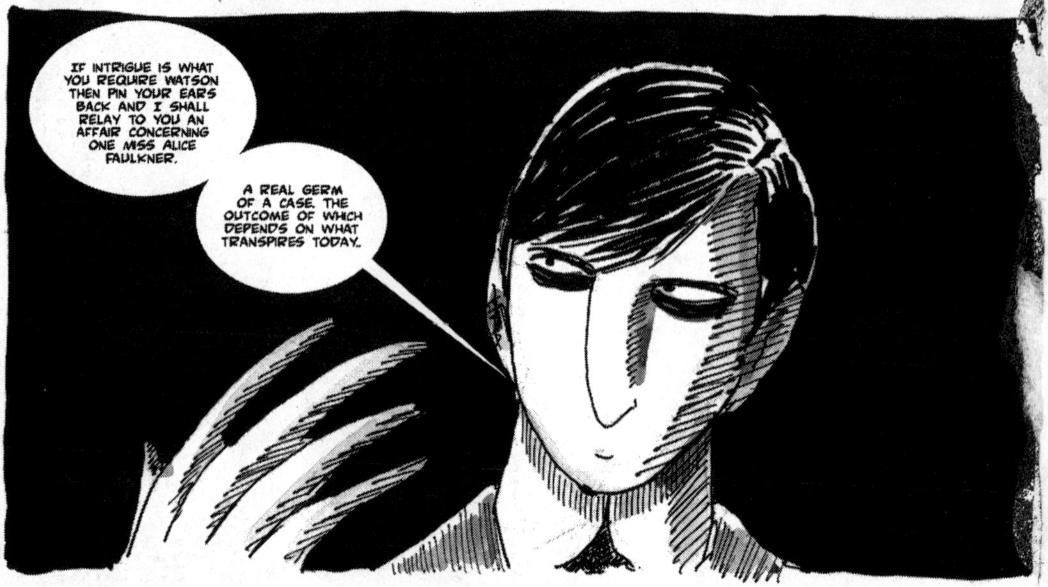
IF INTRIGUE IS WHAT YOU REQUIRE WATSON THEN PIN YOUR EARS BACK AND I SHALL RELAY TO YOU AN AFFAIR CONCERNING ONE MISS ALICE FAULKNER.
A REAL GERM OF A CASE. THE OUTCOME OF WHICH DEPENDS ON WHAT TRANSPIRES TODAY..

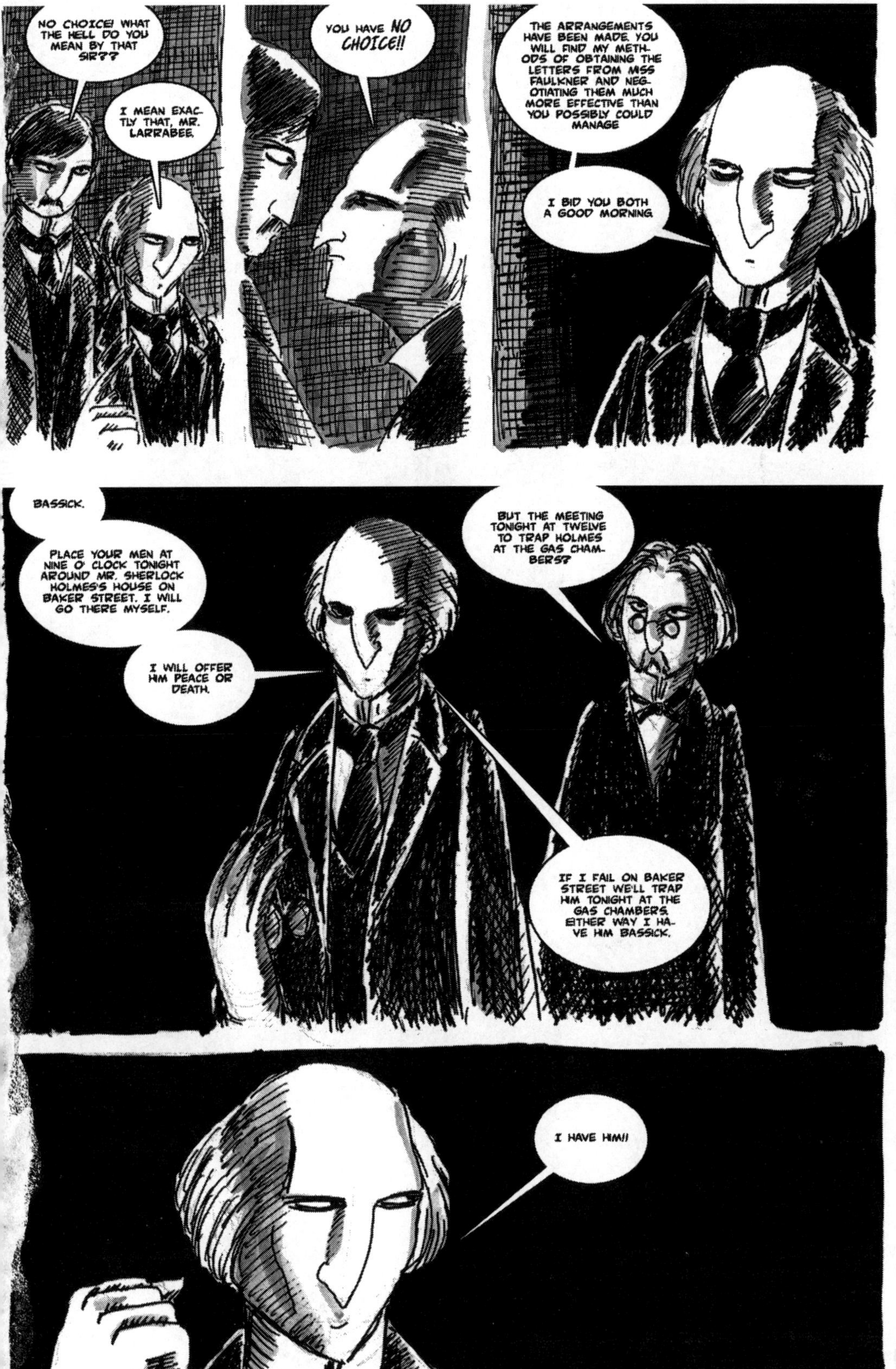
NO CHOICE! WHAT THE HELL DO YOU MEAN BY THAT SIR??
I MEAN EXACTLY THAT, MR. LARRABEE.
YOU HAVE NO CHOICE!!
THE ARRANGEMENTS HAVE BEEN MADE. YOU WILL FIND MY METHODS OF OBTAINING THE LETTERS FROM MISS FAULKNER AND NEGOTIATING THEM MUCH MORE EFFECTIVE THAN YOU POSSIBLY COULD MANAGE
I BID YOU BOTH A GOOD MORNING.
BASSICK.
PLACE YOUR MEN AT NINE O' CLOCK TONIGHT AROUND MR. SHERLOCK HOLMES'S HOUSE ON BAKER STREET. I WILL GO THERE MYSELF.
I WILL OFFER HIM PEACE OR DEATH.
BUT THE MEETING TONIGHT AT TWELVE TO TRAP HOLMES AT THE GAS CHAMBERS?
IF I FAIL ON BAKER STREET WE'LL TRAP HIM TONIGHT AT THE GAS CHAMBERS. EITHER WAY I HAVE HIM BASSICK.
I HAVE HIM!!

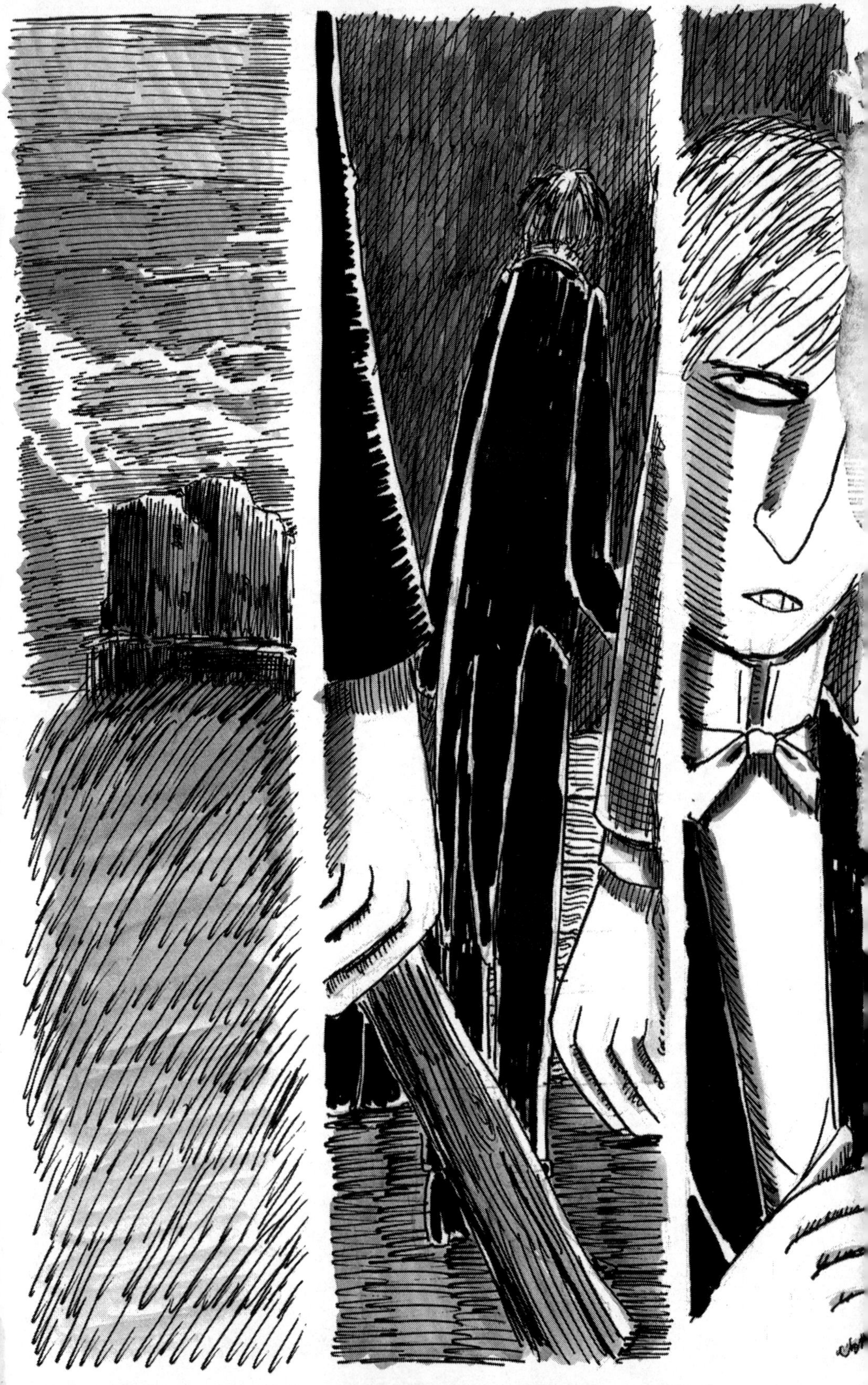

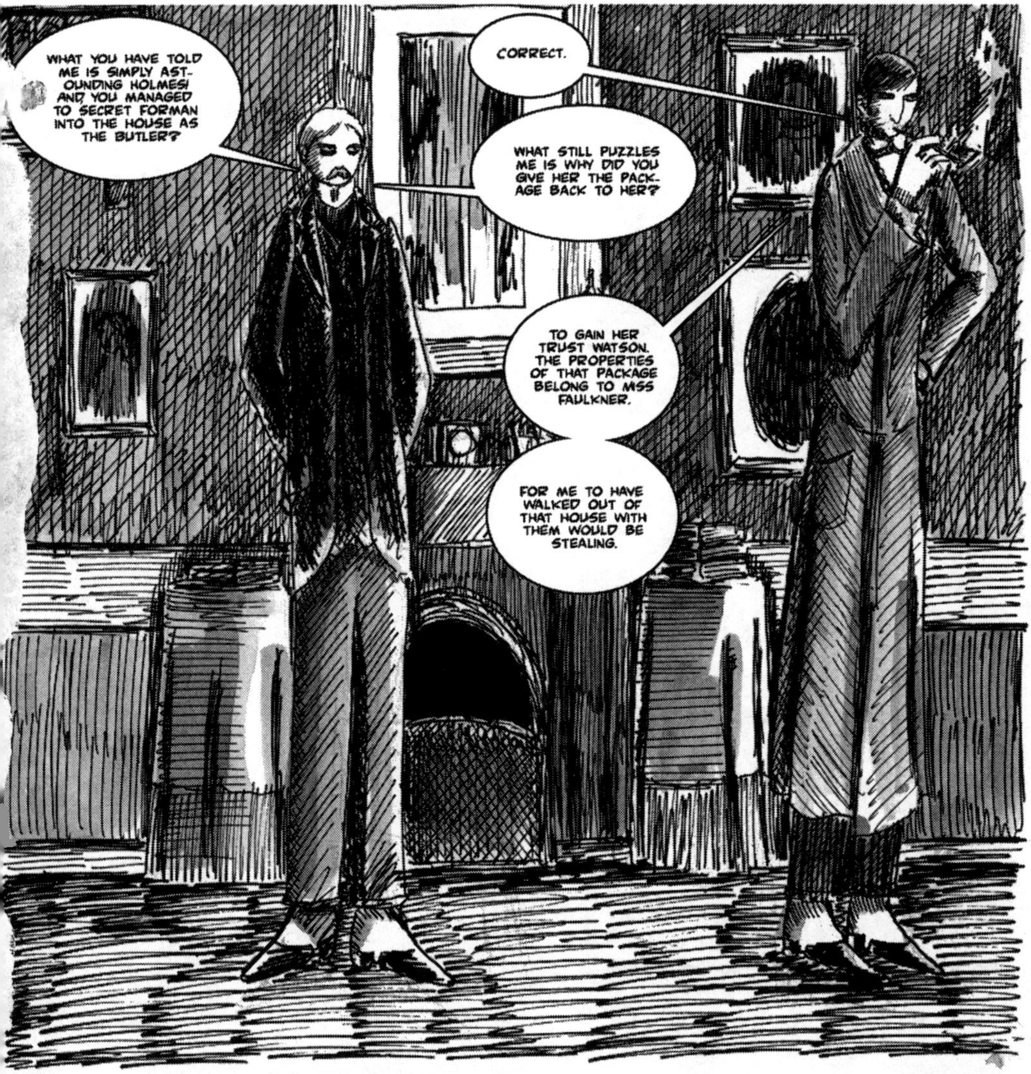
WHAT YOU HAVE TOLD ME IS SIMPLY AST-OUNDING HOLMES! AND YOU MANAGED TO SECRET FORMAN INTO THE HOUSE AS THE BUTLER?
CORRECT.
WHAT STILL PUZZLES ME IS WHY DID YOU GIVE HER THE PACK-AGE BACK TO HER?
TO GAIN HER TRUST WATSON. THE PROPERTIES OF THAT PACKAGE BELONG TO MISS FAULKNER.
FOR ME TO HAVE WALKED OUT OF THAT HOUSE WITH THEM WOULD BE STEALING.

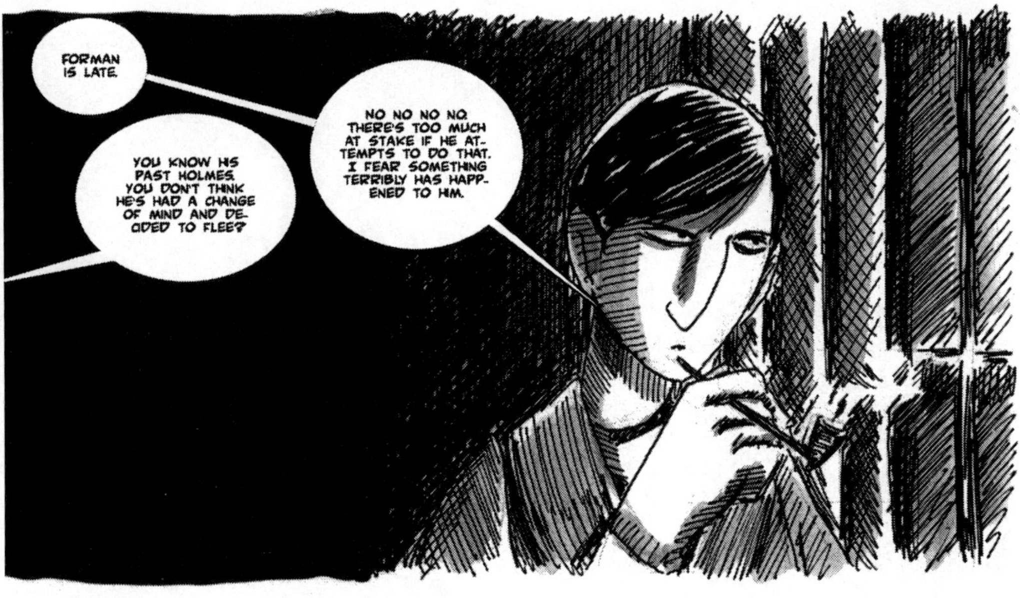
FORMAN IS LATE.
YOU KNOW HIS PAST HOLMES. YOU DON'T THINK HE'S HAD A CHANGE OF MIND AND DE-CIDED TO FLEE?
NO NO NO NO. THERE'S TOO MUCH AT STAKE IF HE AT-TEMPTS TO DO THAT. I FEAR SOMETHING TERRIBLY HAS HAPP-ENED TO HIM.

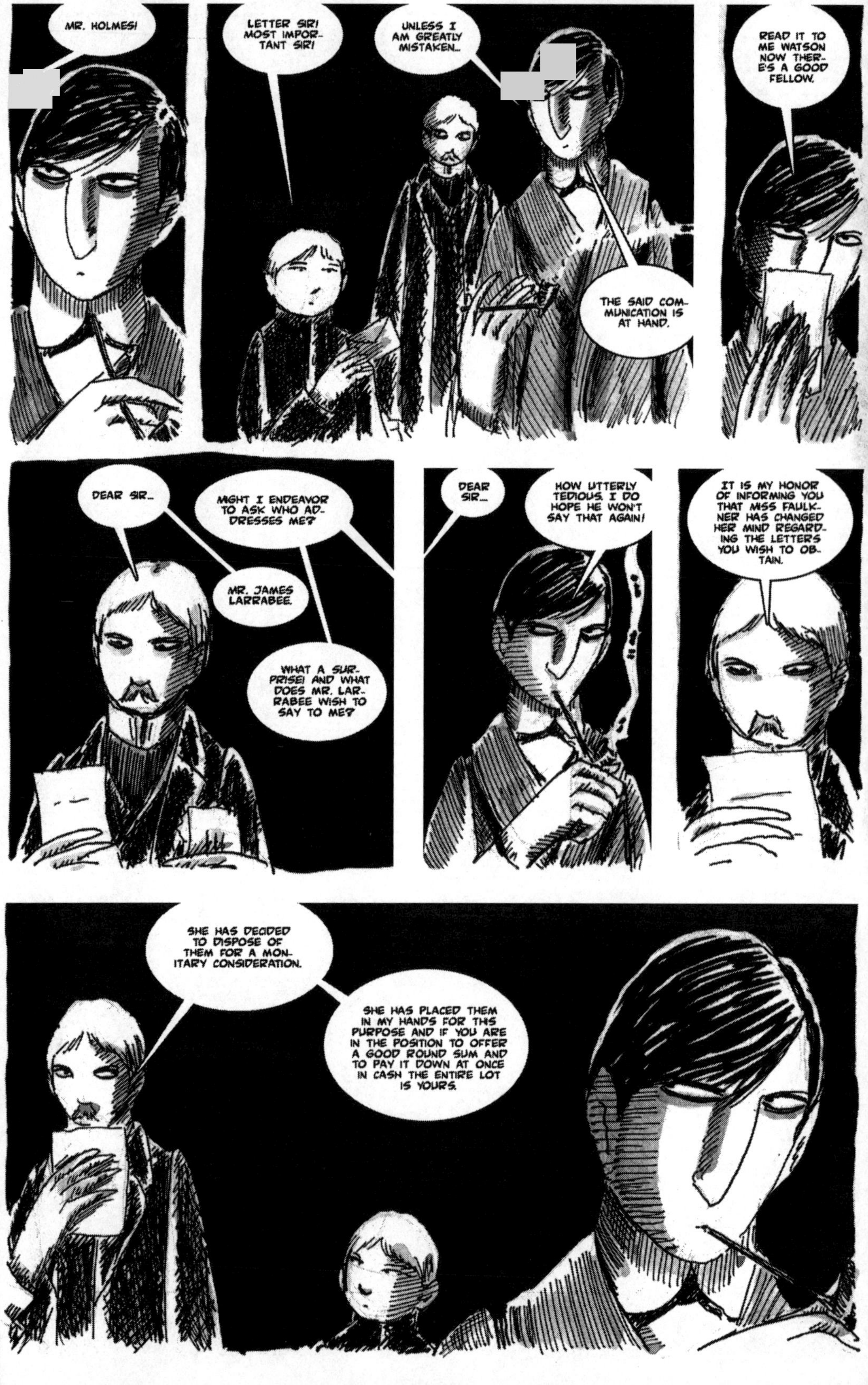
MR. HOLMES!
LETTER SIR! MOST IMPORTANT SIR!
UNLESS I AM GREATLY MISTAKEN...
THE SAID COMMUNICATION IS AT HAND.
READ IT TO ME WATSON NOW THERE'S A GOOD FELLOW.
DEAR SIR...
MIGHT I ENDEAVOR TO ASK WHO ADDRESSES ME?
MR. JAMES LARRABEE.
WHAT A SURPRISE! AND WHAT DOES MR. LARRABEE WISH TO SAY TO ME?
DEAR SIR...
HOW UTTERLY TEDIOUS. I DO HOPE HE WON'T SAY THAT AGAIN!
IT IS MY HONOR OF INFORMING YOU THAT MISS FAULKNER HAS CHANGED HER MIND REGARDING THE LETTERS YOU WISH TO OBTAIN.
SHE HAS DECIDED TO DISPOSE OF THEM FOR A MONITARY CONSIDERATION.
SHE HAS PLACED THEM IN MY HANDS FOR THIS PURPOSE AND IF YOU ARE IN THE POSITION TO OFFER A GOOD ROUND SUM AND TO PAY IT DOWN AT ONCE IN CASH THE ENTIRE LOT IS YOURS.

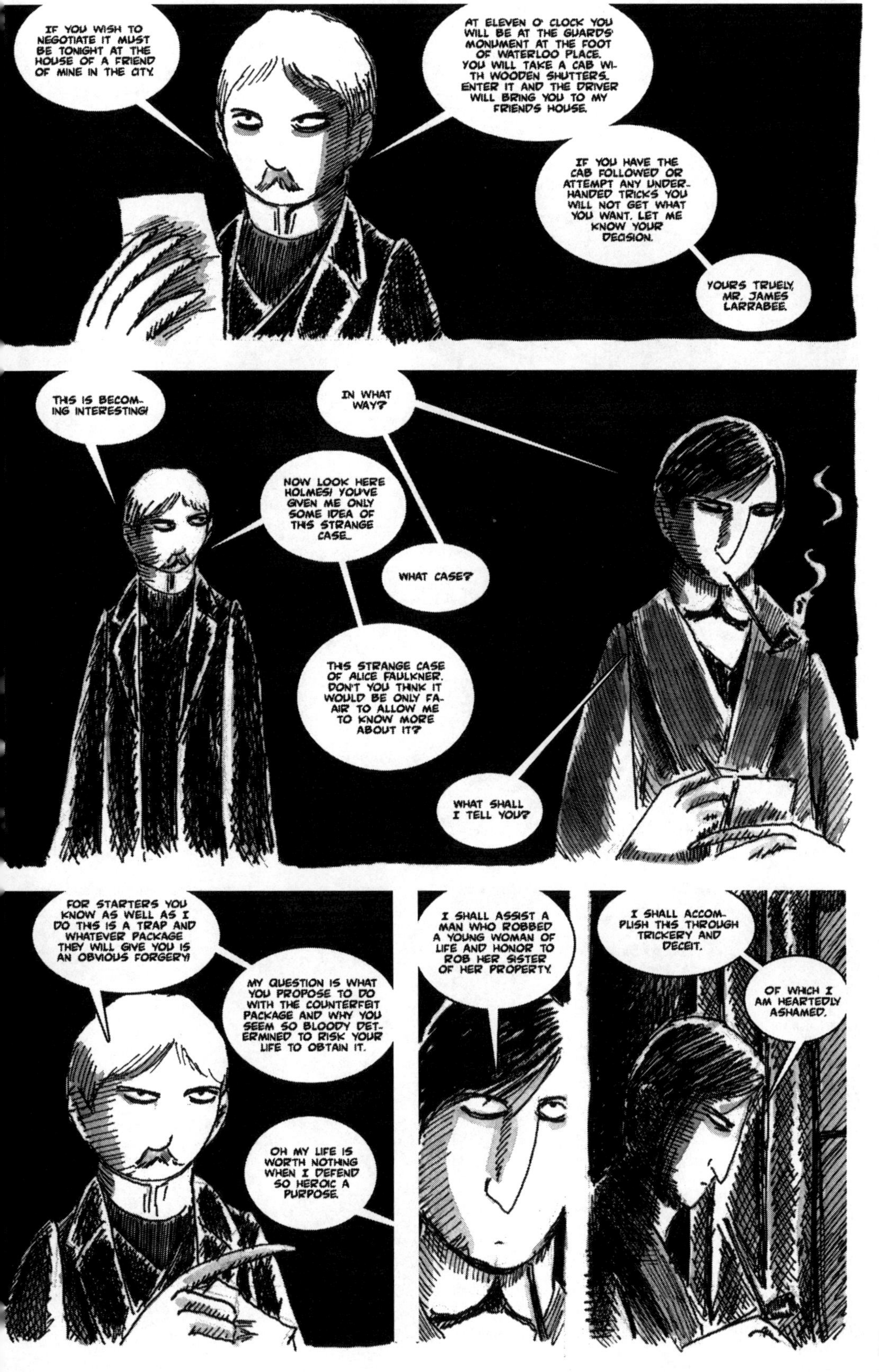
IF YOU WISH TO NEGOTIATE IT MUST BE TONIGHT AT THE HOUSE OF A FRIEND OF MINE IN THE CITY.
AT ELEVEN O' CLOCK YOU WILL BE AT THE GUARDS' MONUMENT AT THE FOOT OF WATERLOO PLACE. YOU WILL TAKE A CAB WI- TH WOODEN SHUTTERS. ENTER IT AND THE DRIVER WILL BRING YOU TO MY FRIENDS HOUSE.
IF YOU HAVE THE CAB FOLLOWED OR ATTEMPT ANY UNDER- HANDED TRICKS YOU WILL NOT GET WHAT YOU WANT. LET ME KNOW YOUR DECISION.
YOURS TRUELY, MR. JAMES LARRABEE.
THIS IS BECOM- ING INTERESTING!
IN WHAT WAY?
NOW LOOK HERE HOLMES! YOU'VE GIVEN ME ONLY SOME IDEA OF THIS STRANGE CASE..
WHAT CASE?
THIS STRANGE CASE OF ALICE FAULKNER. DON'T YOU THINK IT WOULD BE ONLY FA- AIR TO ALLOW ME TO KNOW MORE ABOUT IT?
WHAT SHALL I TELL YOU?
FOR STARTERS YOU KNOW AS WELL AS I DO THIS IS A TRAP AND WHATEVER PACKAGE THEY WILL GIVE YOU IS AN OBVIOUS FORGERY!
MY QUESTION IS WHAT YOU PROPOSE TO DO WITH THE COUNTERFEIT PACKAGE AND WHY YOU SEEM SO BLOODY DET- ERMINED TO RISK YOUR LIFE TO OBTAIN IT.
OH MY LIFE IS WORTH NOTHING WHEN I DEFEND SO HEROIC A PURPOSE.
I SHALL ASSIST A MAN WHO ROBBED A YOUNG WOMAN OF LIFE AND HONOR TO ROB HER SISTER OF HER PROPERTY.
I SHALL ACCOM- PLISH THIS THROUGH TRICKERY AND DECEIT.
OF WHICH I AM HEARTEDLY ASHAMED.

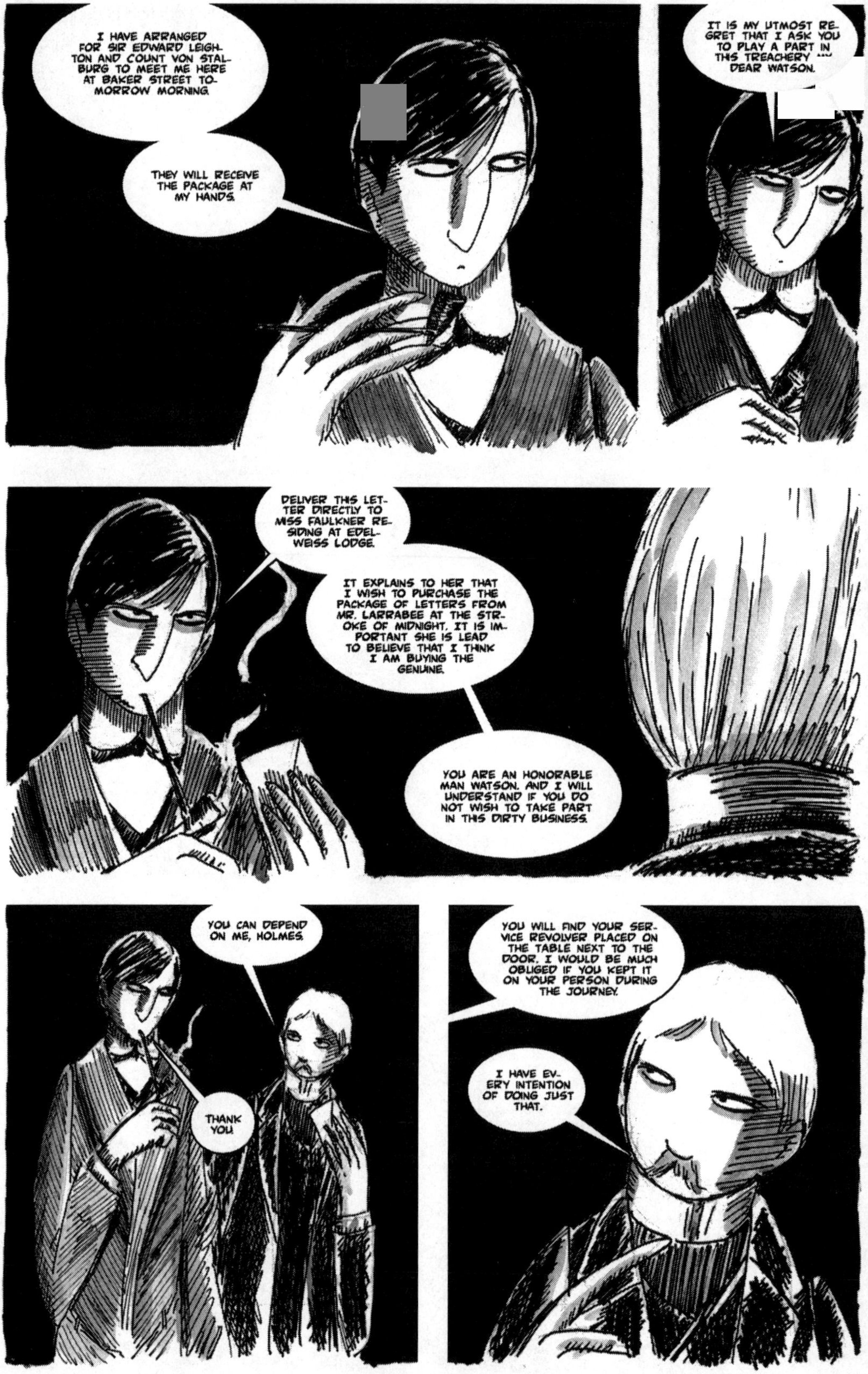
I HAVE ARRANGED FOR SIR EDWARD LEIGH-TON AND COUNT VON STAL-BURG TO MEET ME HERE AT BAKER STREET TO-MORROW MORNING.
THEY WILL RECEIVE THE PACKAGE AT MY HANDS.
IT IS MY UTMOST RE-GRET THAT I ASK YOU TO PLAY A PART IN THIS TREACHERY
DEAR WATSON.
DELIVER THIS LET-TER DIRECTLY TO MISS FAULKNER RE-SIDING AT EDEL-WEISS LODGE.
IT EXPLAINS TO HER THAT I WISH TO PURCHASE THE PACKAGE OF LETTERS FROM MR. LARRABEE AT THE STR-OKE OF MIDNIGHT. IT IS IM-PORTANT SHE IS LEAD TO BELIEVE THAT I THINK I AM BUYING THE GENUINE.
YOU ARE AN HONORABLE MAN WATSON. AND I WILL UNDERSTAND IF YOU DO NOT WISH TO TAKE PART IN THIS DIRTY BUSINESS.
YOU CAN DEPEND ON ME, HOLMES.
THANK YOU.
YOU WILL FIND YOUR SER-VICE REVOLVER PLACED ON THE TABLE NEXT TO THE DOOR. I WOULD BE MUCH OBLIGED IF YOU KEPT IT ON YOUR PERSON DURING THE JOURNEY.
I HAVE EV-ERY INTENTION OF DOING JUST THAT.

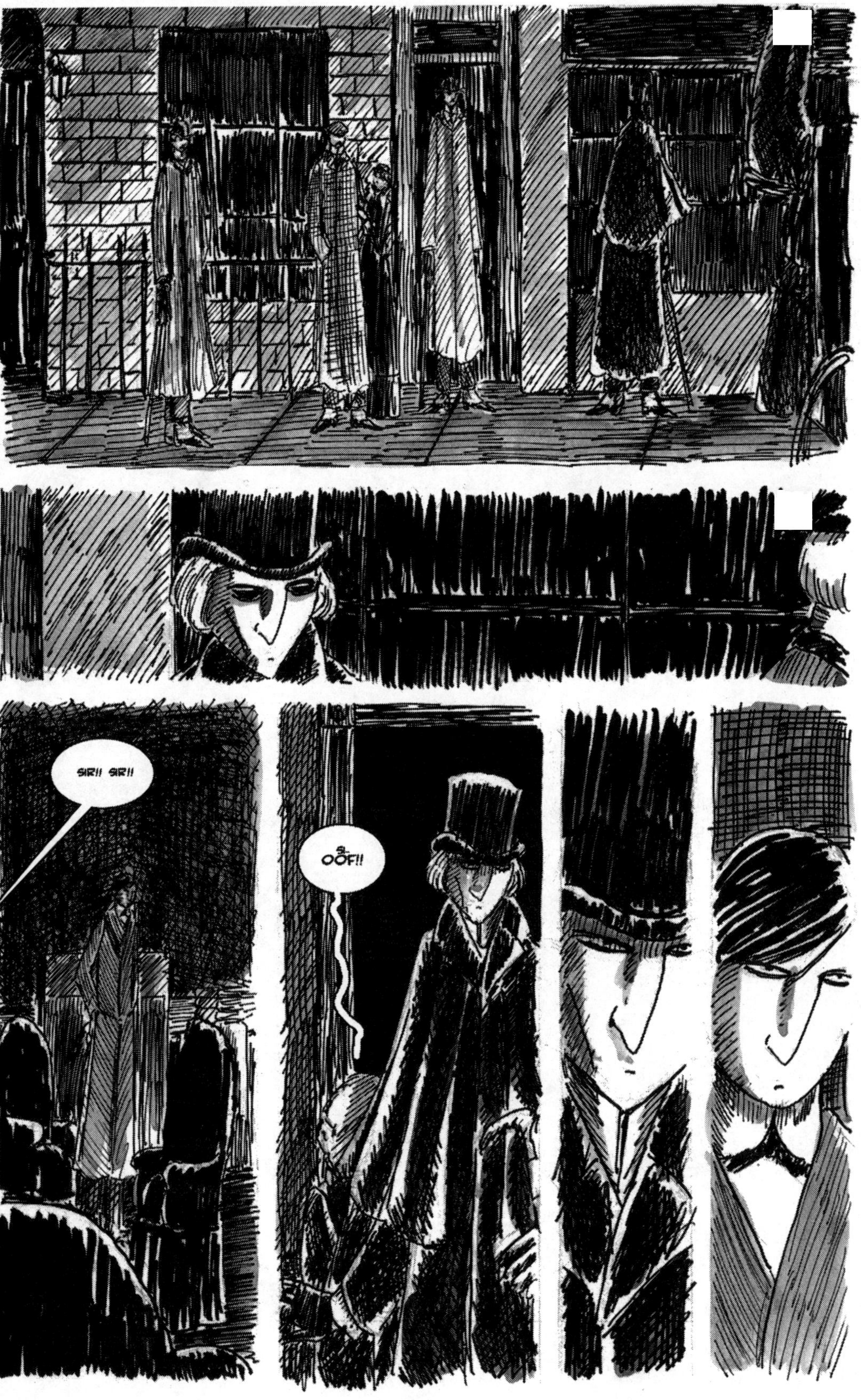
SIR!! SIR!!
SI-
OOF!!

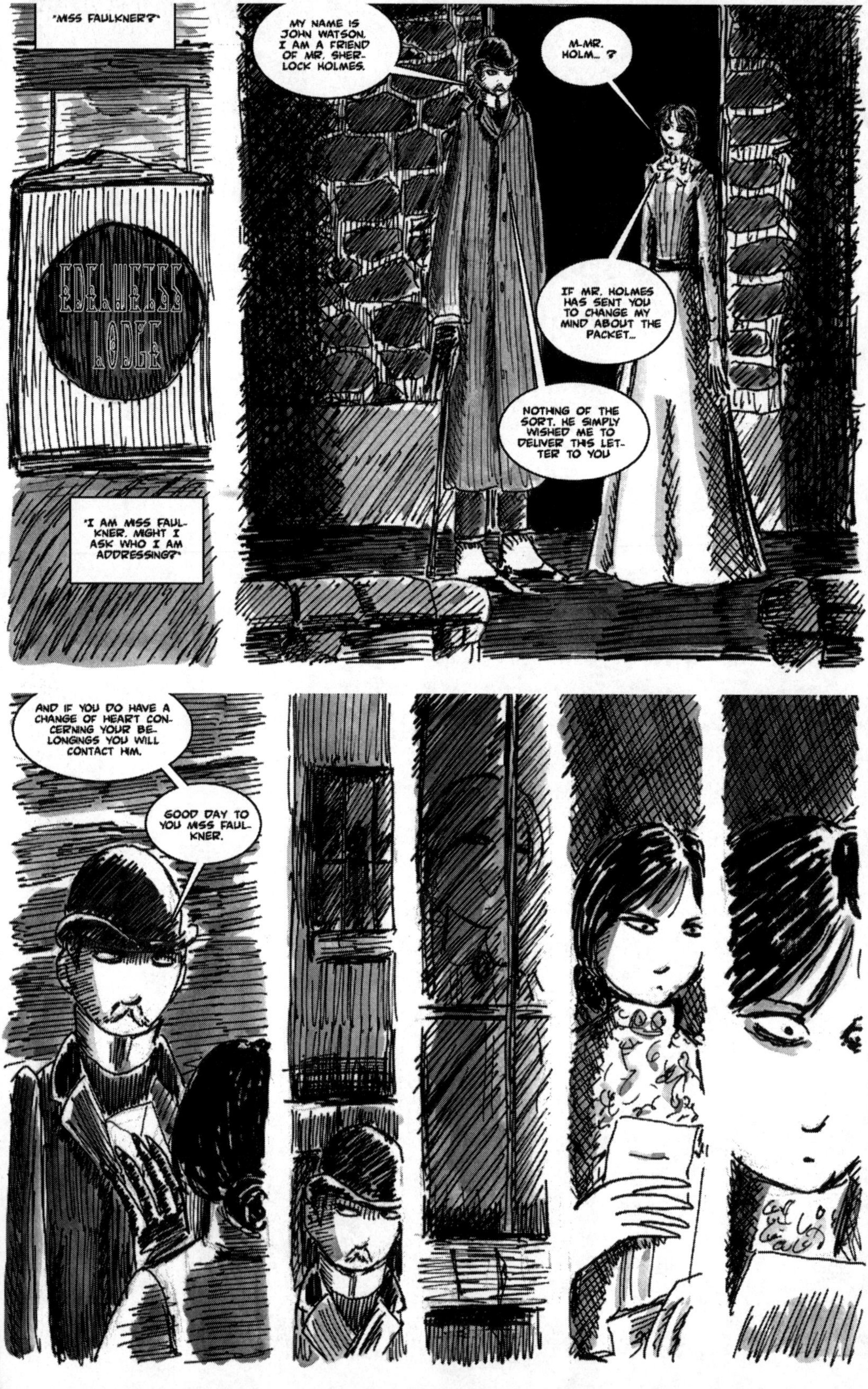
"MISS FAULKNER?"
EDELWEISS LODGE
"I AM MISS FAULKNER. MIGHT I ASK WHO I AM ADDRESSING?"
MY NAME IS JOHN WATSON. I AM A FRIEND OF MR. SHERLOCK HOLMES.
M-MR. HOLM... ?
IF MR. HOLMES HAS SENT YOU TO CHANGE MY MIND ABOUT THE PACKET...
NOTHING OF THE SORT. HE SIMPLY WISHED ME TO DELIVER THIS LETTER TO YOU
AND IF YOU DO HAVE A CHANGE OF HEART CONCERNING YOUR BELONGINGS YOU WILL CONTACT HIM.
GOOD DAY TO YOU MISS FAULKNER.

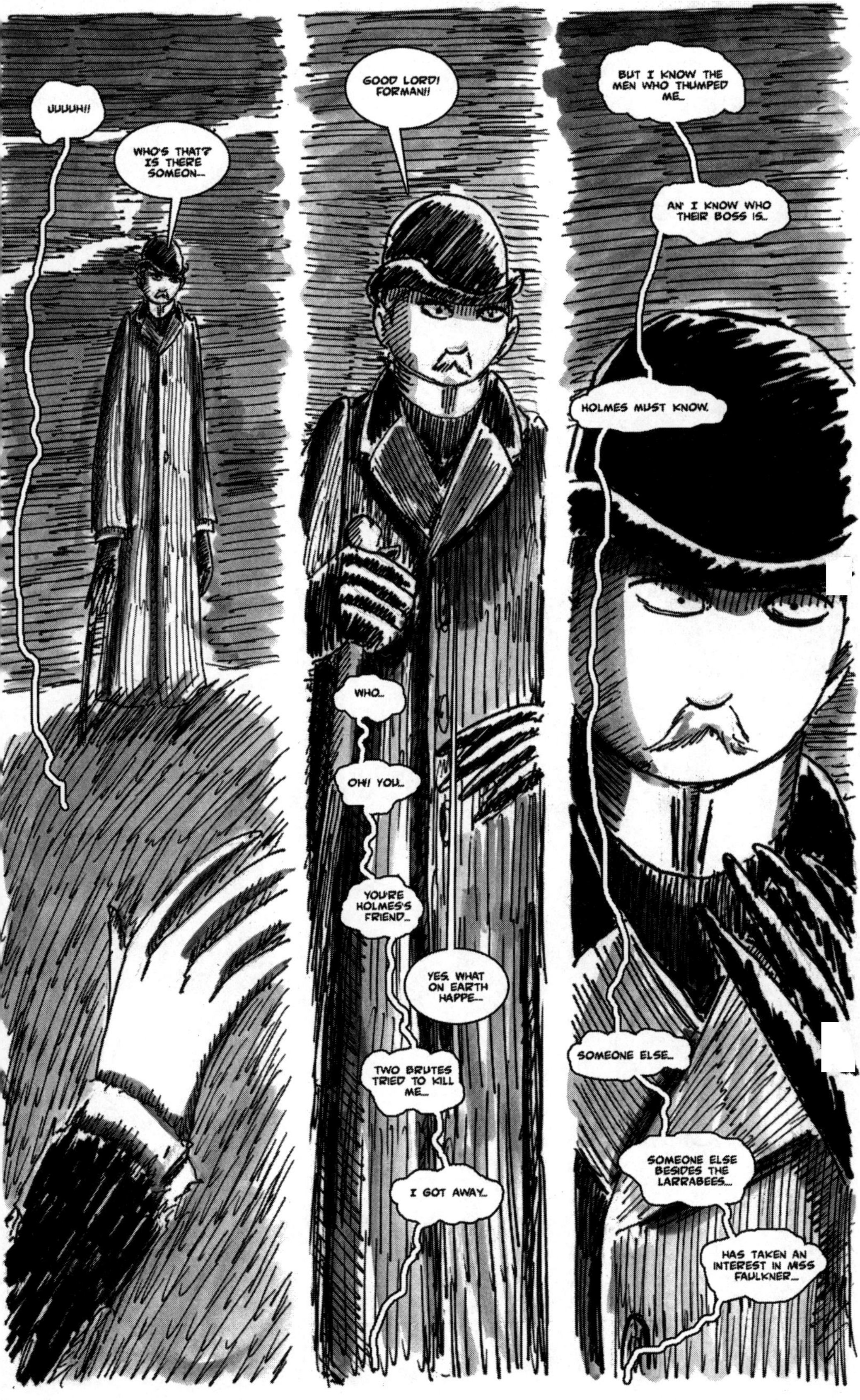
UUUUH!!
WHO'S THAT? IS THERE SOMEON...
GOOD LORD! FORMAN!!
WHO...
OH! YOU...
YOU'RE HOLMES'S FRIEND...
YES. WHAT ON EARTH HAPPE...
TWO BRUTES TRIED TO KILL ME...
I GOT AWAY...
BUT I KNOW THE MEN WHO THUMPED ME...
AN' I KNOW WHO THEIR BOSS IS...
HOLMES MUST KNOW.
SOMEONE ELSE...
SOMEONE ELSE BESIDES THE LARRABEES...
HAS TAKEN AN INTEREST IN MISS FAULKNER...

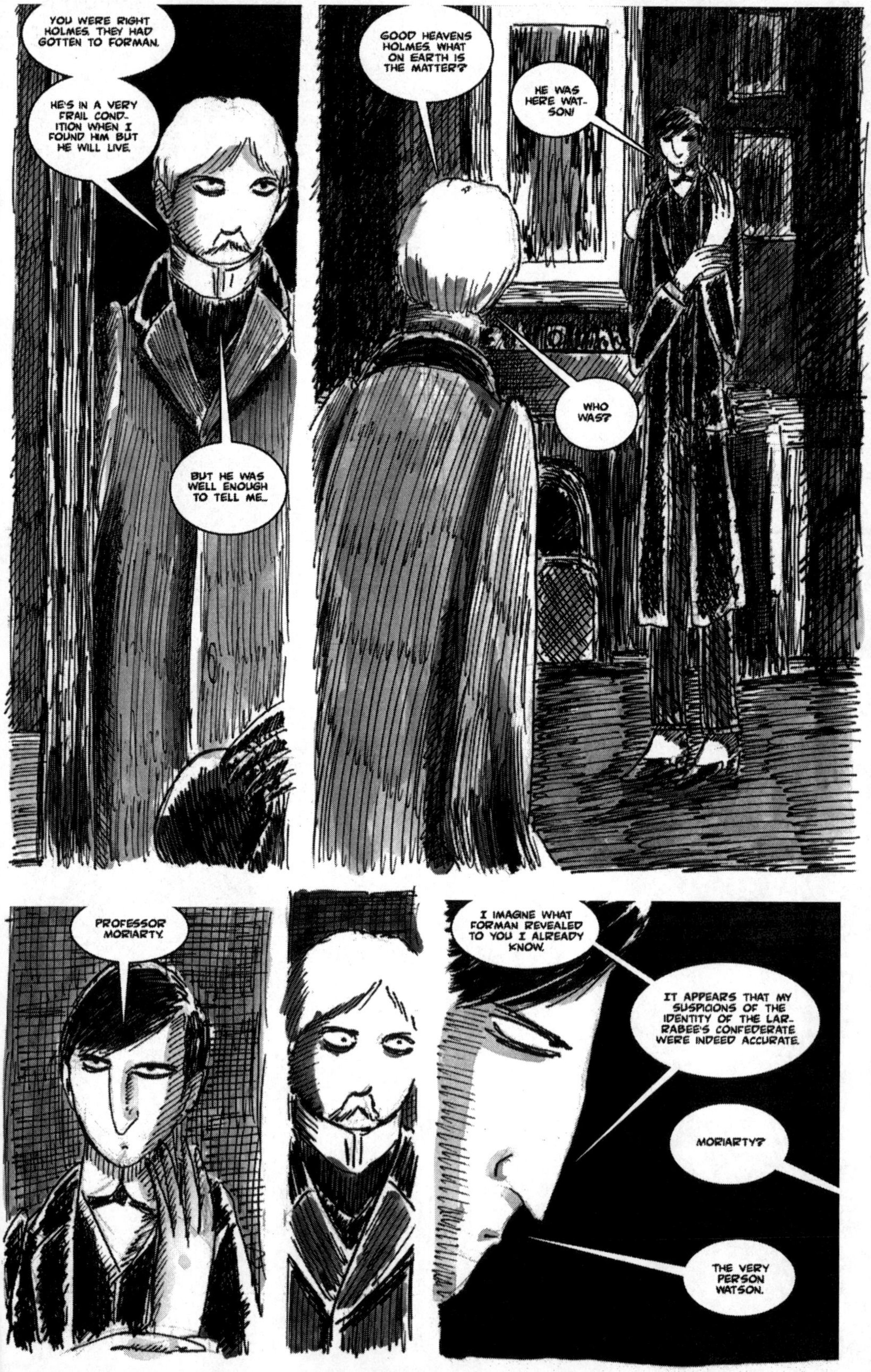
YOU WERE RIGHT HOLMES. THEY HAD GOTTEN TO FORMAN.
HE'S IN A VERY FRAIL CONDITION WHEN I FOUND HIM BUT HE WILL LIVE.
BUT HE WAS WELL ENOUGH TO TELL ME...
GOOD HEAVENS HOLMES. WHAT ON EARTH IS THE MATTER?
HE WAS HERE WATSON!
WHO WAS?
PROFESSOR MORIARTY.
I IMAGINE WHAT FORMAN REVEALED TO YOU I ALREADY KNOW.
IT APPEARS THAT MY SUSPICIONS OF THE IDENTITY OF THE LARRABEE'S CONFEDERATE WERE INDEED ACCURATE.
MORIARTY?
THE VERY PERSON WATSON.

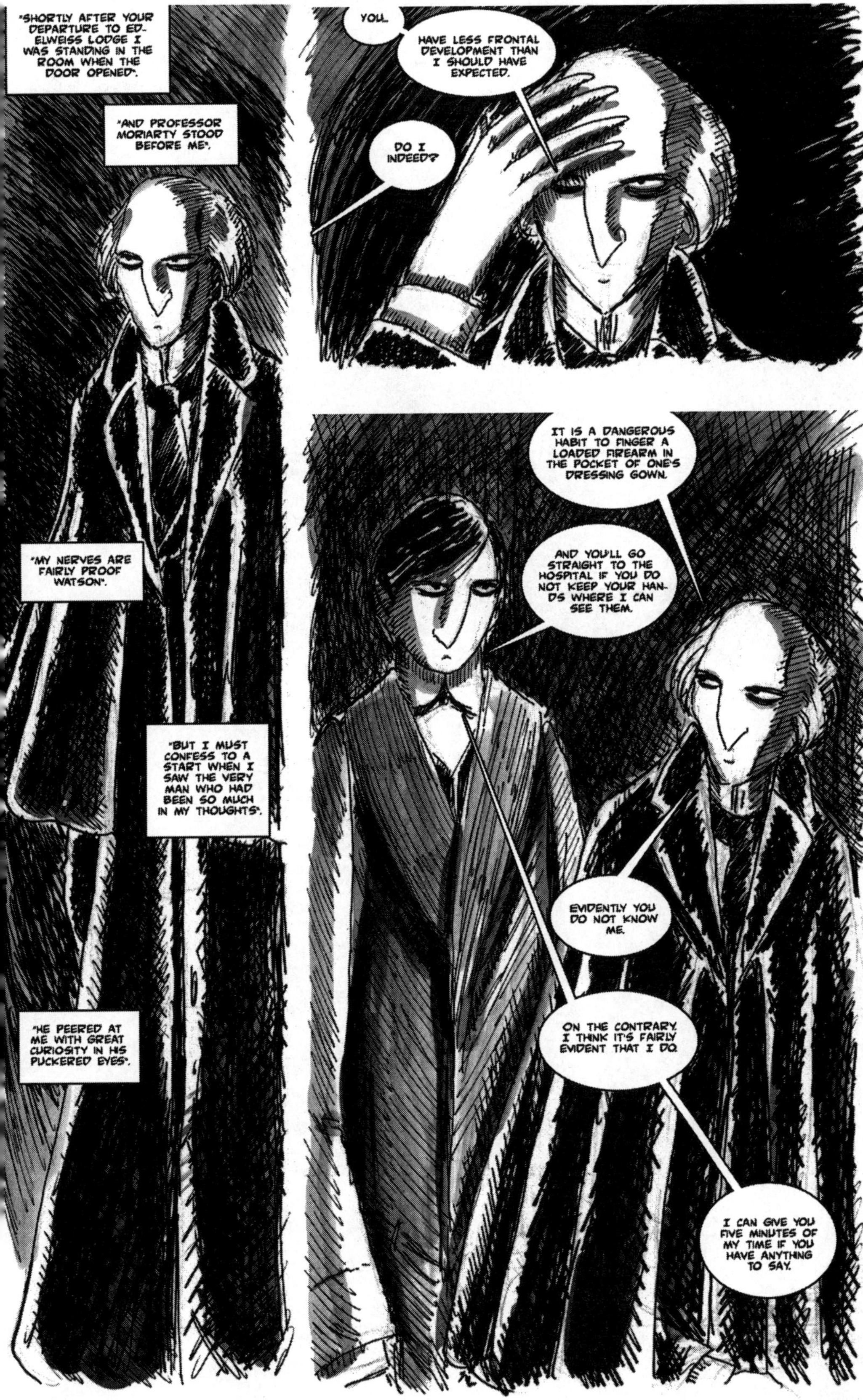
"SHORTLY AFTER YOUR DEPARTURE TO ED-ELWEISS LODGE I WAS STANDING IN THE ROOM WHEN THE DOOR OPENED".
"AND PROFESSOR MORIARTY STOOD BEFORE ME".
"MY NERVES ARE FAIRLY PROOF WATSON".
"BUT I MUST CONFESS TO A START WHEN I SAW THE VERY MAN WHO HAD BEEN SO MUCH IN MY THOUGHTS".
"HE PEERED AT ME WITH GREAT CURIOSITY IN HIS PUCKERED EYES".
YOU..
HAVE LESS FRONTAL DEVELOPMENT THAN I SHOULD HAVE EXPECTED.
DO I INDEED?
IT IS A DANGEROUS HABIT TO FINGER A LOADED FIREARM IN THE POCKET OF ONE'S DRESSING GOWN.
AND YOU'LL GO STRAIGHT TO THE HOSPITAL IF YOU DO NOT KEEP YOUR HAN-DS WHERE I CAN SEE THEM.
EVIDENTLY YOU DO NOT KNOW ME.
ON THE CONTRARY. I THINK IT'S FAIRLY EVIDENT THAT I DO.
I CAN GIVE YOU FIVE MINUTES OF MY TIME IF YOU HAVE ANYTHING TO SAY.

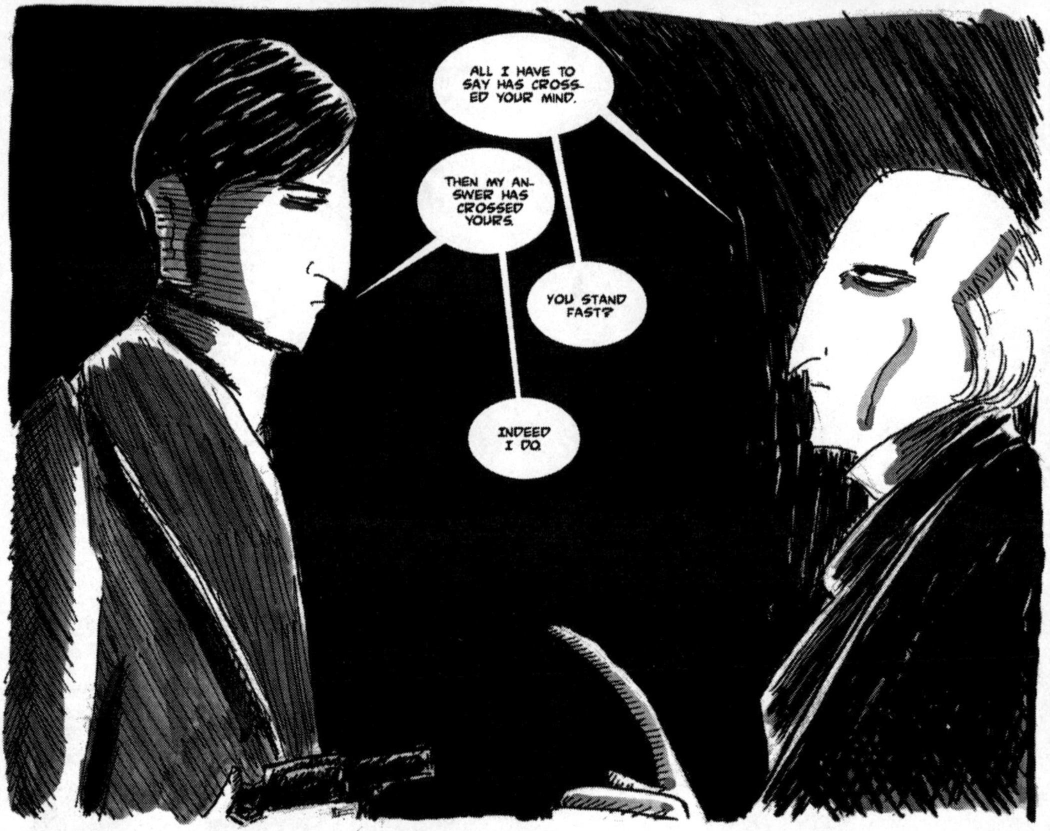
ALL I HAVE TO SAY HAS CROSS-ED YOUR MIND.
THEN MY AN-SWER HAS CROSSED YOURS.
YOU STAND FAST?
INDEED I DO.

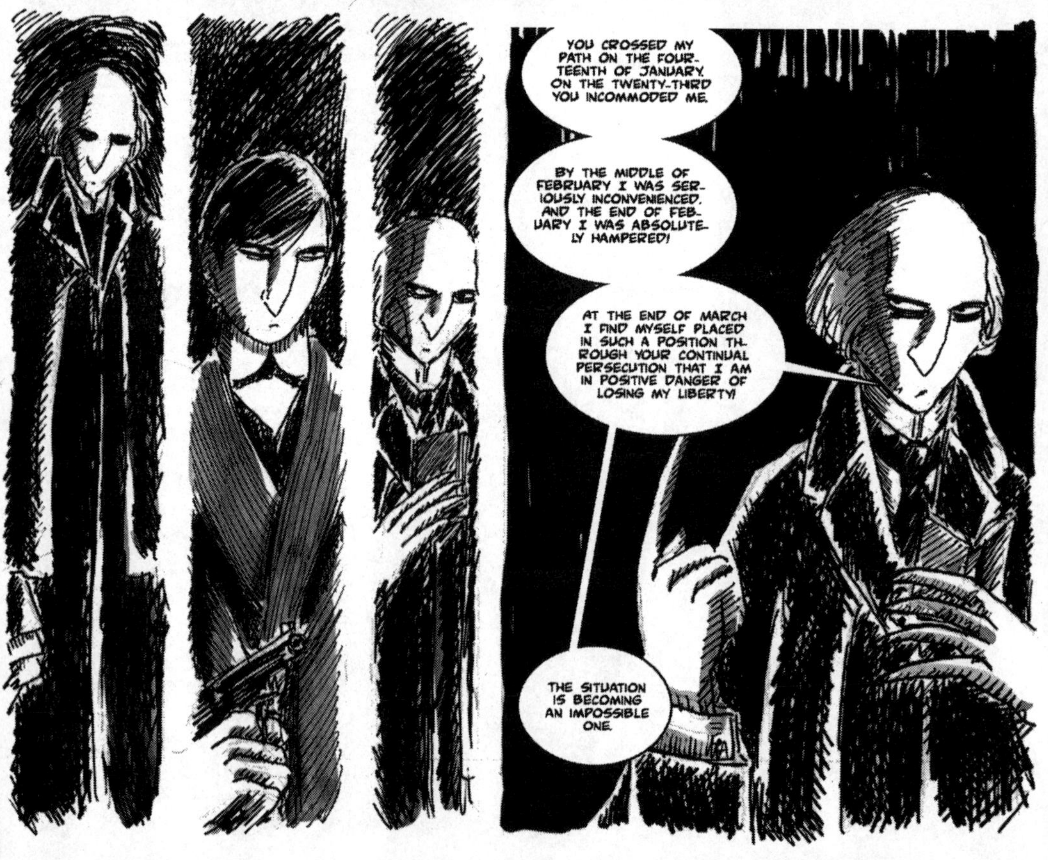
YOU CROSSED MY PATH ON THE FOUR-TEENTH OF JANUARY. ON THE TWENTY-THIRD YOU INCOMMODED ME.
BY THE MIDDLE OF FEBRUARY I WAS SER-IOUSLY INCONVENIENCED. AND THE END OF FEB-UARY I WAS ABSOLUTE-LY HAMPERED!
AT THE END OF MARCH I FIND MYSELF PLACED IN SUCH A POSITION TH-ROUGH YOUR CONTINUAL PERSECUTION THAT I AM IN POSITIVE DANGER OF LOSING MY LIBERTY!
THE SITUATION IS BECOMING AN IMPOSSIBLE ONE.

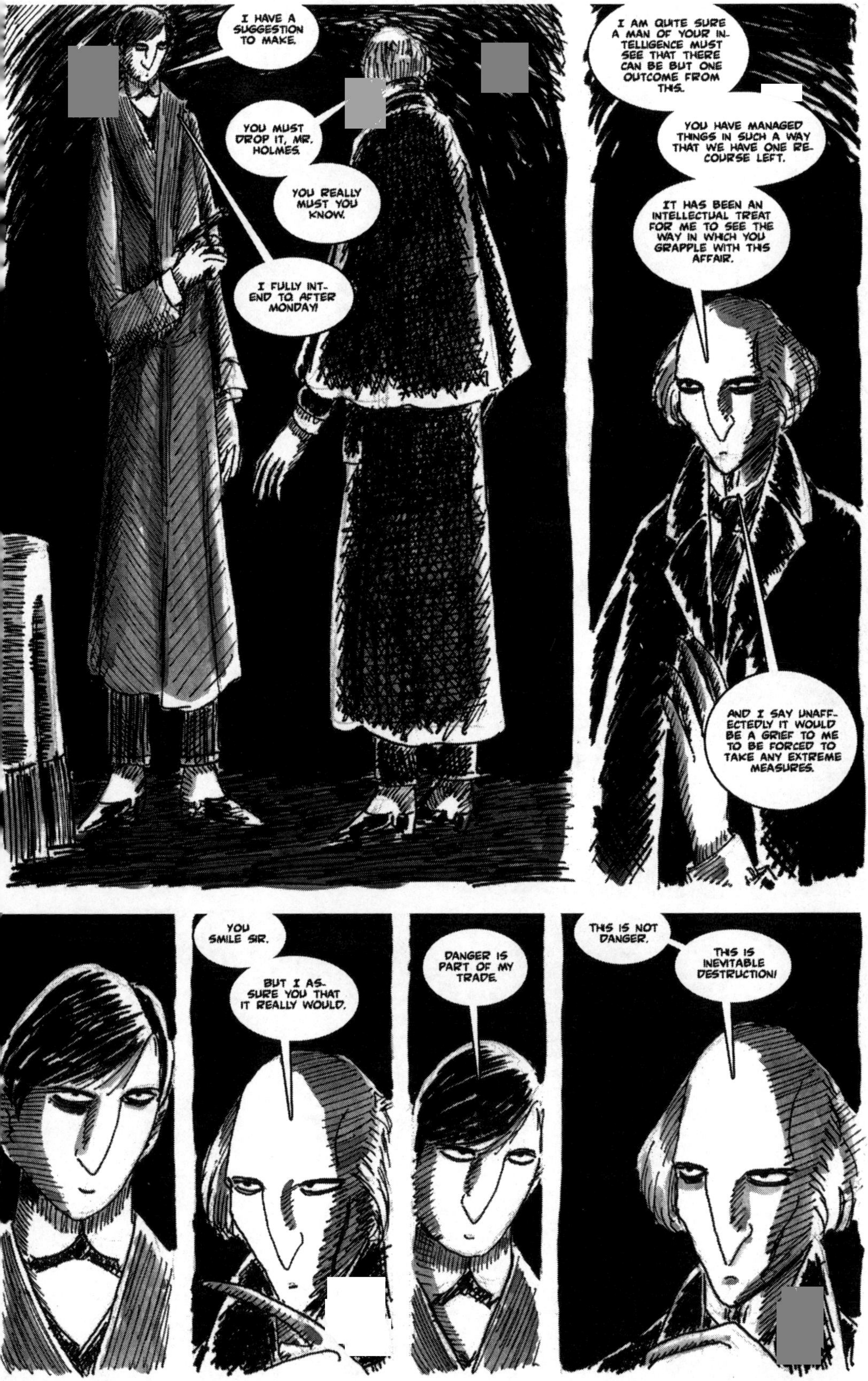
I HAVE A SUGGESTION TO MAKE.
YOU MUST DROP IT, MR. HOLMES.
YOU REALLY MUST YOU KNOW.
I FULLY INT-END TO, AFTER MONDAY!
I AM QUITE SURE A MAN OF YOUR IN-TELLIGENCE MUST SEE THAT THERE CAN BE BUT ONE OUTCOME FROM THIS.
YOU HAVE MANAGED THINGS IN SUCH A WAY THAT WE HAVE ONE RE-COURSE LEFT.
IT HAS BEEN AN INTELLECTUAL TREAT FOR ME TO SEE THE WAY IN WHICH YOU GRAPPLE WITH THIS AFFAIR.
AND I SAY UNAFF-ECTEDLY IT WOULD BE A GRIEF TO ME TO BE FORCED TO TAKE ANY EXTREME MEASURES.
YOU SMILE SIR.
BUT I AS-SURE YOU THAT IT REALLY WOULD.
DANGER IS PART OF MY TRADE.
THIS IS NOT DANGER.
THIS IS INEVITABLE DESTRUCTION!

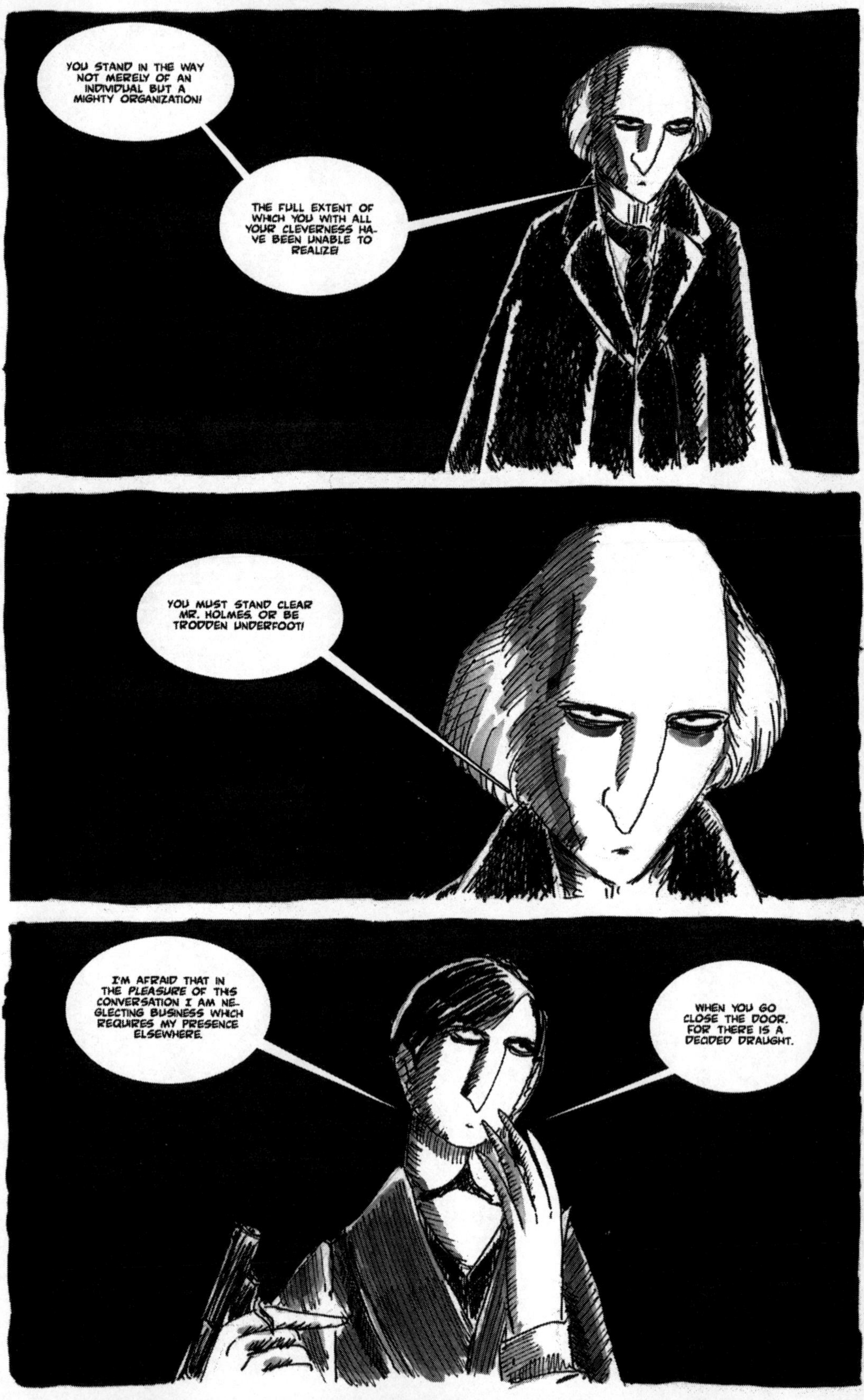
YOU STAND IN THE WAY NOT MERELY OF AN INDIVIDUAL BUT A MIGHTY ORGANIZATION!
THE FULL EXTENT OF WHICH YOU WITH ALL YOUR CLEVERNESS HA-VE BEEN UNABLE TO REALIZE!
YOU MUST STAND CLEAR MR. HOLMES, OR BE TRODDEN UNDERFOOT!
I'M AFRAID THAT IN THE *PLEASURE* OF THIS CONVERSATION I AM NE-GLECTING BUSINESS WHICH REQUIRES MY PRESENCE ELSEWHERE.
WHEN YOU GO CLOSE THE DOOR, FOR THERE IS A DECIDED DRAUGHT.

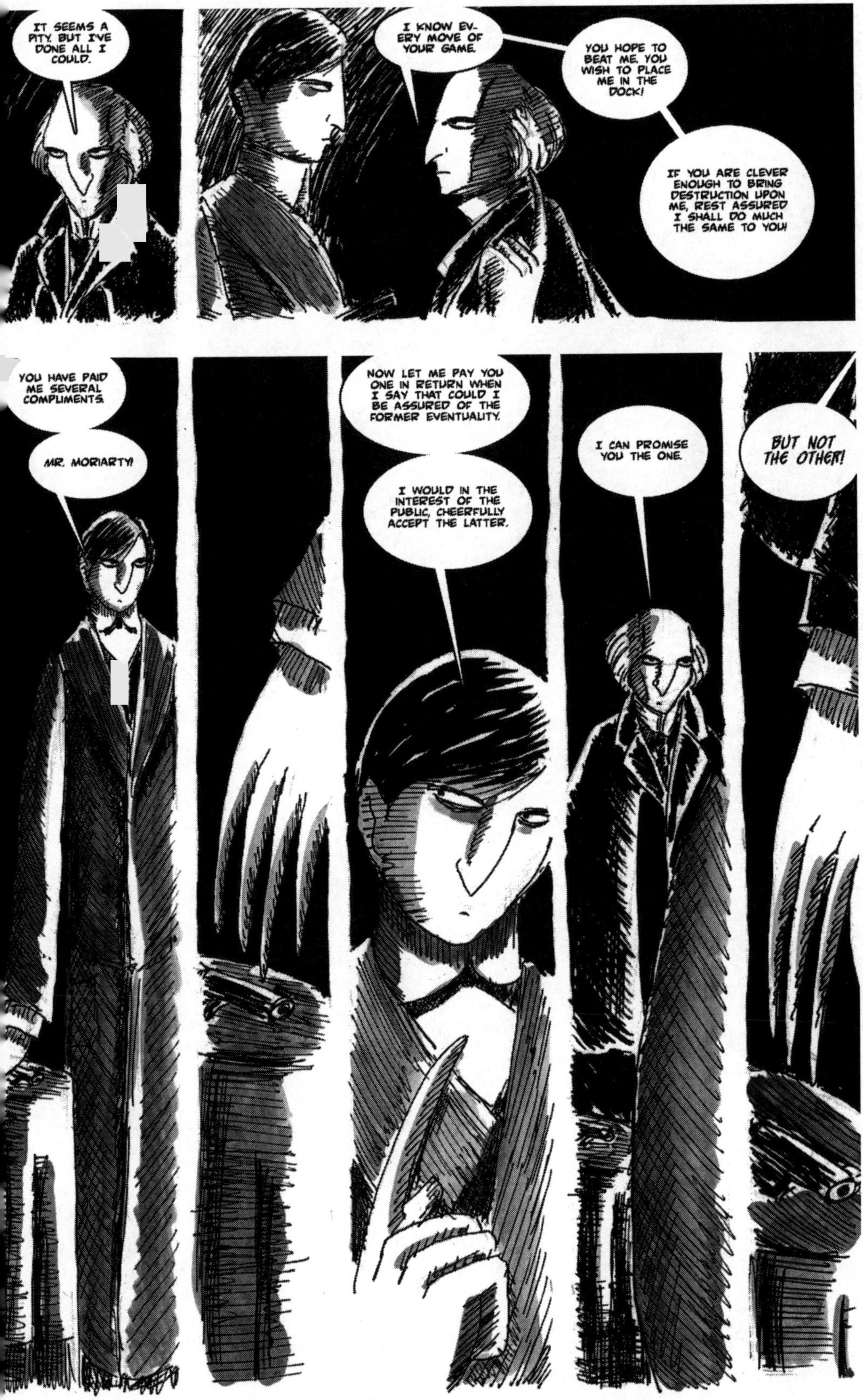
IT SEEMS A PITY. BUT I'VE DONE ALL I COULD.
I KNOW EVERY MOVE OF YOUR GAME.
YOU HOPE TO BEAT ME. YOU WISH TO PLACE ME IN THE DOCK!
IF YOU ARE CLEVER ENOUGH TO BRING DESTRUCTION UPON ME, REST ASSURED I SHALL DO MUCH THE SAME TO YOU!
YOU HAVE PAID ME SEVERAL COMPLIMENTS.
MR. MORIARTY!
NOW LET ME PAY YOU ONE IN RETURN WHEN I SAY THAT COULD I BE ASSURED OF THE FORMER EVENTUALITY.
I WOULD IN THE INTEREST OF THE PUBLIC, CHEERFULLY ACCEPT THE LATTER.
I CAN PROMISE YOU THE ONE.
BUT NOT THE OTHER!

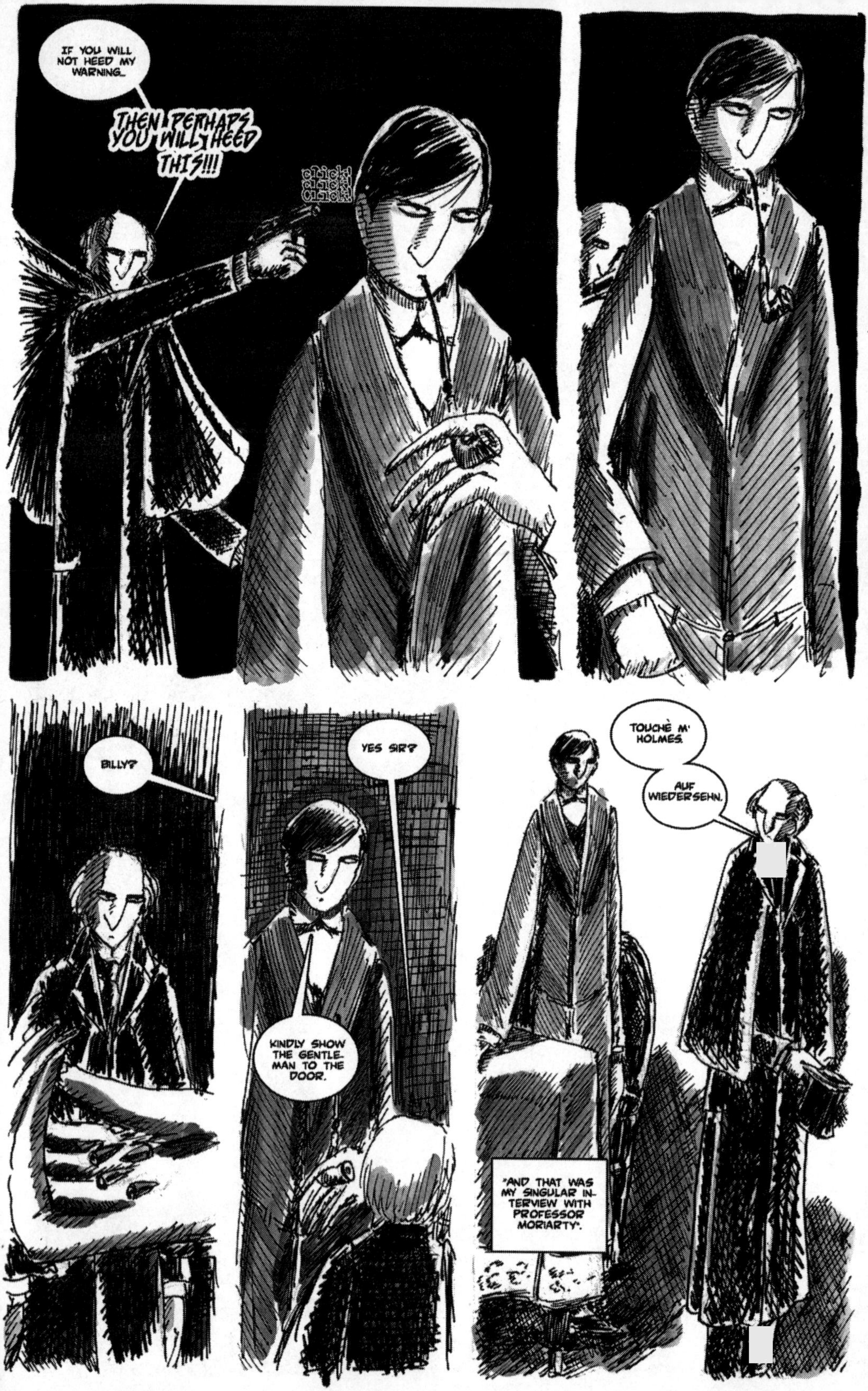
IF YOU WILL NOT HEED MY WARNING...
THEN PERHAPS YOU WILL HEED THIS!!!
click! click! click!
BILLY?
YES SIR?
KINDLY SHOW THE GENTLE-MAN TO THE DOOR.
TOUCHÈ M' HOLMES.
AUF WIEDERSEHN.
"AND THAT WAS MY SINGULAR IN-TERVIEW WITH PROFESSOR MORIARTY".

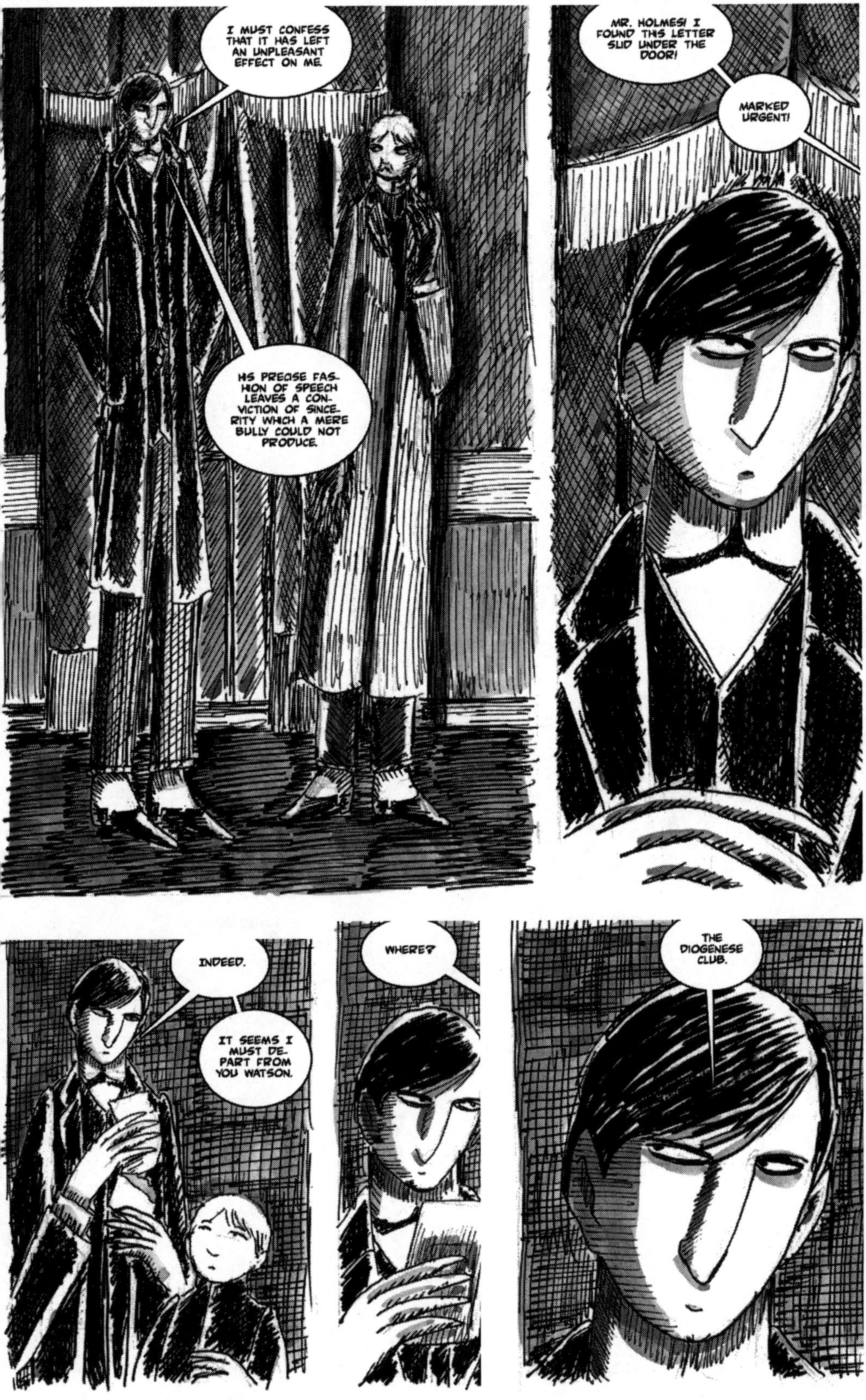
I MUST CONFESS THAT IT HAS LEFT AN UNPLEASANT EFFECT ON ME.
HIS PRECISE FASHION OF SPEECH LEAVES A CONVICTION OF SINCERITY WHICH A MERE BULLY COULD NOT PRODUCE.
MR. HOLMES! I FOUND THIS LETTER SLID UNDER THE DOOR!
MARKED URGENT!
INDEED.
IT SEEMS I MUST DEPART FROM YOU WATSON.
WHERE?
THE DIOGENESE CLUB.

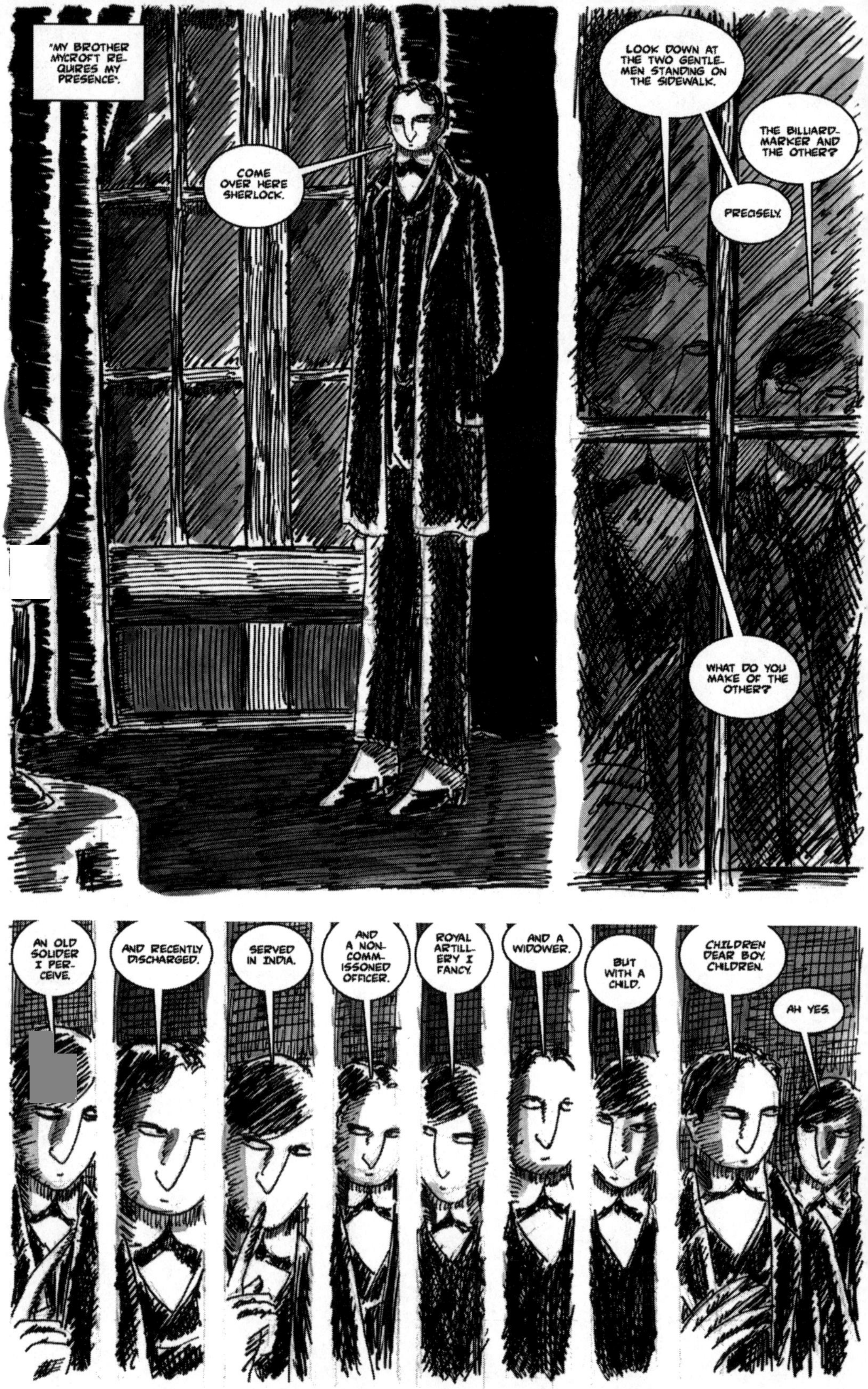
"MY BROTHER MYCROFT REQUIRES MY PRESENCE".
COME OVER HERE SHERLOCK.
LOOK DOWN AT THE TWO GENTLEMEN STANDING ON THE SIDEWALK.
THE BILLIARD-MARKER AND THE OTHER?
PRECISELY.
WHAT DO YOU MAKE OF THE OTHER?
AN OLD SOLIDER I PERCEIVE.
AND RECENTLY DISCHARGED.
SERVED IN INDIA.
AND A NON-COMMISSONED OFFICER.
ROYAL ARTILLERY I FANCY.
AND A WIDOWER.
BUT WITH A CHILD.
CHILDREN DEAR BOY. CHILDREN.
AH YES.

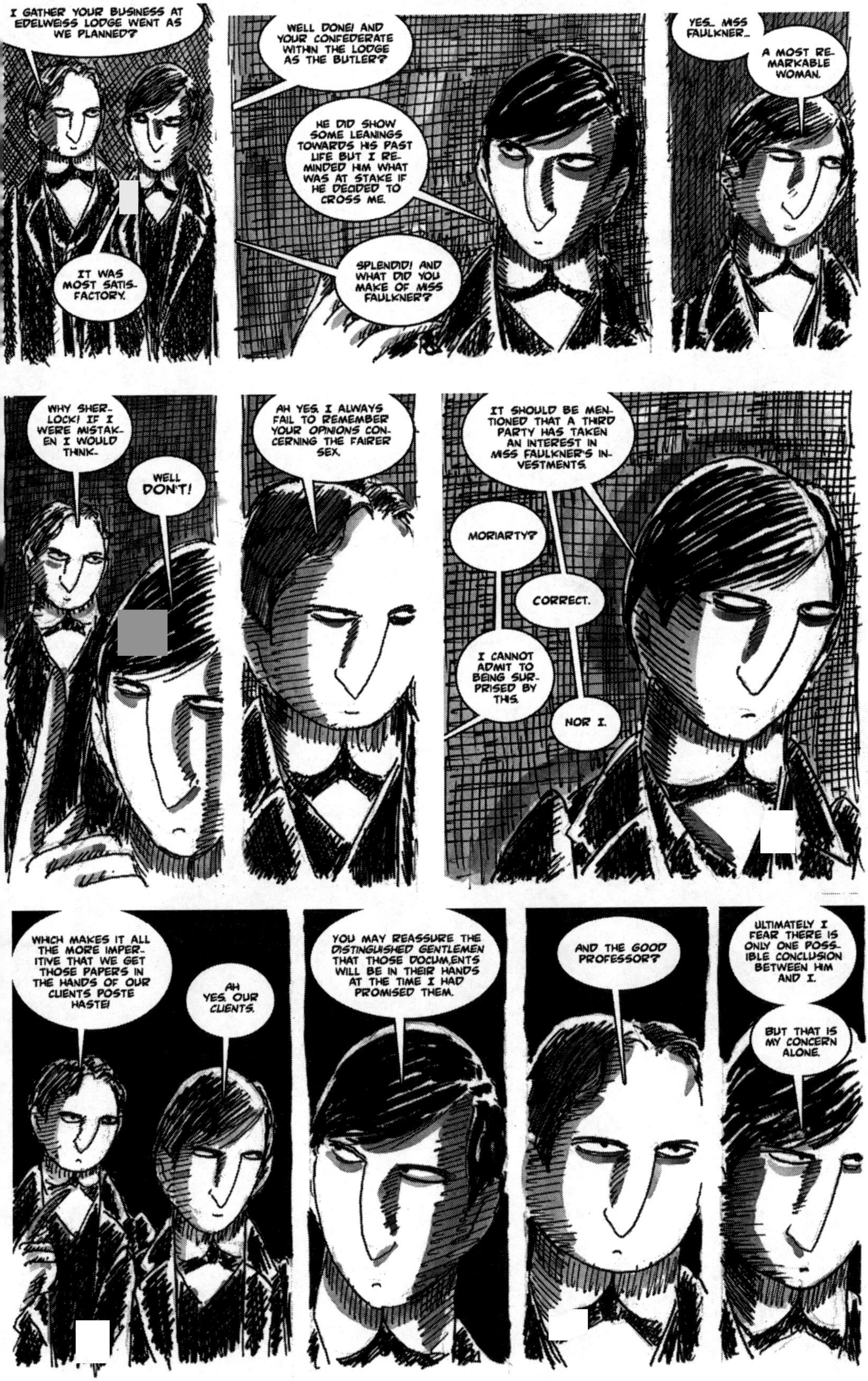
I GATHER YOUR BUSINESS AT EDELWEISS LODGE WENT AS WE PLANNED?
IT WAS MOST SATIS-FACTORY.
WELL DONE! AND YOUR CONFEDERATE WITHIN THE LODGE AS THE BUTLER?
HE DID SHOW SOME LEANINGS TOWARDS HIS PAST LIFE BUT I RE-MINDED HIM WHAT WAS AT STAKE IF HE DECIDED TO CROSS ME.
SPLENDID! AND WHAT DID YOU MAKE OF MISS FAULKNER?
YES... MISS FAULKNER...
A MOST RE-MARKABLE WOMAN.
WHY SHER-LOCK! IF I WERE MISTAK-EN I WOULD THINK...
WELL DON'T!
AH YES. I ALWAYS FAIL TO REMEMBER YOUR OPINIONS CON-CERNING THE FAIRER SEX.
IT SHOULD BE MEN-TIONED THAT A THIRD PARTY HAS TAKEN AN INTEREST IN MISS FAULKNER'S IN-VESTMENTS.
MORIARTY?
CORRECT.
I CANNOT ADMIT TO BEING SUR-PRISED BY THIS.
NOR I.
WHICH MAKES IT ALL THE MORE IMPER-ITIVE THAT WE GET THOSE PAPERS IN THE HANDS OF OUR CLIENTS POSTE HASTE!
AH YES. OUR CLIENTS.
YOU MAY REASSURE THE DISTINGUISHED GENTLEMEN THAT THOSE DOCUMENTS WILL BE IN THEIR HANDS AT THE TIME I HAD PROMISED THEM.
AND THE GOOD PROFESSOR?
ULTIMATELY I FEAR THERE IS ONLY ONE POSS-IBLE CONCLUSION BETWEEN HIM AND I.
BUT THAT IS MY CONCERN ALONE.

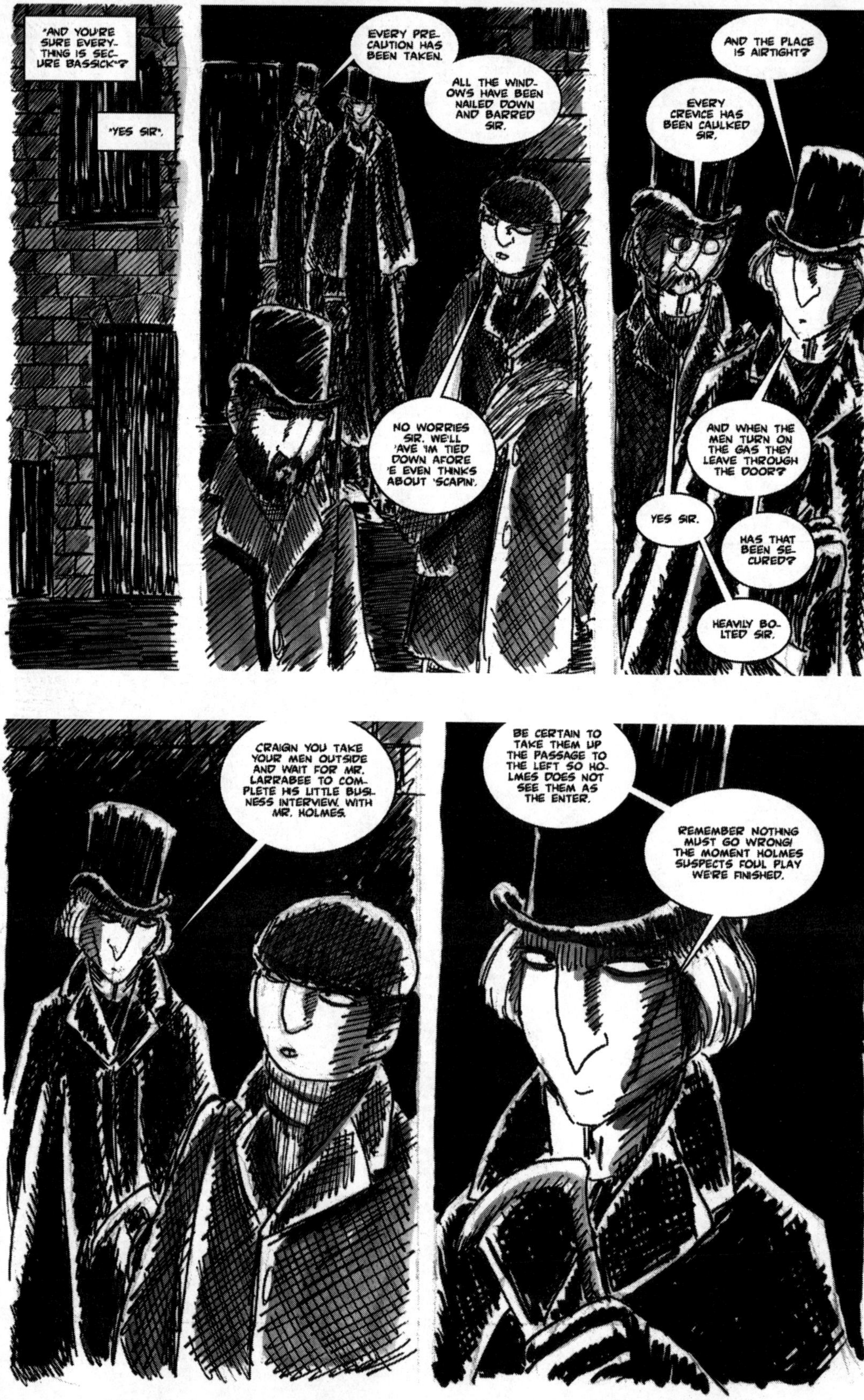
"AND YOU'RE SURE EVERYTHING IS SECURE BASSICK"?
"YES SIR".
EVERY PRECAUTION HAS BEEN TAKEN.
ALL THE WINDOWS HAVE BEEN NAILED DOWN AND BARRED SIR.
NO WORRIES SIR. WE'LL 'AVE 'IM TIED DOWN AFORE 'E EVEN THINKS ABOUT 'SCAPIN'.
AND THE PLACE IS AIRTIGHT?
EVERY CREVICE HAS BEEN CAULKED SIR.
AND WHEN THE MEN TURN ON THE GAS THEY LEAVE THROUGH THE DOOR?
YES SIR.
HAS THAT BEEN SECURED?
HEAVILY BOLTED SIR.
CRAIGIN YOU TAKE YOUR MEN OUTSIDE AND WAIT FOR MR. LARRABEE TO COMPLETE HIS LITTLE BUSINESS INTERVIEW WITH MR. HOLMES.
BE CERTAIN TO TAKE THEM UP THE PASSAGE TO THE LEFT SO HOLMES DOES NOT SEE THEM AS THE ENTER.
REMEMBER NOTHING MUST GO WRONG! THE MOMENT HOLMES SUSPECTS FOUL PLAY WE'RE FINISHED.

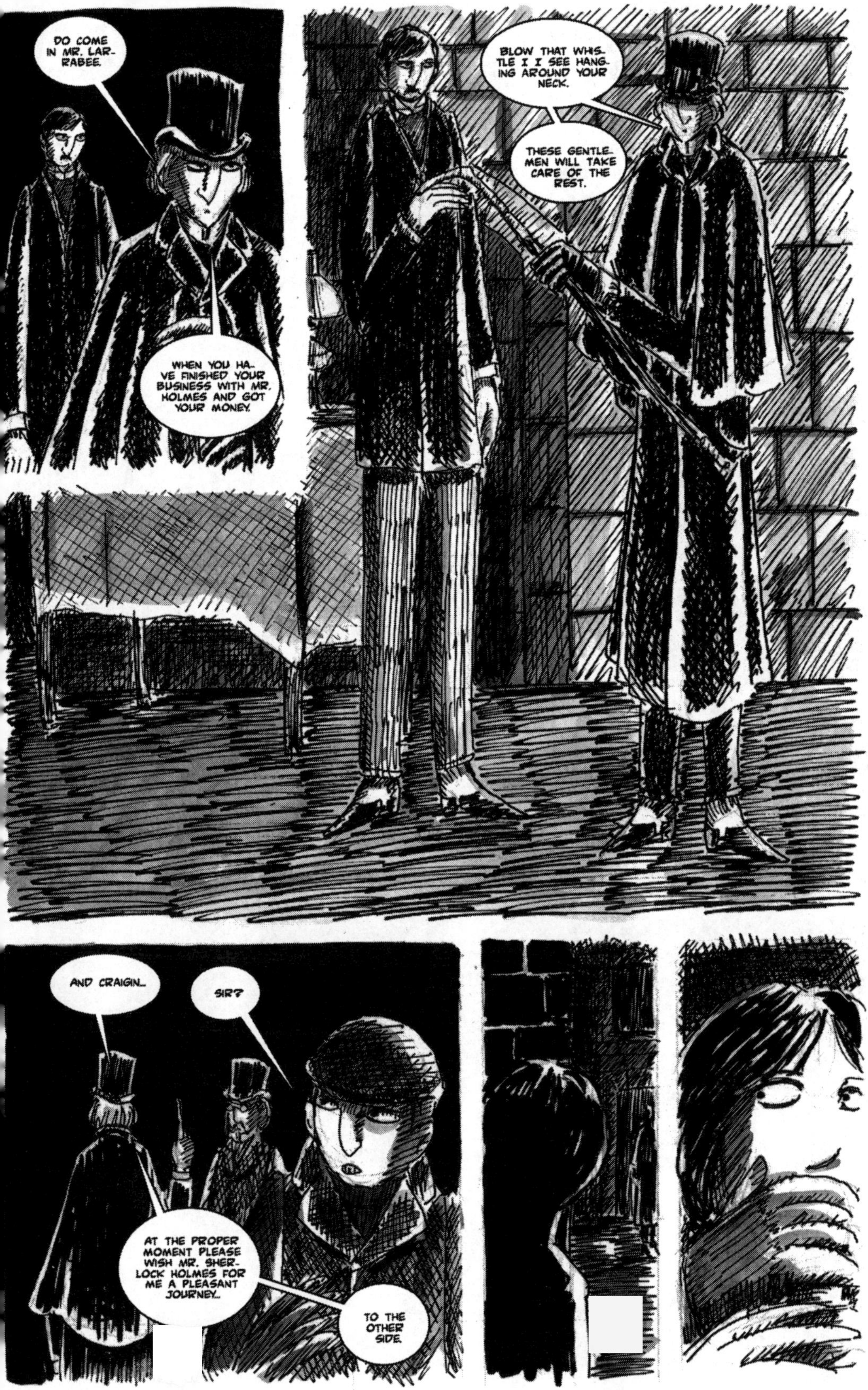
DO COME IN MR. LARRABEE.
WHEN YOU HAVE FINISHED YOUR BUSINESS WITH MR. HOLMES AND GOT YOUR MONEY.
BLOW THAT WHISTLE I I SEE HANGING AROUND YOUR NECK.
THESE GENTLEMEN WILL TAKE CARE OF THE REST.
AND CRAIGIN...
SIR?
AT THE PROPER MOMENT PLEASE WISH MR. SHERLOCK HOLMES FOR ME A PLEASANT JOURNEY...
TO THE OTHER SIDE.

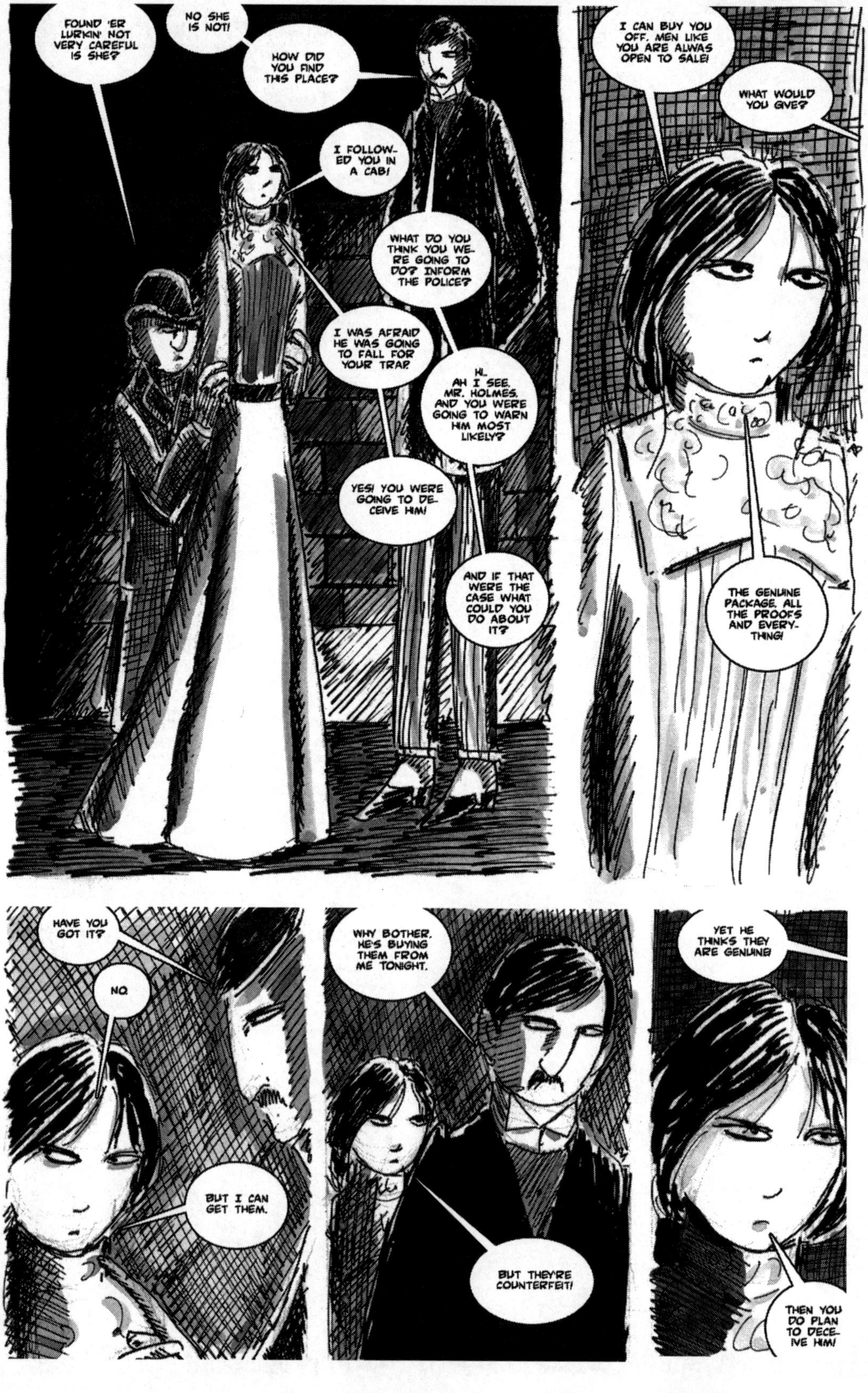
FOUND 'ER LURKIN' NOT VERY CAREFUL IS SHE?
NO SHE IS NOT!
HOW DID YOU FIND THIS PLACE?
I FOLLOW-ED YOU IN A CAB!
WHAT DO YOU THINK YOU WE-RE GOING TO DO? INFORM THE POLICE?
I WAS AFRAID HE WAS GOING TO FALL FOR YOUR TRAP.
HI. AH I SEE. MR. HOLMES. AND YOU WERE GOING TO WARN HIM MOST LIKELY?
YES! YOU WERE GOING TO DE-CEIVE HIM!
AND IF THAT WERE THE CASE WHAT COULD YOU DO ABOUT IT?
I CAN BUY YOU OFF. MEN LIKE YOU ARE ALWAYS OPEN TO SALE!
WHAT WOULD YOU GIVE?
THE GENUINE PACKAGE. ALL THE PROOFS AND EVERY-THING!
HAVE YOU GOT IT?
NO.
BUT I CAN GET THEM.
WHY BOTHER. HE'S BUYING THEM FROM ME TONIGHT.
BUT THEY'RE COUNTERFEIT!
YET HE THINKS THEY ARE GENUINE!
THEN YOU DO PLAN TO DECE-IVE HIM!

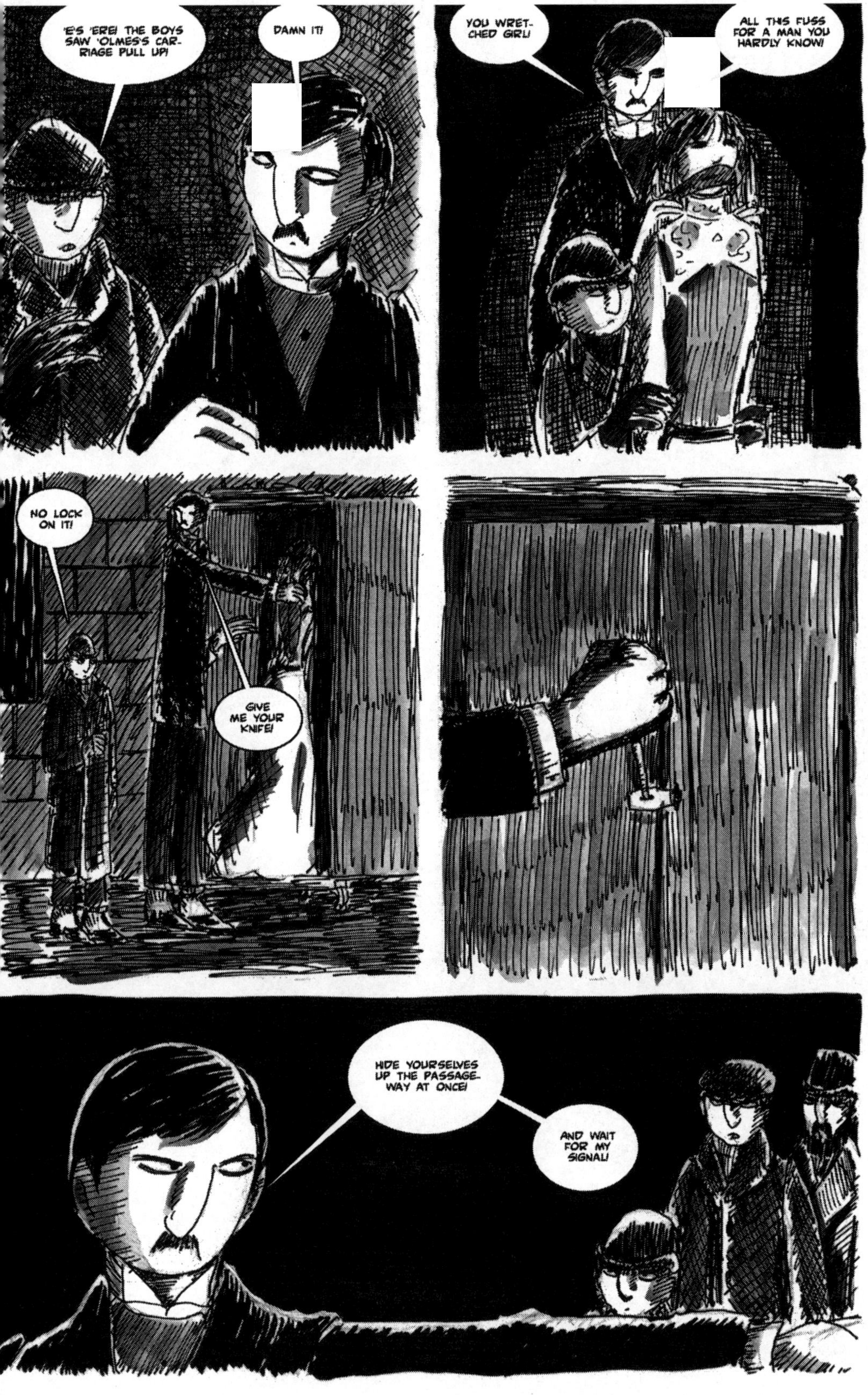
'E'S 'ERE! THE BOYS SAW 'OLMES'S CAR-RIAGE PULL UP!
DAMN IT!
YOU WRET-CHED GIRL!
ALL THIS FUSS FOR A MAN YOU HARDLY KNOW!
NO LOCK ON IT!
GIVE ME YOUR KNIFE!
HIDE YOURSELVES UP THE PASSAGE-WAY AT ONCE!
AND WAIT FOR MY SIGNAL!

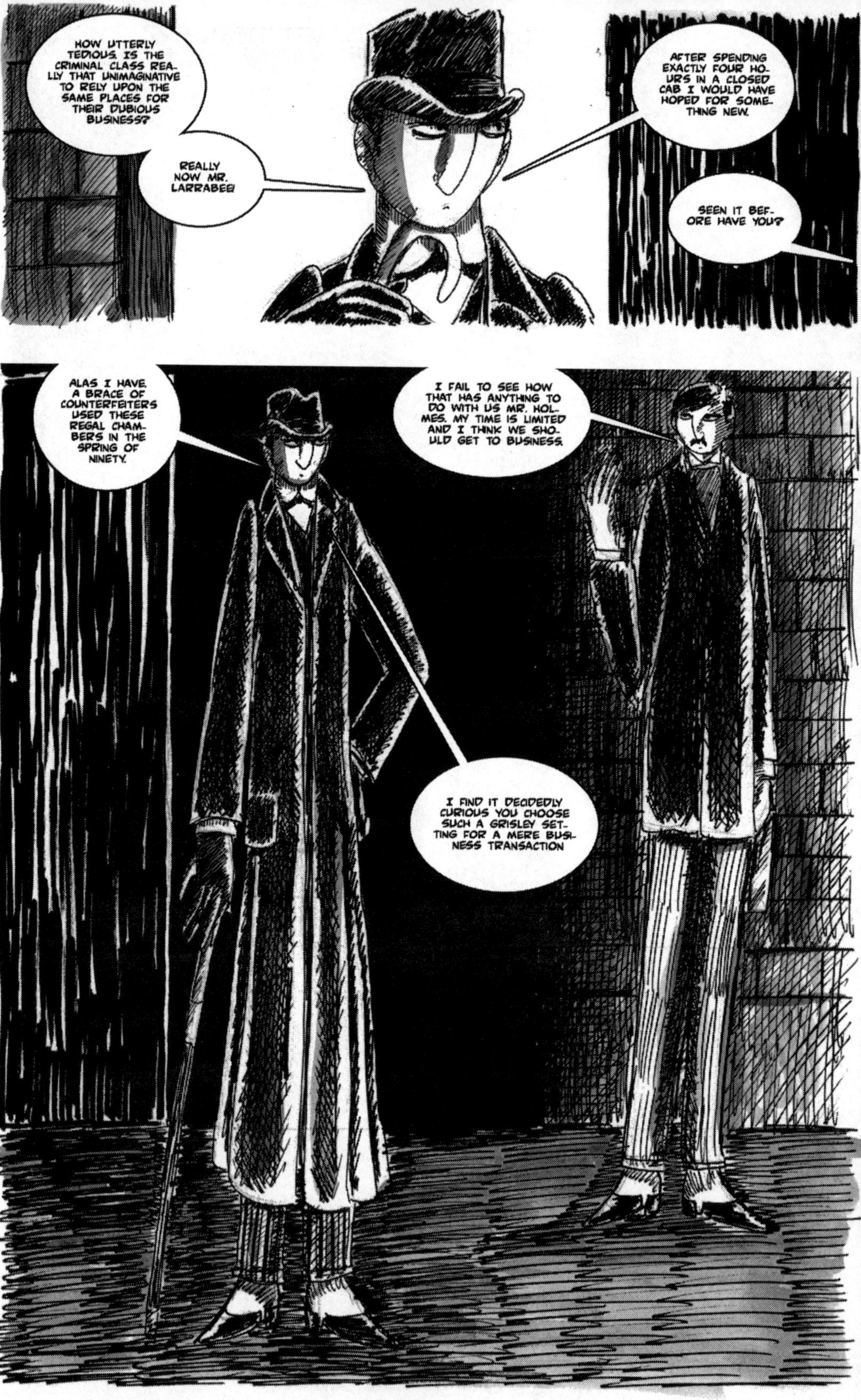
HOW UTTERLY TEDIOUS. IS THE CRIMINAL CLASS REALLY THAT UNIMAGINATIVE TO RELY UPON THE SAME PLACES FOR THEIR DUBIOUS BUSINESS?
REALLY NOW MR. LARRABEE!
AFTER SPENDING EXACTLY FOUR HOURS IN A CLOSED CAB I WOULD HAVE HOPED FOR SOMETHING NEW.
SEEN IT BEFORE HAVE YOU?
ALAS I HAVE. A BRACE OF COUNTERFEITERS USED THESE REGAL CHAMBERS IN THE SPRING OF NINETY.
I FAIL TO SEE HOW THAT HAS ANYTHING TO DO WITH US MR. HOLMES. MY TIME IS LIMITED AND I THNK WE SHOULD GET TO BUSINESS.
I FIND IT DECIDEDLY CURIOUS YOU CHOOSE SUCH A GRISLEY SETTING FOR A MERE BUSINESS TRANSACTION

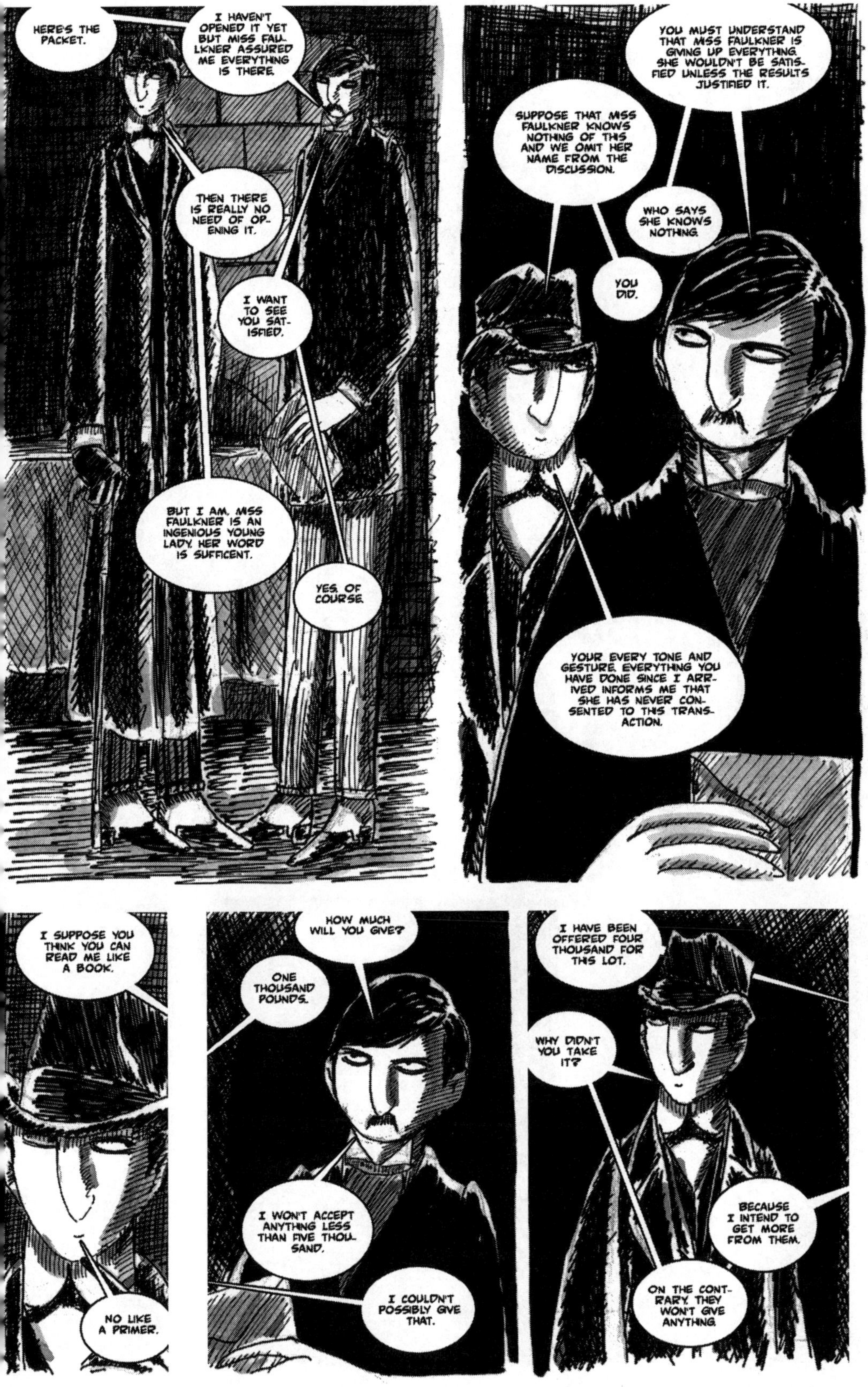
HERE'S THE PACKET.
I HAVEN'T OPENED IT YET BUT MISS FAULKNER ASSURED ME EVERYTHING IS THERE.
THEN THERE IS REALLY NO NEED OF OPENING IT.
I WANT TO SEE YOU SATISFIED.
BUT I AM. MISS FAULKNER IS AN INGENIOUS YOUNG LADY. HER WORD IS SUFFICENT.
YES, OF COURSE.
SUPPOSE THAT MISS FAULKNER KNOWS NOTHING OF THIS AND WE OMIT HER NAME FROM THE DISCUSSION.
YOU MUST UNDERSTAND THAT MISS FAULKNER IS GIVING UP EVERYTHING. SHE WOULDN'T BE SATISFIED UNLESS THE RESULTS JUSTIFIED IT.
WHO SAYS SHE KNOWS NOTHING.
YOU DID.
YOUR EVERY TONE AND GESTURE, EVERYTHING YOU HAVE DONE SINCE I ARRIVED INFORMS ME THAT SHE HAS NEVER CONSENTED TO THIS TRANSACTION.
I SUPPOSE YOU THINK YOU CAN READ ME LIKE A BOOK.
NO LIKE A PRIMER.
HOW MUCH WILL YOU GIVE?
ONE THOUSAND POUNDS.
I WON'T ACCEPT ANYTHING LESS THAN FIVE THOUSAND.
I COULDN'T POSSIBLY GIVE THAT.
I HAVE BEEN OFFERED FOUR THOUSAND FOR THIS LOT.
WHY DIDN'T YOU TAKE IT?
BECAUSE I INTEND TO GET MORE FROM THEM.
ON THE CONTRARY, THEY WON'T GIVE ANYTHING.

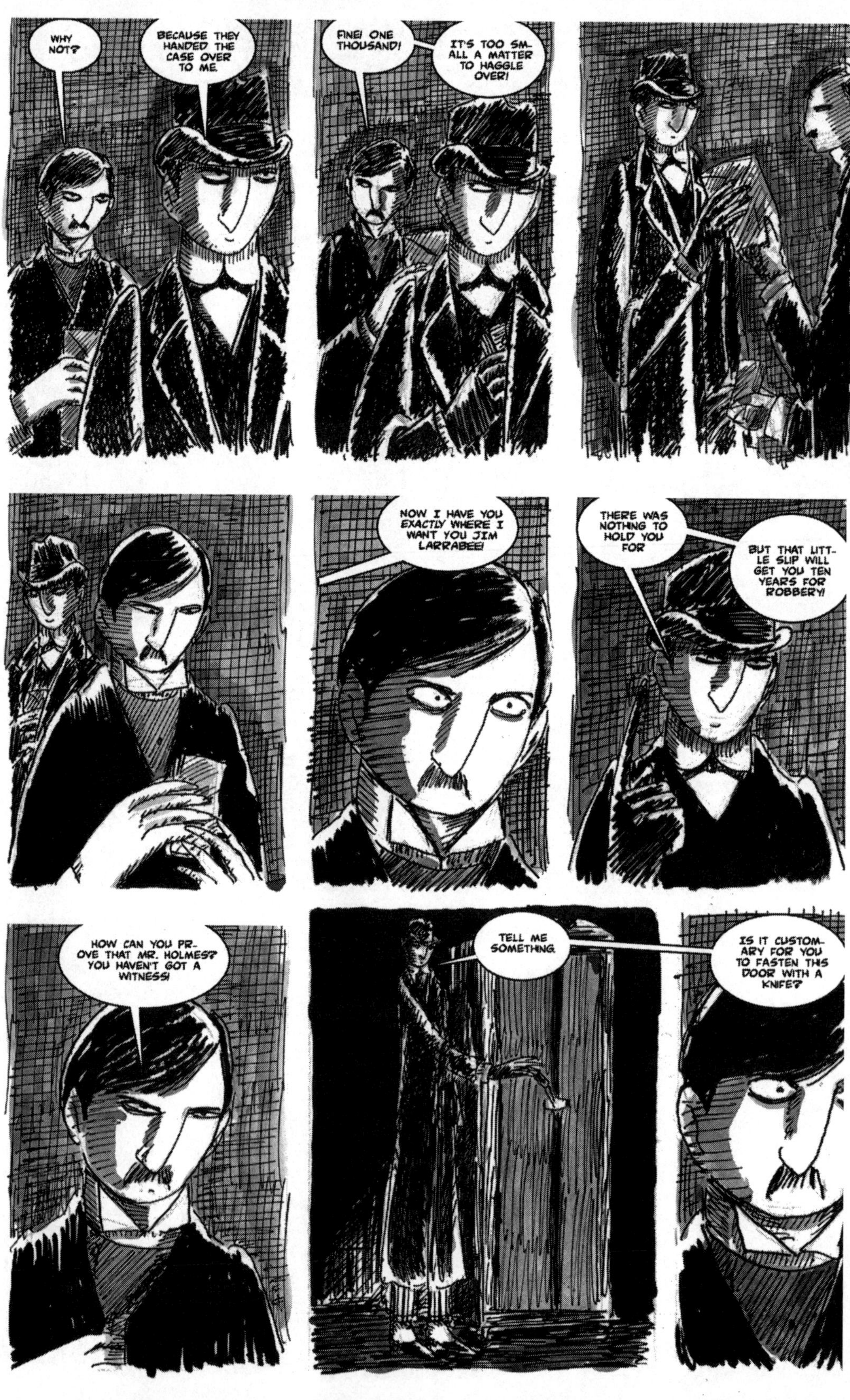
WHY NOT?
BECAUSE THEY HANDED THE CASE OVER TO ME.
FINE! ONE THOUSAND!
IT'S TOO SM- ALL A MATTER TO HAGGLE OVER!
NOW I HAVE YOU EXACTLY WHERE I WANT YOU JIM LARRABEE!
THERE WAS NOTHING TO HOLD YOU FOR
BUT THAT LITT- LE SLIP WILL GET YOU TEN YEARS FOR ROBBERY!
HOW CAN YOU PR- OVE THAT MR. HOLMES? YOU HAVEN'T GOT A WITNESS!
TELL ME SOMETHING.
IS IT CUSTOM- ARY FOR YOU TO FASTEN THIS DOOR WITH A KNIFE?

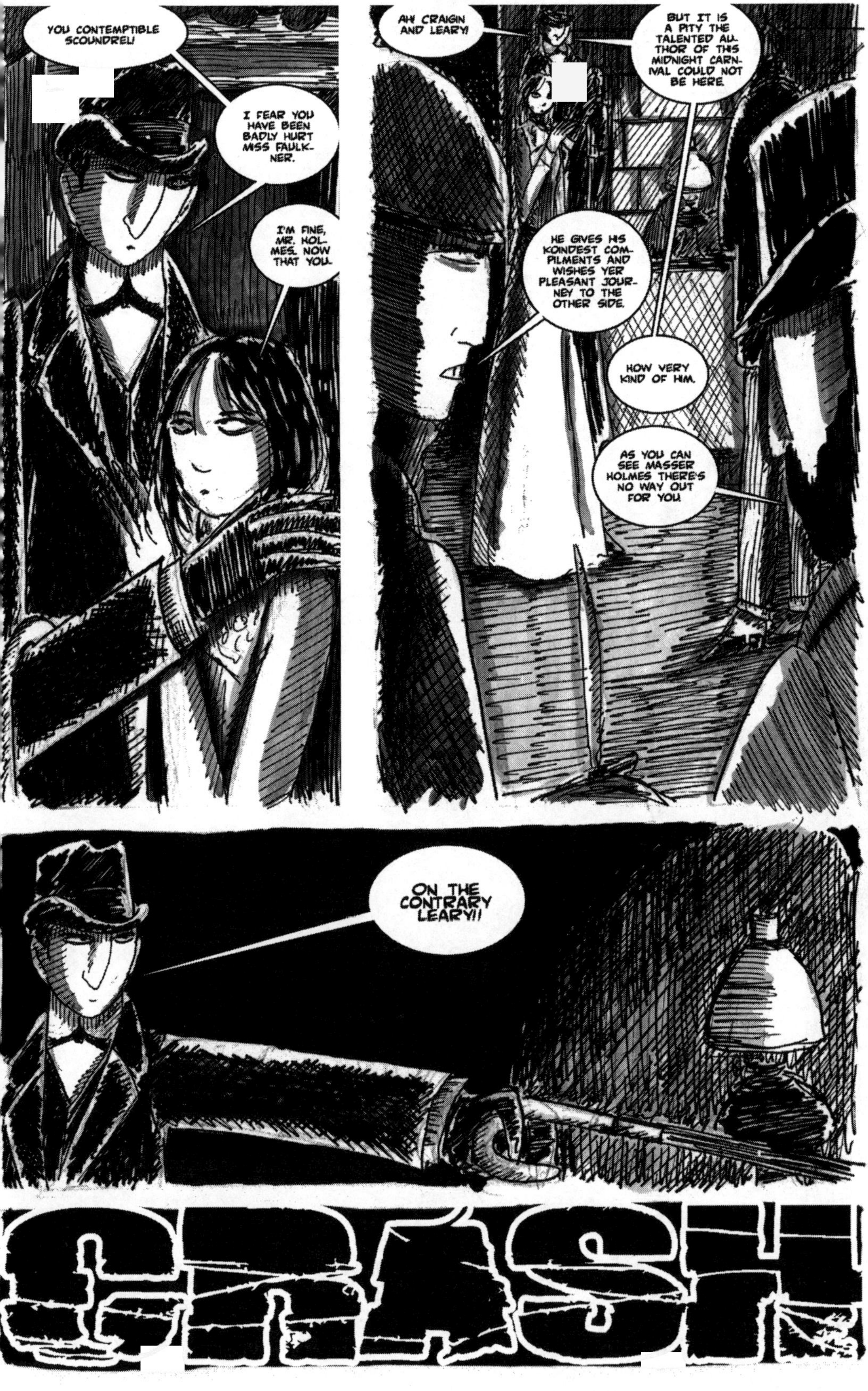
YOU CONTEMPTIBLE SCOUNDREL!
I FEAR YOU HAVE BEEN BADLY HURT MISS FAULKNER.
I'M FINE, MR. HOLMES. NOW THAT YOU...
AH! CRAIGIN AND LEARY!
BUT IT IS A PITY THE TALENTED AUTHOR OF THIS MIDNIGHT CARNIVAL COULD NOT BE HERE.
HE GIVES HIS KOINDEST COMPILMENTS AND WISHES YER PLEASANT JOURNEY TO THE OTHER SIDE.
HOW VERY KIND OF HIM.
AS YOU CAN SEE MASSER HOLMES THERE'S NO WAY OUT FOR YOU.
ON THE CONTRARY LEARY!!
CRASH

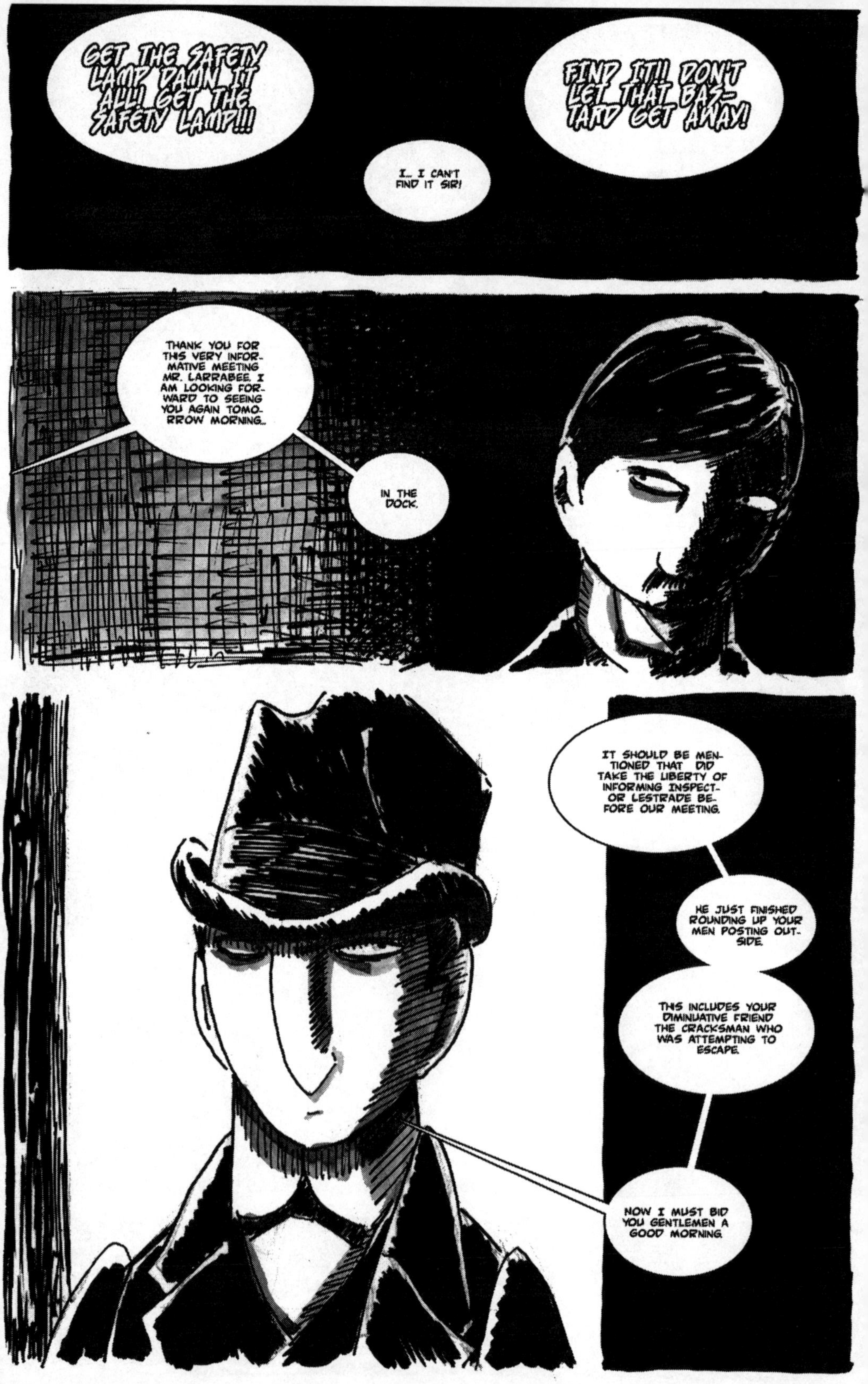
GET THE SAFETY LAMP DAMN IT ALL! GET THE SAFETY LAMP!!!
FIND IT!! DON'T LET THAT BASTARD GET AWAY!
I... I CAN'T FIND IT SIR!
THANK YOU FOR THIS VERY INFORMATIVE MEETING MR. LARRABEE. I AM LOOKING FORWARD TO SEEING YOU AGAIN TOMORROW MORNING...
IN THE DOCK.
IT SHOULD BE MENTIONED THAT DID TAKE THE LIBERTY OF INFORMING INSPECTOR LESTRADE BEFORE OUR MEETING.
HE JUST FINISHED ROUNDING UP YOUR MEN POSTING OUTSIDE.
THIS INCLUDES YOUR DIMINUATIVE FRIEND THE CRACKSMAN WHO WAS ATTEMPTING TO ESCAPE.
NOW I MUST BID YOU GENTLEMEN A GOOD MORNING.

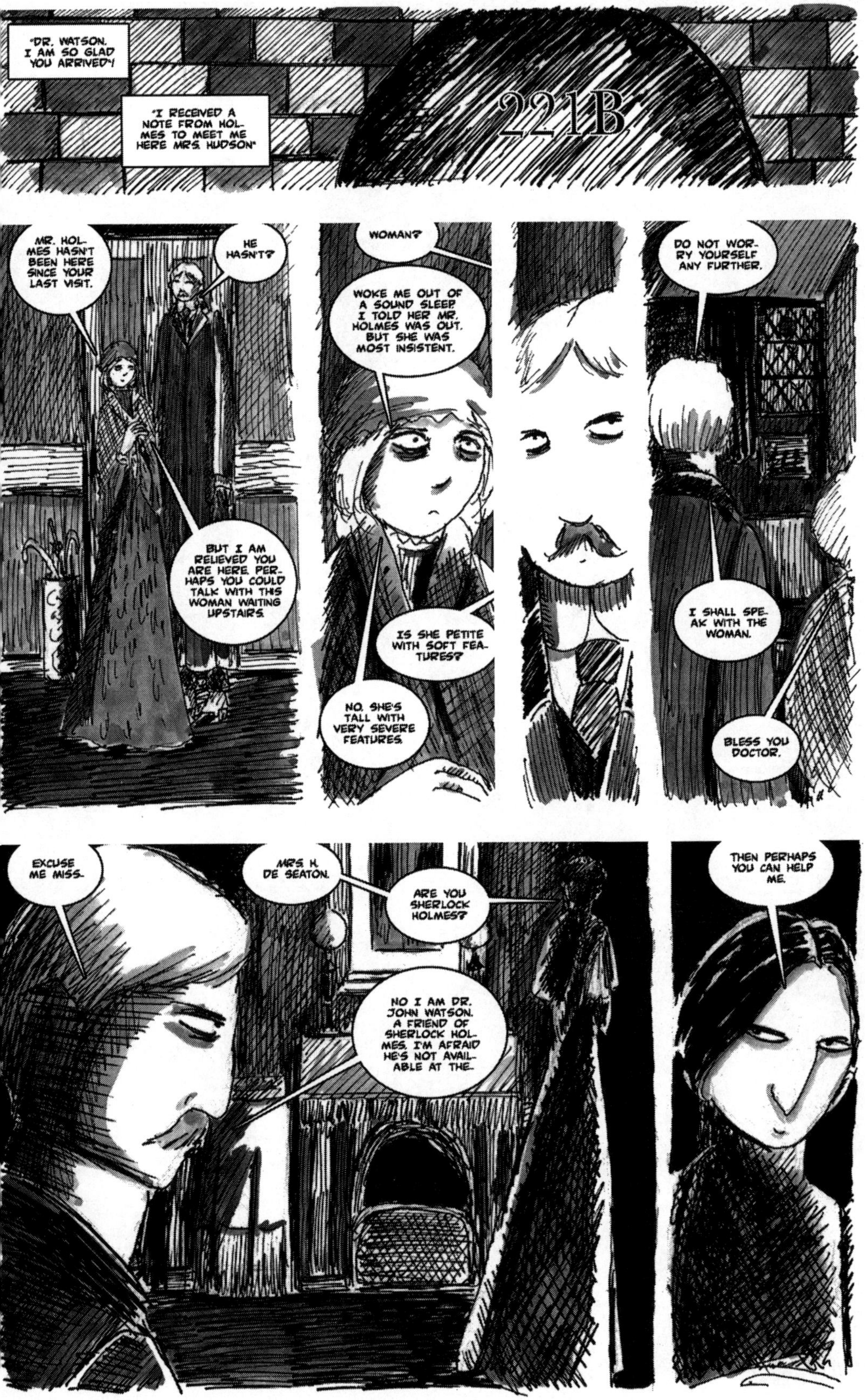
"DR. WATSON. I AM SO GLAD YOU ARRIVED"!
"I RECEIVED A NOTE FROM HOLMES TO MEET ME HERE MRS. HUDSON"
221B
MR. HOLMES HASN'T BEEN HERE SINCE YOUR LAST VISIT.
HE HASN'T?
BUT I AM RELIEVED YOU ARE HERE. PERHAPS YOU COULD TALK WITH THIS WOMAN WAITING UPSTAIRS.
WOMAN?
WOKE ME OUT OF A SOUND SLEEP. I TOLD HER MR. HOLMES WAS OUT. BUT SHE WAS MOST INSISTENT.
IS SHE PETITE WITH SOFT FEATURES?
NO. SHE'S TALL WITH VERY SEVERE FEATURES.
DO NOT WORRY YOURSELF ANY FURTHER.
I SHALL SPEAK WITH THE WOMAN.
BLESS YOU DOCTOR.
EXCUSE ME MISS.
MRS. H. DE SEATON.
ARE YOU SHERLOCK HOLMES?
NO I AM DR. JOHN WATSON. A FRIEND OF SHERLOCK HOLMES. I'M AFRAID HE'S NOT AVAILABLE AT THE.
THEN PERHAPS YOU CAN HELP ME.

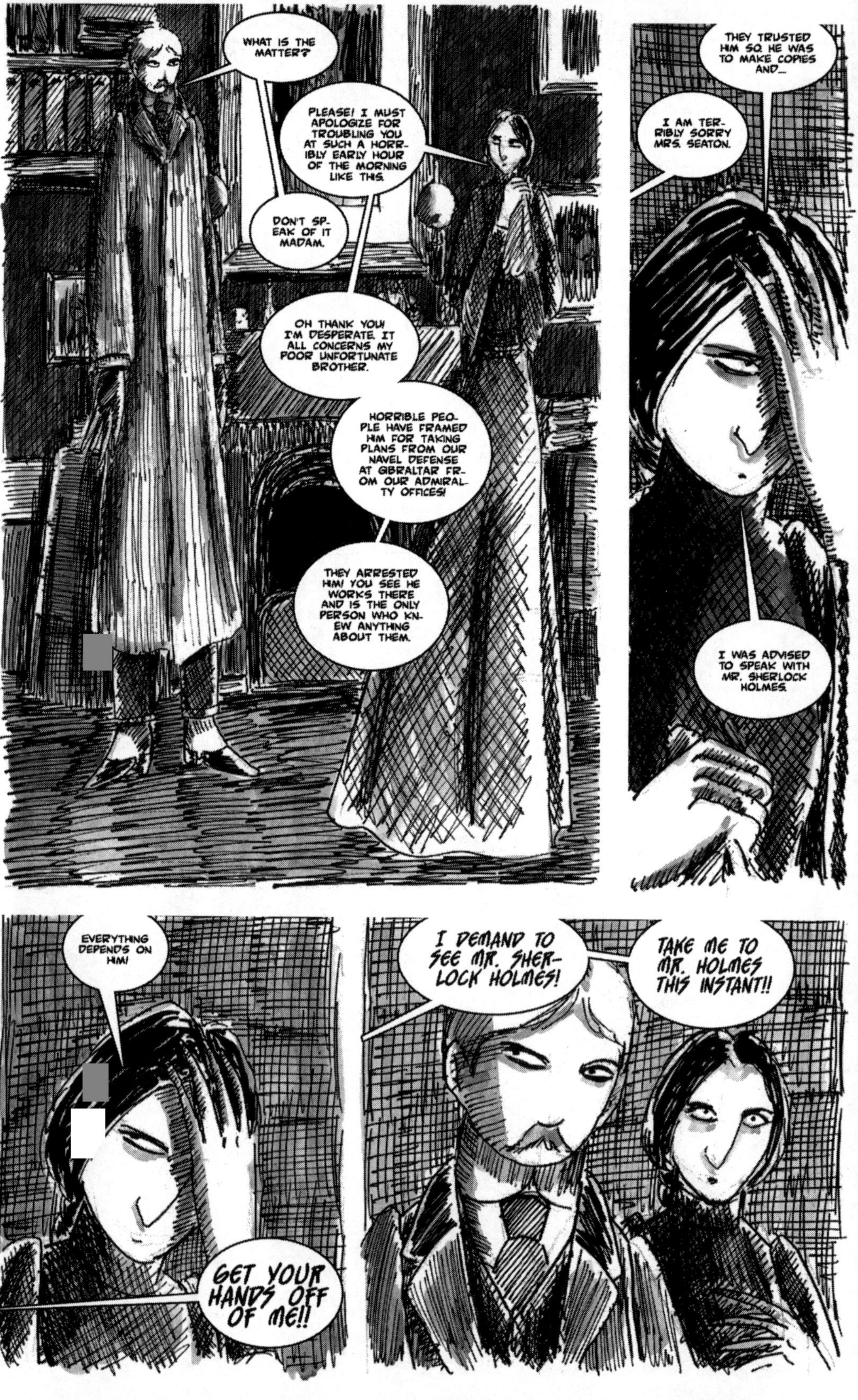
WHAT IS THE MATTER?
PLEASE! I MUST APOLOGIZE FOR TROUBLING YOU AT SUCH A HORRIBLY EARLY HOUR OF THE MORNING LIKE THIS.
DON'T SPEAK OF IT MADAM.
OH THANK YOU! I'M DESPERATE. IT ALL CONCERNS MY POOR UNFORTUNATE BROTHER.
HORRIBLE PEOPLE HAVE FRAMED HIM FOR TAKING PLANS FROM OUR NAVEL DEFENSE AT GIBRALTAR FROM OUR ADMIRALTY OFFICES!
THEY ARRESTED HIM! YOU SEE HE WORKS THERE AND IS THE ONLY PERSON WHO KNEW ANYTHING ABOUT THEM.
THEY TRUSTED HIM SO. HE WAS TO MAKE COPIES AND...
I AM TERRIBLY SORRY MRS. SEATON.
I WAS ADVISED TO SPEAK WITH MR. SHERLOCK HOLMES.
EVERYTHING DEPENDS ON HIM!
GET YOUR HANDS OFF OF ME!!
I DEMAND TO SEE MR. SHERLOCK HOLMES!
TAKE ME TO MR. HOLMES THIS INSTANT!!

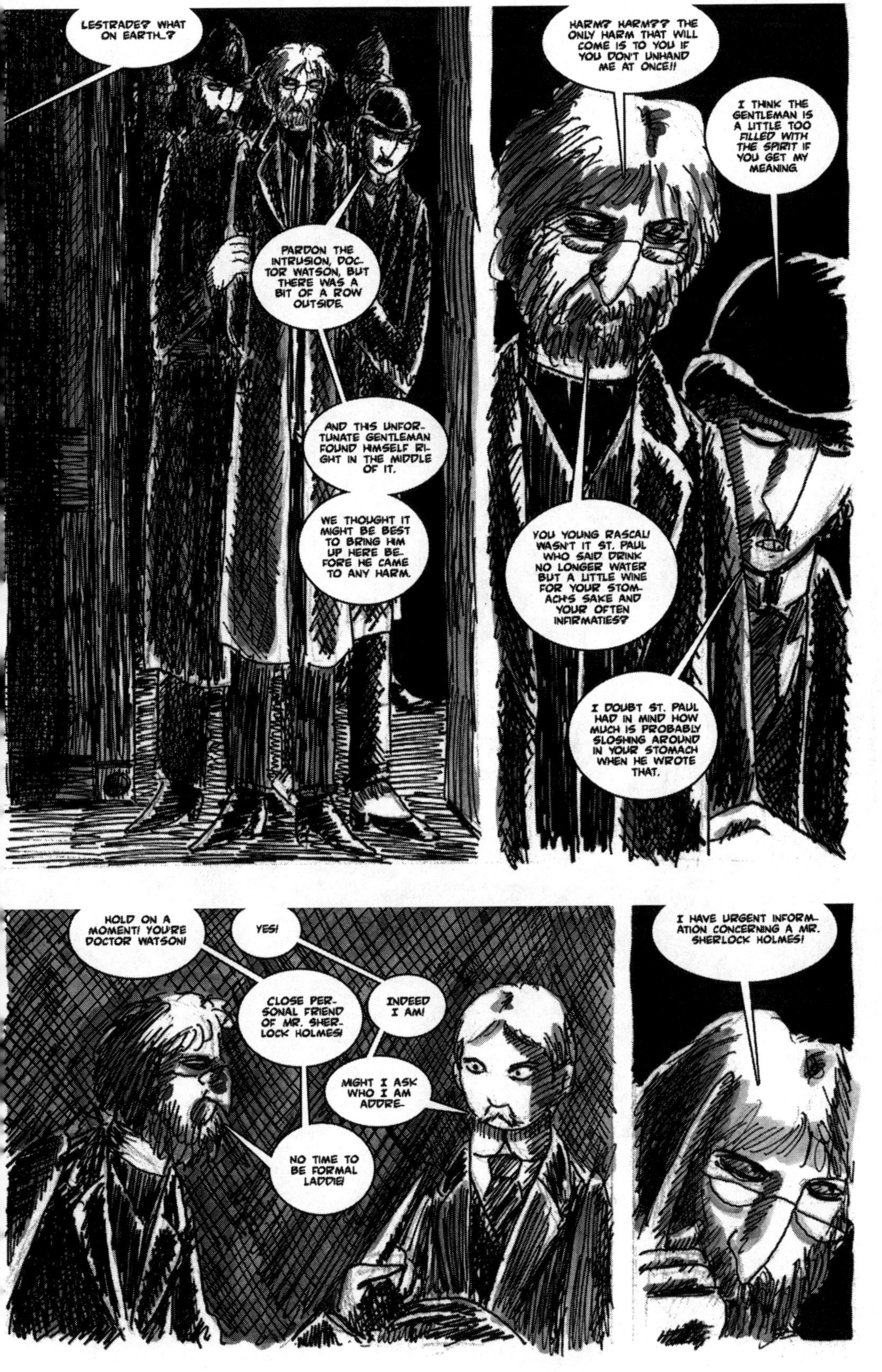
LESTRADE? WHAT ON EARTH...?
PARDON THE INTRUSION, DOCTOR WATSON, BUT THERE WAS A BIT OF A ROW OUTSIDE.
AND THIS UNFORTUNATE GENTLEMAN FOUND HIMSELF RIGHT IN THE MIDDLE OF IT.
WE THOUGHT IT MIGHT BE BEST TO BRING HIM UP HERE BEFORE HE CAME TO ANY HARM.
HARM? HARM?? THE ONLY HARM THAT WILL COME IS TO YOU IF YOU DON'T UNHAND ME AT ONCE!!
I THINK THE GENTLEMAN IS A LITTLE TOO FILLED WITH THE SPIRIT IF YOU GET MY MEANING.
YOU YOUNG RASCAL! WASN'T IT ST. PAUL WHO SAID DRINK NO LONGER WATER BUT A LITTLE WINE FOR YOUR STOMACH'S SAKE AND YOUR OFTEN INFIRMATIES?
I DOUBT ST. PAUL HAD IN MIND HOW MUCH IS PROBABLY SLOSHING AROUND IN YOUR STOMACH WHEN HE WROTE THAT.
HOLD ON A MOMENT! YOU'RE DOCTOR WATSON!
YES!
CLOSE PERSONAL FRIEND OF MR. SHERLOCK HOLMES!
INDEED I AM!
MIGHT I ASK WHO I AM ADDRE-
NO TIME TO BE FORMAL LADDIE!
I HAVE URGENT INFORMATION CONCERNING A MR. SHERLOCK HOLMES!

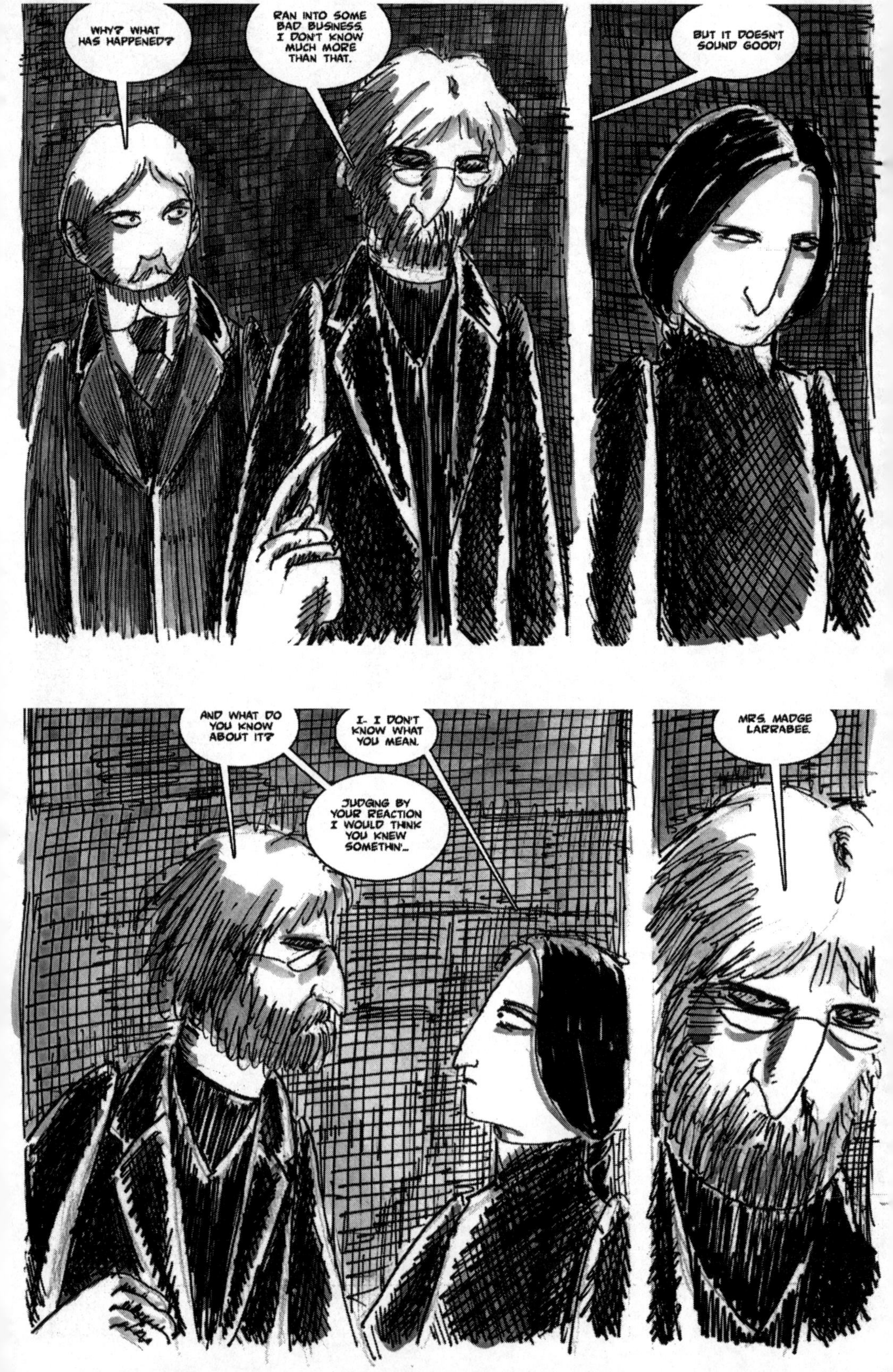
WHY? WHAT HAS HAPPENED?
RAN INTO SOME BAD BUSINESS. I DON'T KNOW MUCH MORE THAN THAT.
BUT IT DOESN'T SOUND GOOD!
AND WHAT DO YOU KNOW ABOUT IT?
I- I DON'T KNOW WHAT YOU MEAN.
JUDGING BY YOUR REACTION I WOULD THINK YOU KNEW SOMETHIN'...
MRS. MADGE LARRABEE.

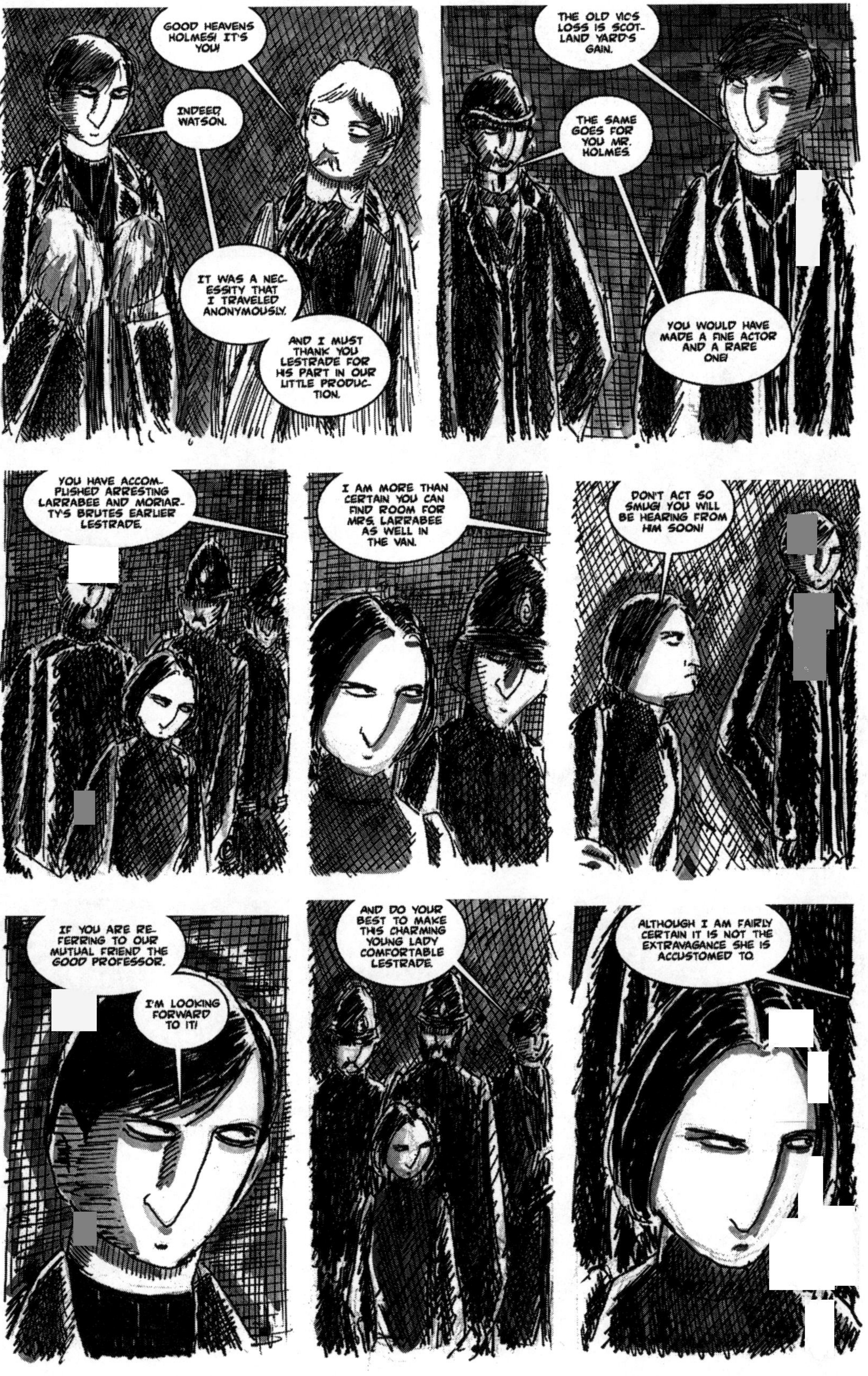
GOOD HEAVENS HOLMES! IT'S YOU!
INDEED WATSON.
IT WAS A NECESSITY THAT I TRAVELED ANONYMOUSLY.
AND I MUST THANK YOU LESTRADE FOR HIS PART IN OUR LITTLE PRODUCTION.
THE OLD VIC'S LOSS IS SCOTLAND YARD'S GAIN.
THE SAME GOES FOR YOU MR. HOLMES.
YOU WOULD HAVE MADE A FINE ACTOR AND A RARE ONE!
YOU HAVE ACCOMPLISHED ARRESTING LARRABEE AND MORIARTY'S BRUTES EARLIER LESTRADE.
I AM MORE THAN CERTAIN YOU CAN FIND ROOM FOR MRS. LARRABEE AS WELL IN THE VAN.
DON'T ACT SO SMUG! YOU WILL BE HEARING FROM HIM SOON!
IF YOU ARE REFERRING TO OUR MUTUAL FRIEND THE GOOD PROFESSOR.
I'M LOOKING FORWARD TO IT!
AND DO YOUR BEST TO MAKE THIS CHARMING YOUNG LADY COMFORTABLE LESTRADE.
ALTHOUGH I AM FAIRLY CERTAIN IT IS NOT THE EXTRAVAGANCE SHE IS ACCUSTOMED TO.

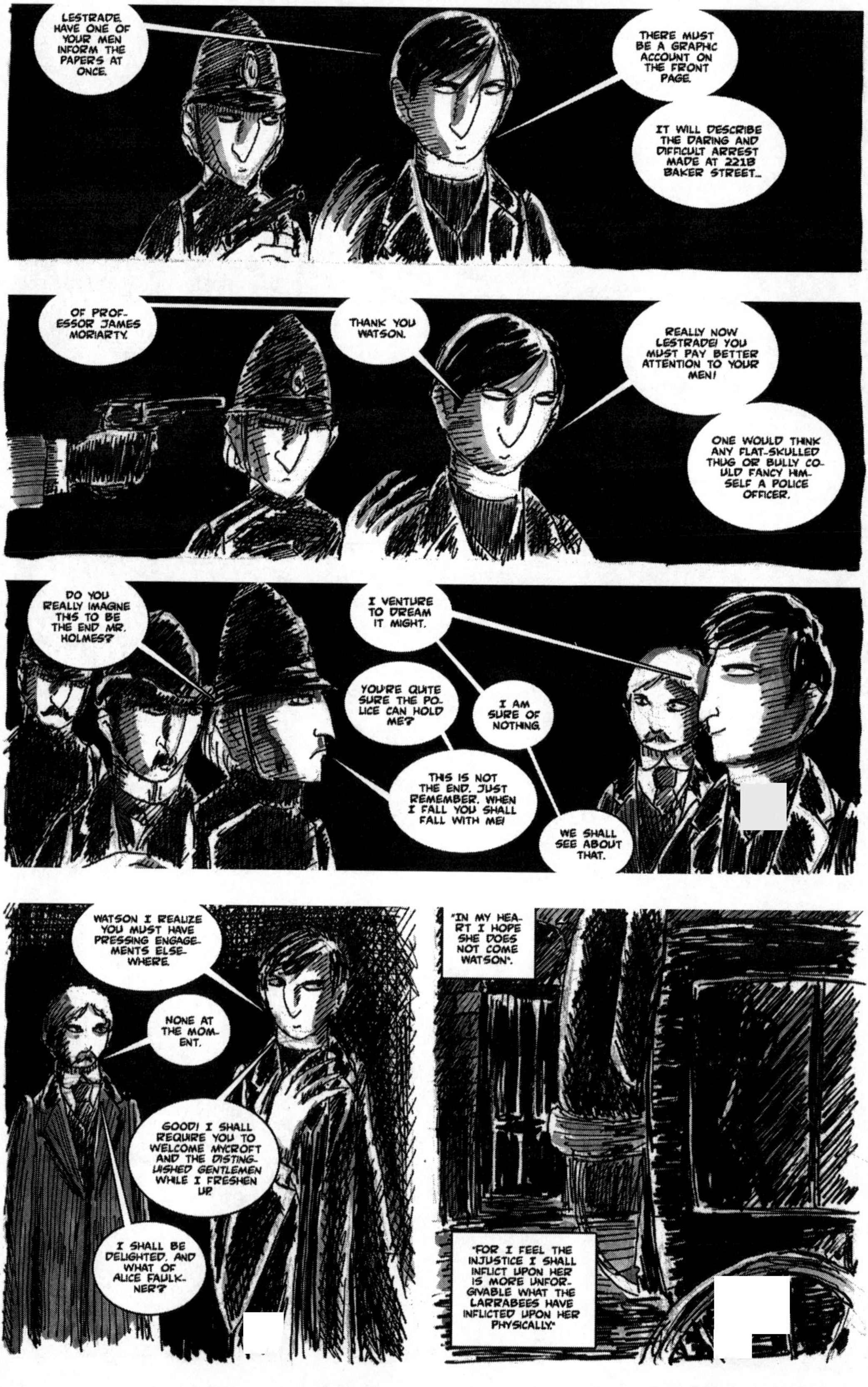
LESTRADE. HAVE ONE OF YOUR MEN INFORM THE PAPERS AT ONCE.
THERE MUST BE A GRAPHIC ACCOUNT ON THE FRONT PAGE.
IT WILL DESCRIBE THE DARING AND DIFFICULT ARREST MADE AT 221B BAKER STREET...
OF PROFESSOR JAMES MORIARTY.
THANK YOU WATSON.
REALLY NOW LESTRADE! YOU MUST PAY BETTER ATTENTION TO YOUR MEN!
ONE WOULD THINK ANY FLAT-SKULLED THUG OR BULLY COULD FANCY HIMSELF A POLICE OFFICER.
DO YOU REALLY IMAGINE THIS TO BE THE END MR. HOLMES?
I VENTURE TO DREAM IT MIGHT.
YOU'RE QUITE SURE THE POLICE CAN HOLD ME?
I AM SURE OF NOTHING.
THIS IS NOT THE END. JUST REMEMBER. WHEN I FALL YOU SHALL FALL WITH ME!
WE SHALL SEE ABOUT THAT.
WATSON I REALIZE YOU MUST HAVE PRESSING ENGAGEMENTS ELSEWHERE.
NONE AT THE MOMENT.
GOOD! I SHALL REQUIRE YOU TO WELCOME MYCROFT AND THE DISTINGUISHED GENTLEMEN WHILE I FRESHEN UP.
I SHALL BE DELIGHTED. AND WHAT OF ALICE FAULKNER?
"IN MY HEART I HOPE SHE DOES NOT COME WATSON".
"FOR I FEEL THE INJUSTICE I SHALL INFLICT UPON HER IS MORE UNFORGIVABLE WHAT THE LARRABEES HAVE INFLICTED UPON HER PHYSICALLY."

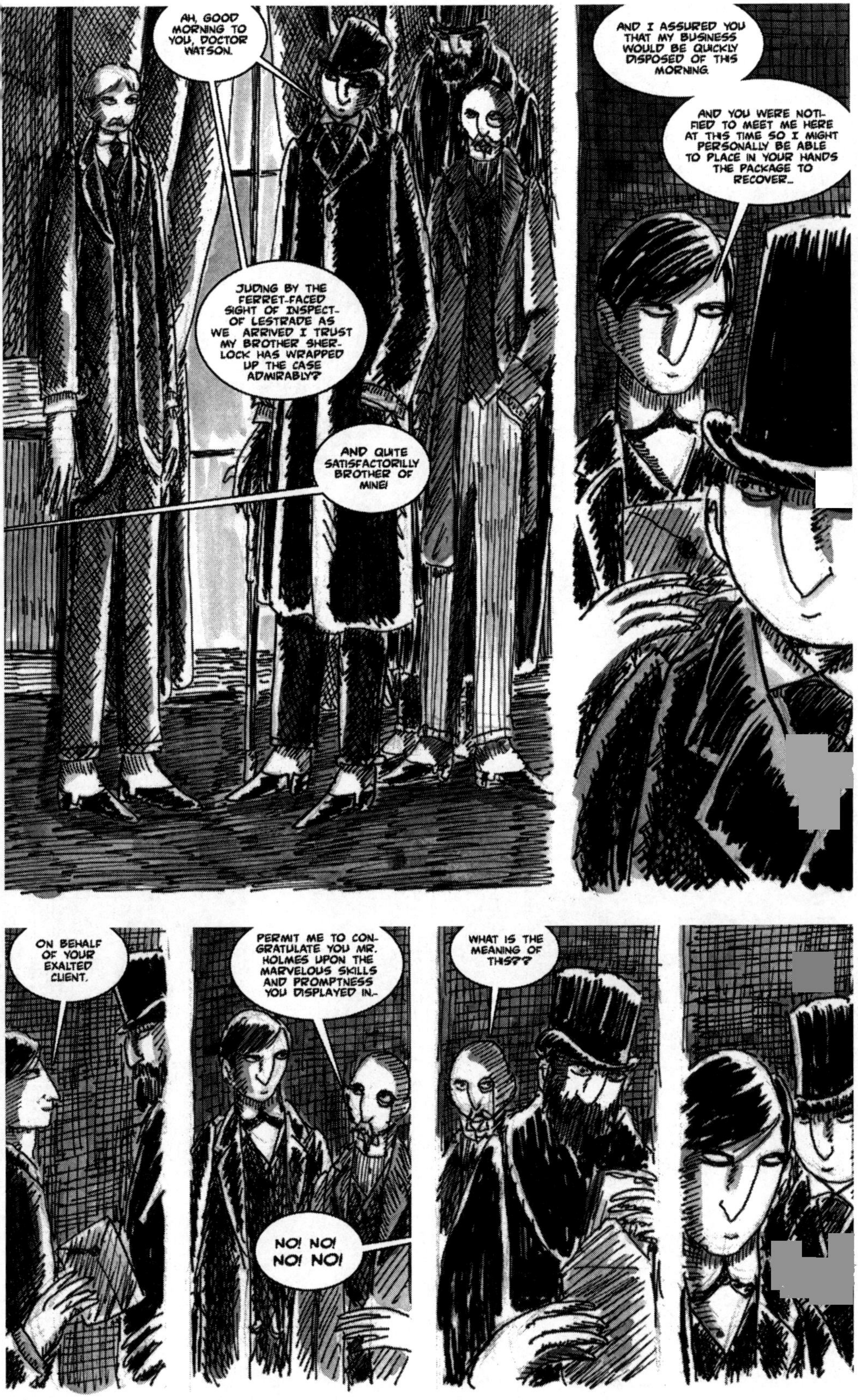
AH, GOOD MORNING TO YOU, DOCTOR WATSON.
JUDING BY THE FERRET-FACED SIGHT OF INSPECT-OR LESTRADE AS WE ARRIVED I TRUST MY BROTHER SHER-LOCK HAS WRAPPED UP THE CASE ADMIRABLY?
AND QUITE SATISFACTORILLY BROTHER OF MINE!
AND I ASSURED YOU THAT MY BUSINESS WOULD BE QUICKLY DISPOSED OF THIS MORNING.
AND YOU WERE NOTI-FIED TO MEET ME HERE AT THIS TIME SO I MIGHT PERSONALLY BE ABLE TO PLACE IN YOUR HANDS THE PACKAGE TO RECOVER...
ON BEHALF OF YOUR EXALTED CLIENT.
PERMIT ME TO CON-GRATULATE YOU MR. HOLMES UPON THE MARVELOUS SKILLS AND PROMPTNESS YOU DISPLAYED IN...
NO! NO! NO! NO!
WHAT IS THE MEANING OF THIS??

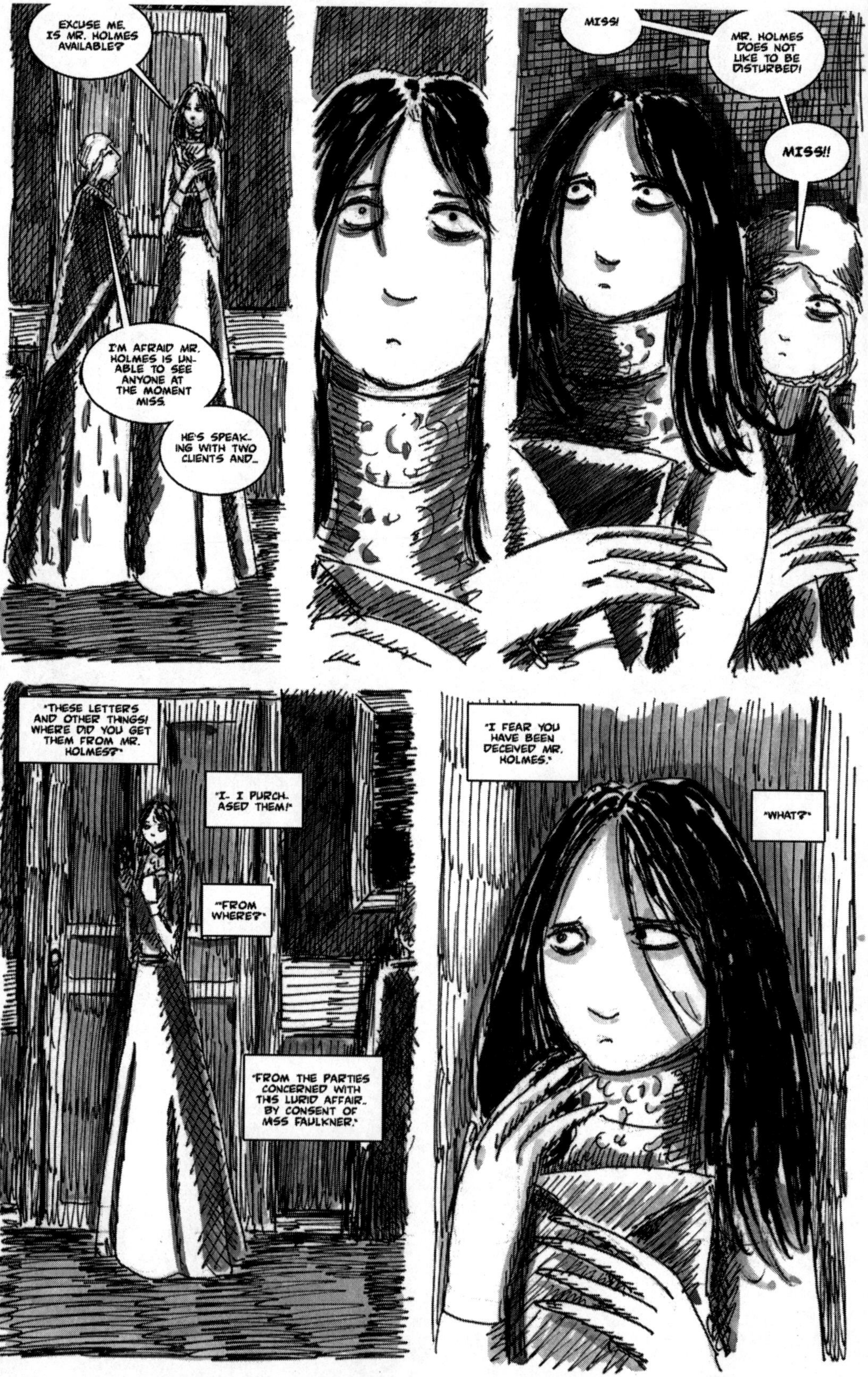
EXCUSE ME. IS MR. HOLMES AVAILABLE?
I'M AFRAID MR. HOLMES IS UNABLE TO SEE ANYONE AT THE MOMENT MISS.
HE'S SPEAKING WITH TWO CLIENTS AND...
MISS!
MR. HOLMES DOES NOT LIKE TO BE DISTURBED!
MISS!!
"THESE LETTERS AND OTHER THINGS! WHERE DID YOU GET THEM FROM MR. HOLMES?"
"I- I PURCHASED THEM!"
"FROM WHERE?"
"FROM THE PARTIES CONCERNED WITH THIS LURID AFFAIR.. BY CONSENT OF MISS FAULKNER."
"I FEAR YOU HAVE BEEN DECEIVED MR. HOLMES."
"WHAT?"

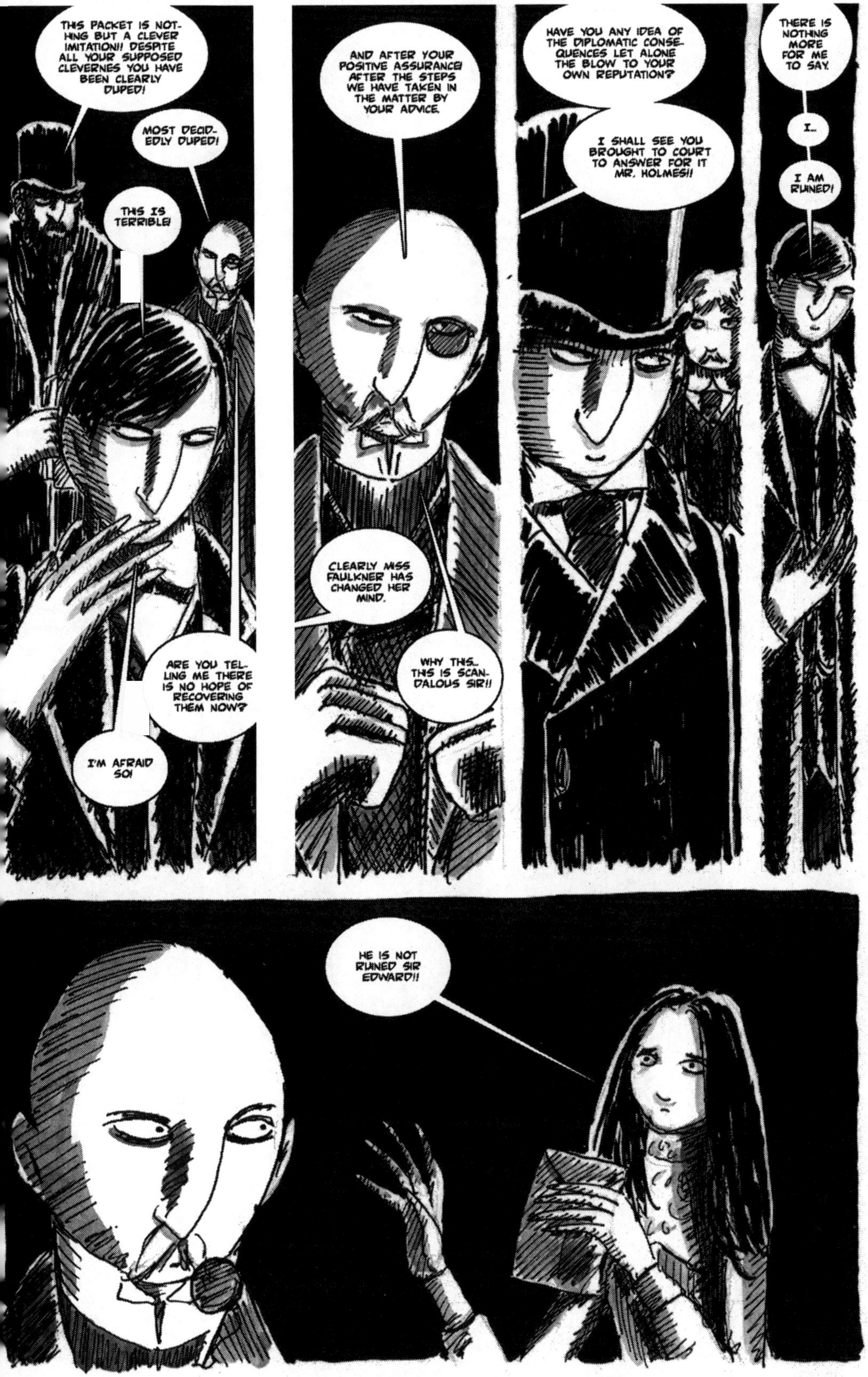
THIS PACKET IS NOTHING BUT A CLEVER IMITATION!! DESPITE ALL YOUR SUPPOSED CLEVERNES YOU HAVE BEEN CLEARLY DUPED!
MOST DECIDEDLY DUPED!
THIS IS TERRIBLE!
ARE YOU TELLING ME THERE IS NO HOPE OF RECOVERING THEM NOW?
I'M AFRAID SO!
AND AFTER YOUR POSITIVE ASSURANCE! AFTER THE STEPS WE HAVE TAKEN IN THE MATTER BY YOUR ADVICE.
CLEARLY MISS FAULKNER HAS CHANGED HER MIND.
WHY THIS.. THIS IS SCANDALOUS SIR!!
HAVE YOU ANY IDEA OF THE DIPLOMATIC CONSEQUENCES LET ALONE THE BLOW TO YOUR OWN REPUTATION?
I SHALL SEE YOU BROUGHT TO COURT TO ANSWER FOR IT MR. HOLMES!!
THERE IS NOTHING MORE FOR ME TO SAY.
I..
I AM RUINED!
HE IS NOT RUINED SIR EDWARD!!

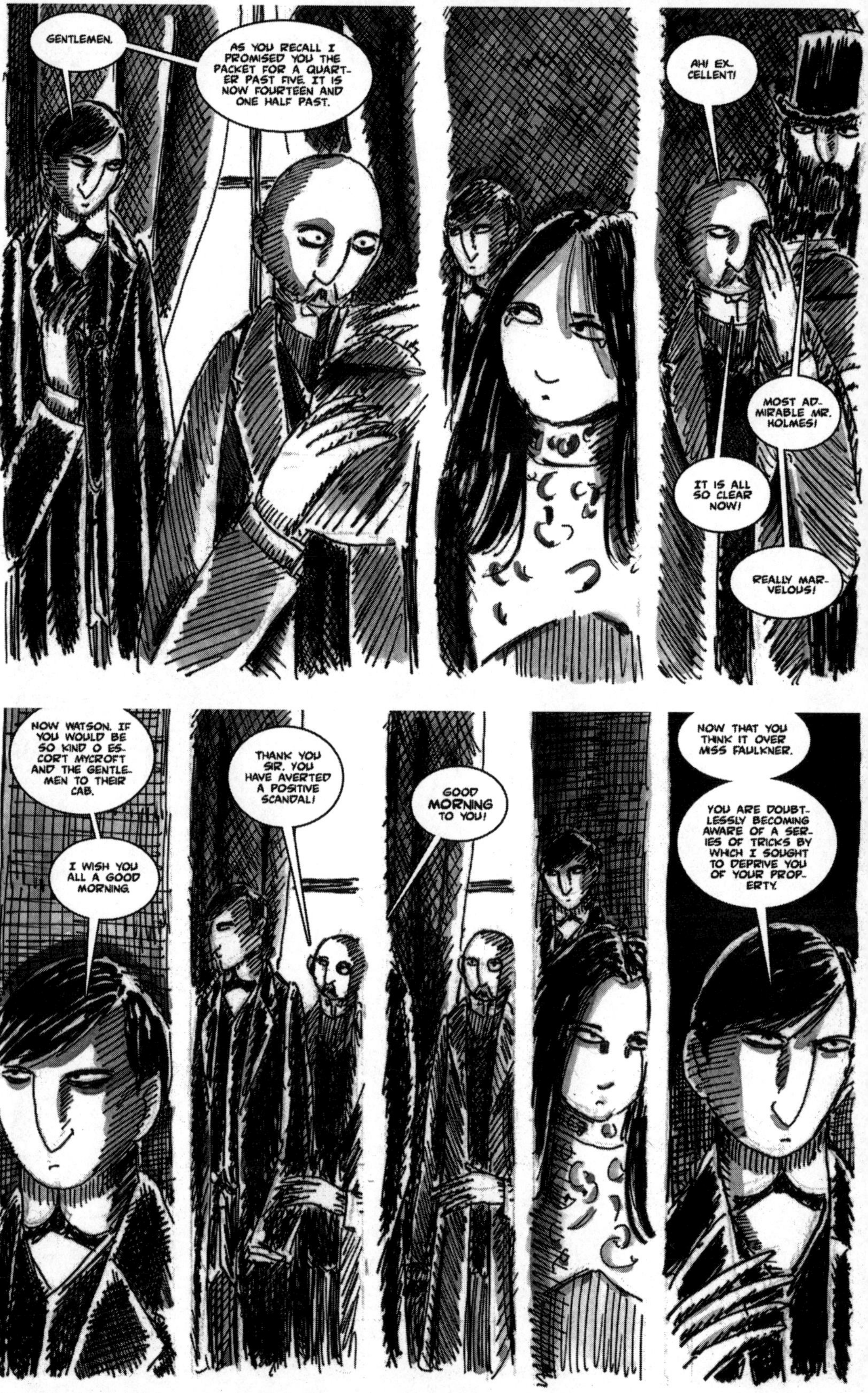
GENTLEMEN.
AS YOU RECALL I PROMISED YOU THE PACKET FOR A QUARTER PAST FIVE. IT IS NOW FOURTEEN AND ONE HALF PAST.
AH! EXCELLENT!
MOST ADMIRABLE MR. HOLMES!
IT IS ALL SO CLEAR NOW!
REALLY MARVELOUS!
NOW WATSON. IF YOU WOULD BE SO KIND O ESCORT MYCROFT AND THE GENTLEMEN TO THEIR CAB.
I WISH YOU ALL A GOOD MORNING.
THANK YOU SIR. YOU HAVE AVERTED A POSITIVE SCANDAL!
GOOD MORNING TO YOU!
NOW THAT YOU THINK IT OVER MSS FAULKNER.
YOU ARE DOUBTLESSLY BECOMING AWARE OF A SERIES OF TRICKS BY WHICH I SOUGHT TO DEPRIVE YOU OF YOUR PROPERTY.

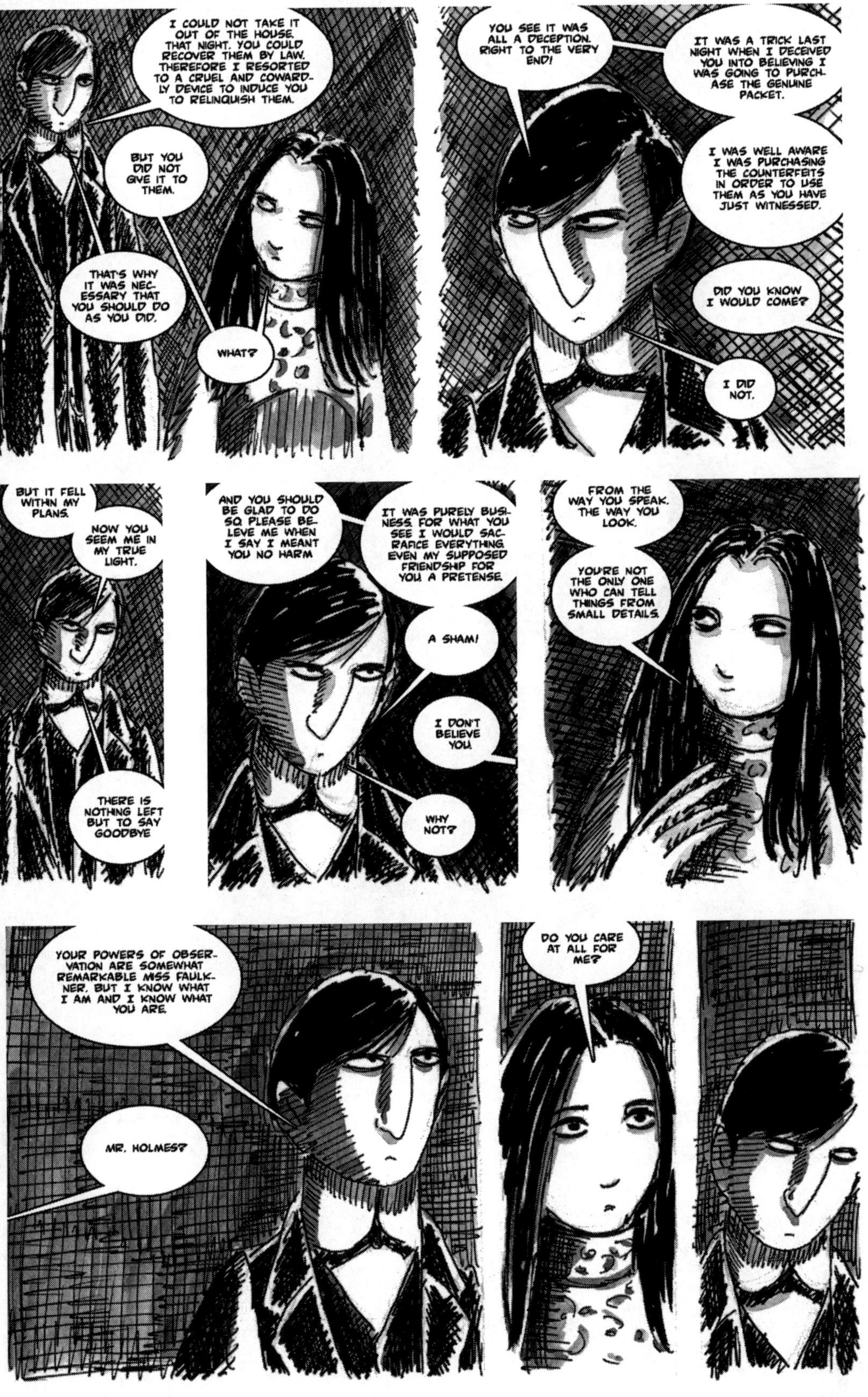
I COULD NOT TAKE IT OUT OF THE HOUSE. THAT NIGHT, YOU COULD RECOVER THEM BY LAW. THEREFORE I RESORTED TO A CRUEL AND COWARDLY DEVICE TO INDUCE YOU TO RELINQUISH THEM.
BUT YOU DID NOT GIVE IT TO THEM.
THAT'S WHY IT WAS NECESSARY THAT YOU SHOULD DO AS YOU DID.
WHAT?
YOU SEE IT WAS ALL A DECEPTION. RIGHT TO THE VERY END!
IT WAS A TRICK LAST NIGHT WHEN I DECEIVED YOU INTO BELIEVING I WAS GOING TO PURCHASE THE GENUINE PACKET.
I WAS WELL AWARE I WAS PURCHASING THE COUNTERFEITS IN ORDER TO USE THEM AS YOU HAVE JUST WITNESSED.
DID YOU KNOW I WOULD COME?
I DID NOT.
BUT IT FELL WITHIN MY PLANS.
NOW YOU SEEM ME IN MY TRUE LIGHT.
THERE IS NOTHING LEFT BUT TO SAY GOODBYE
AND YOU SHOULD BE GLAD TO DO SO. PLEASE BELEVE ME WHEN I SAY I MEANT YOU NO HARM
IT WAS PURELY BUSINESS. FOR WHAT YOU SEE I WOULD SACRAFICE EVERYTHING. EVEN MY SUPPOSED FRIENDSHIP FOR YOU. A PRETENSE.
A SHAM!
I DON'T BELIEVE YOU.
WHY NOT?
FROM THE WAY YOU SPEAK. THE WAY YOU LOOK.
YOU'RE NOT THE ONLY ONE WHO CAN TELL THINGS FROM SMALL DETAILS.
YOUR POWERS OF OBSERVATION ARE SOMEWHAT REMARKABLE MISS FAULKNER. BUT I KNOW WHAT I AM AND I KNOW WHAT YOU ARE.
MR. HOLMES?
DO YOU CARE AT ALL FOR ME?

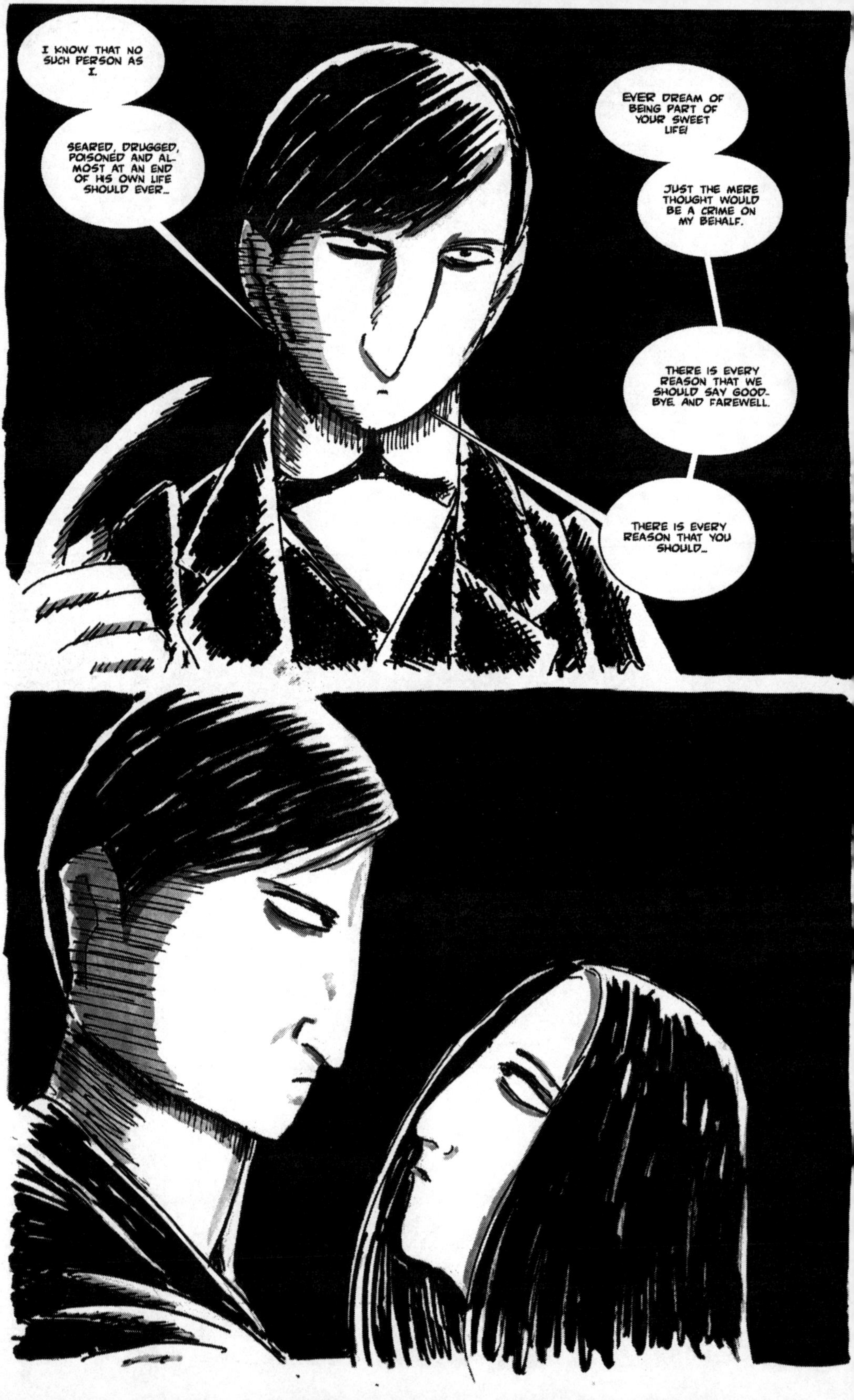
I KNOW THAT NO SUCH PERSON AS I.
SEARED, DRUGGED, POISONED AND AL- MOST AT AN END OF HIS OWN LIFE SHOULD EVER...
EVER DREAM OF BEING PART OF YOUR SWEET LIFE!
JUST THE MERE THOUGHT WOULD BE A CRIME ON MY BEHALF.
THERE IS EVERY REASON THAT WE SHOULD SAY GOOD- BYE AND FAREWELL.
THERE IS EVERY REASON THAT YOU SHOULD...

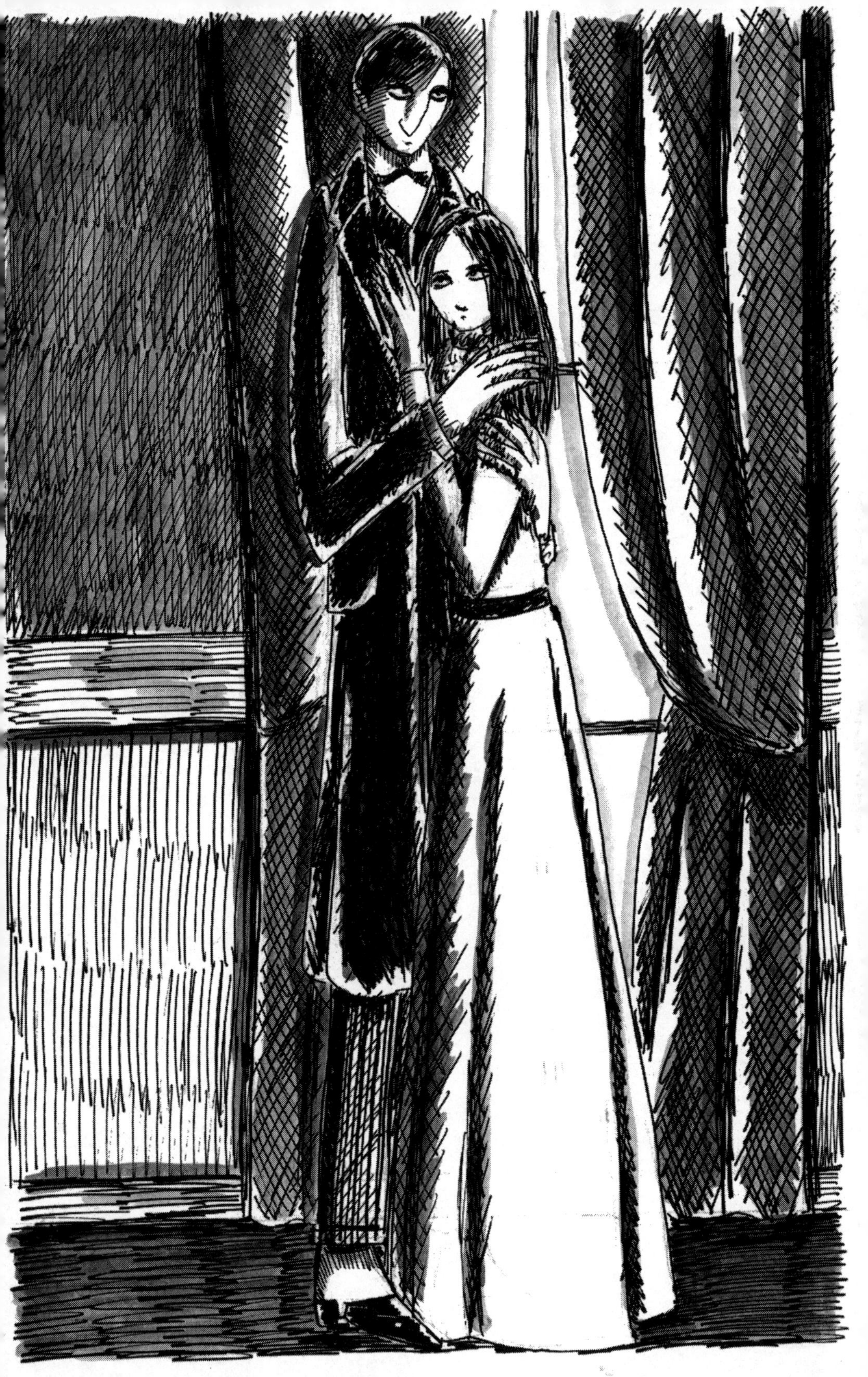

A Study in Sherlock

A gallery of Sherlock Holmes Illustrations throughout the years.

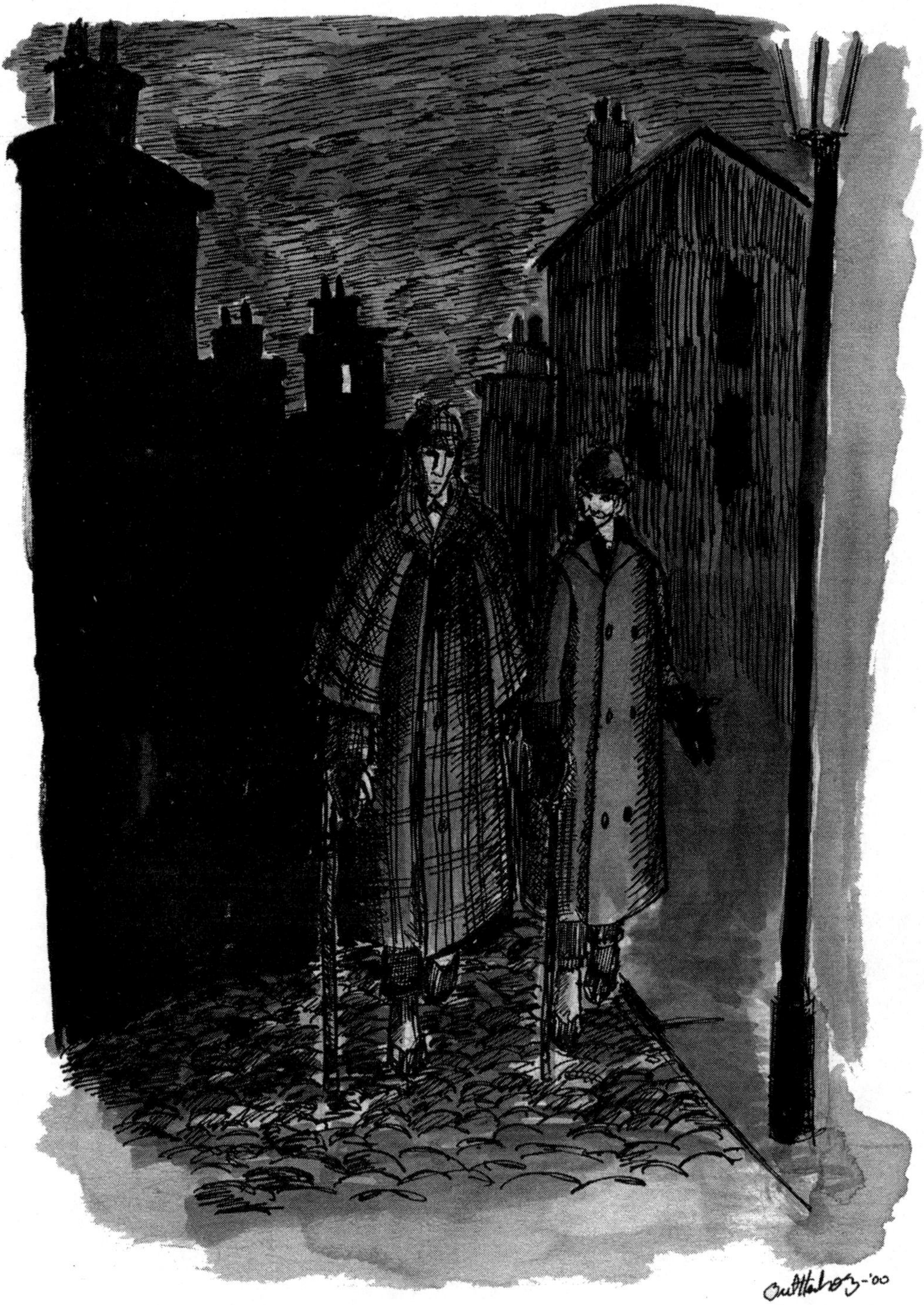

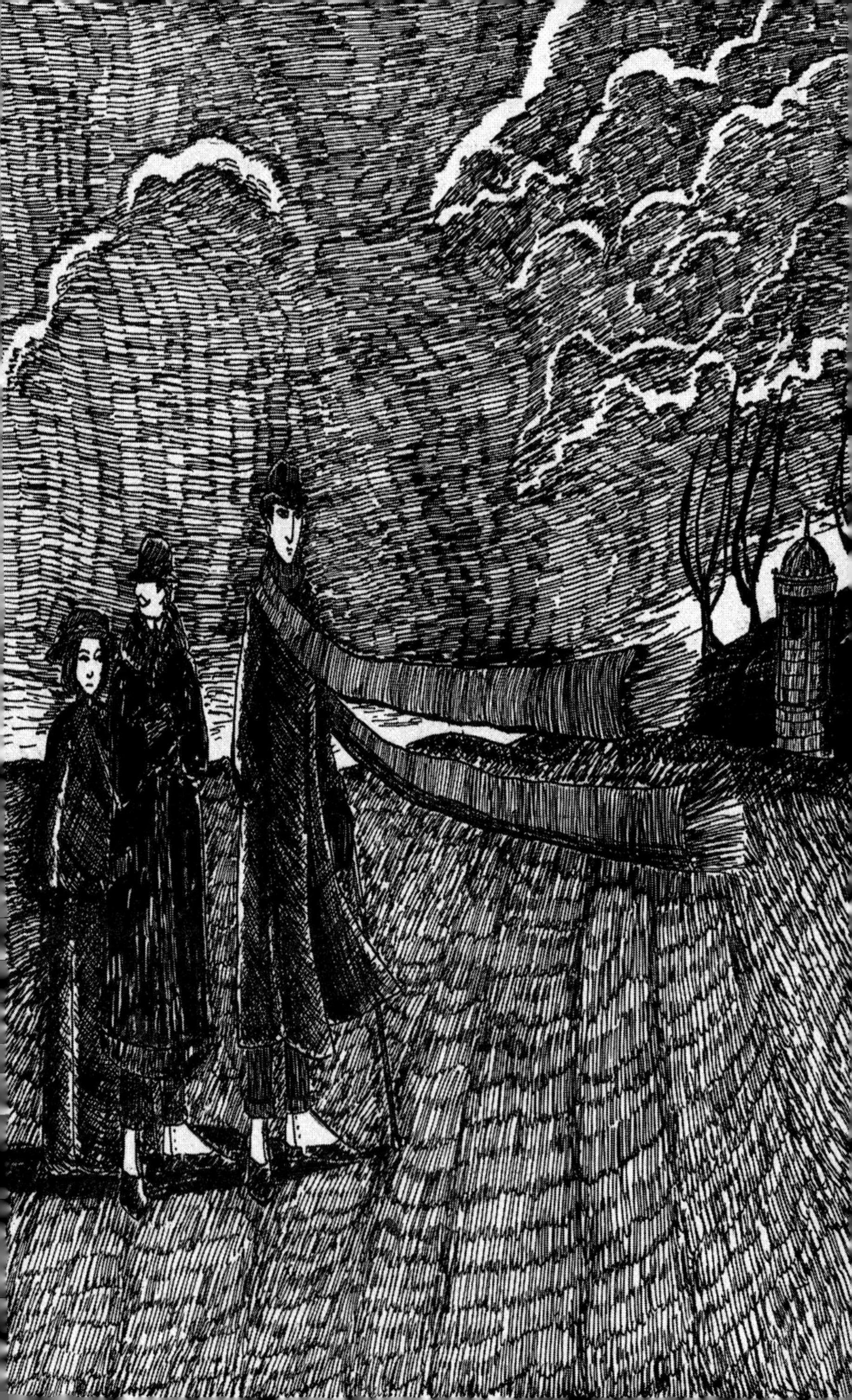

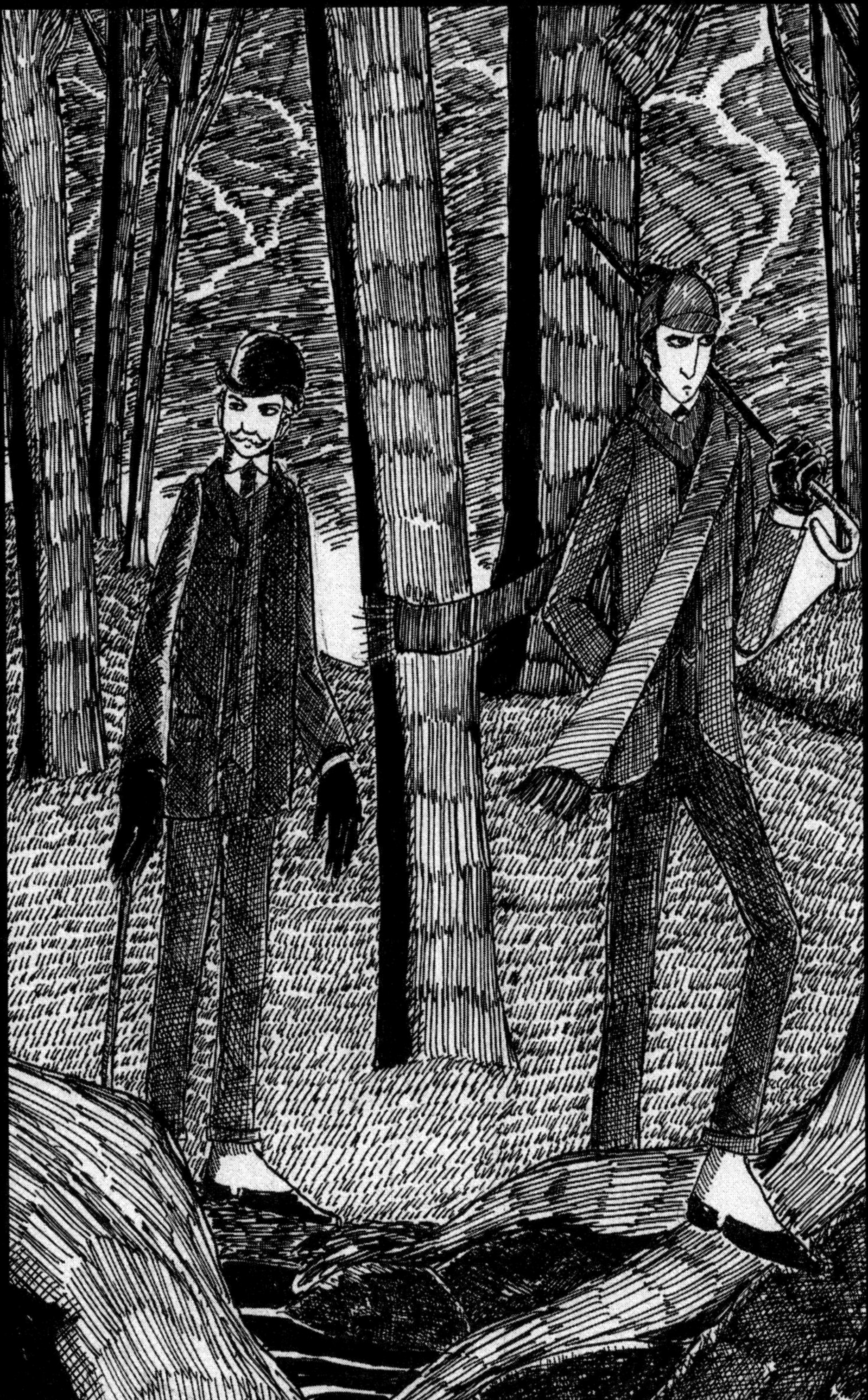

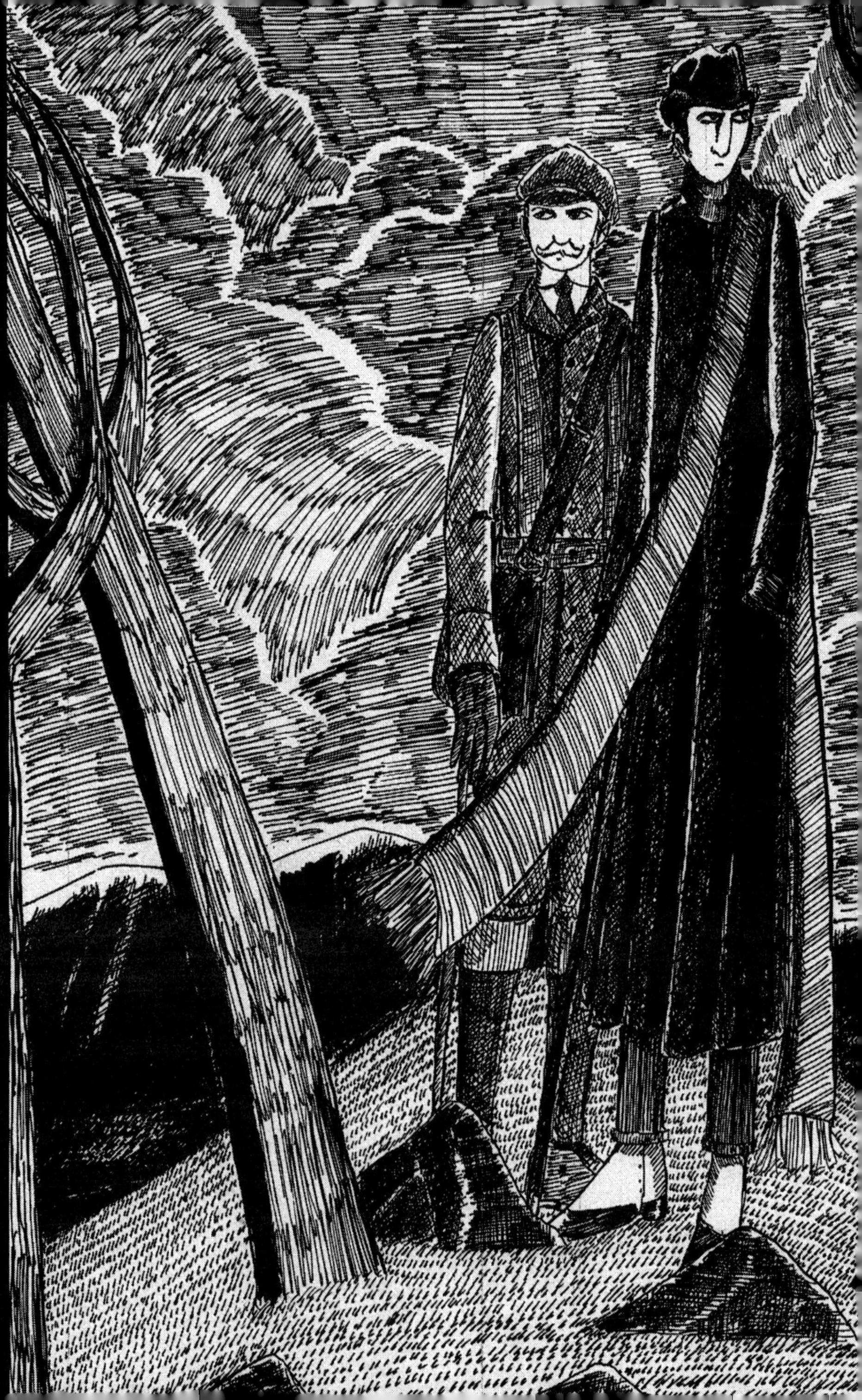

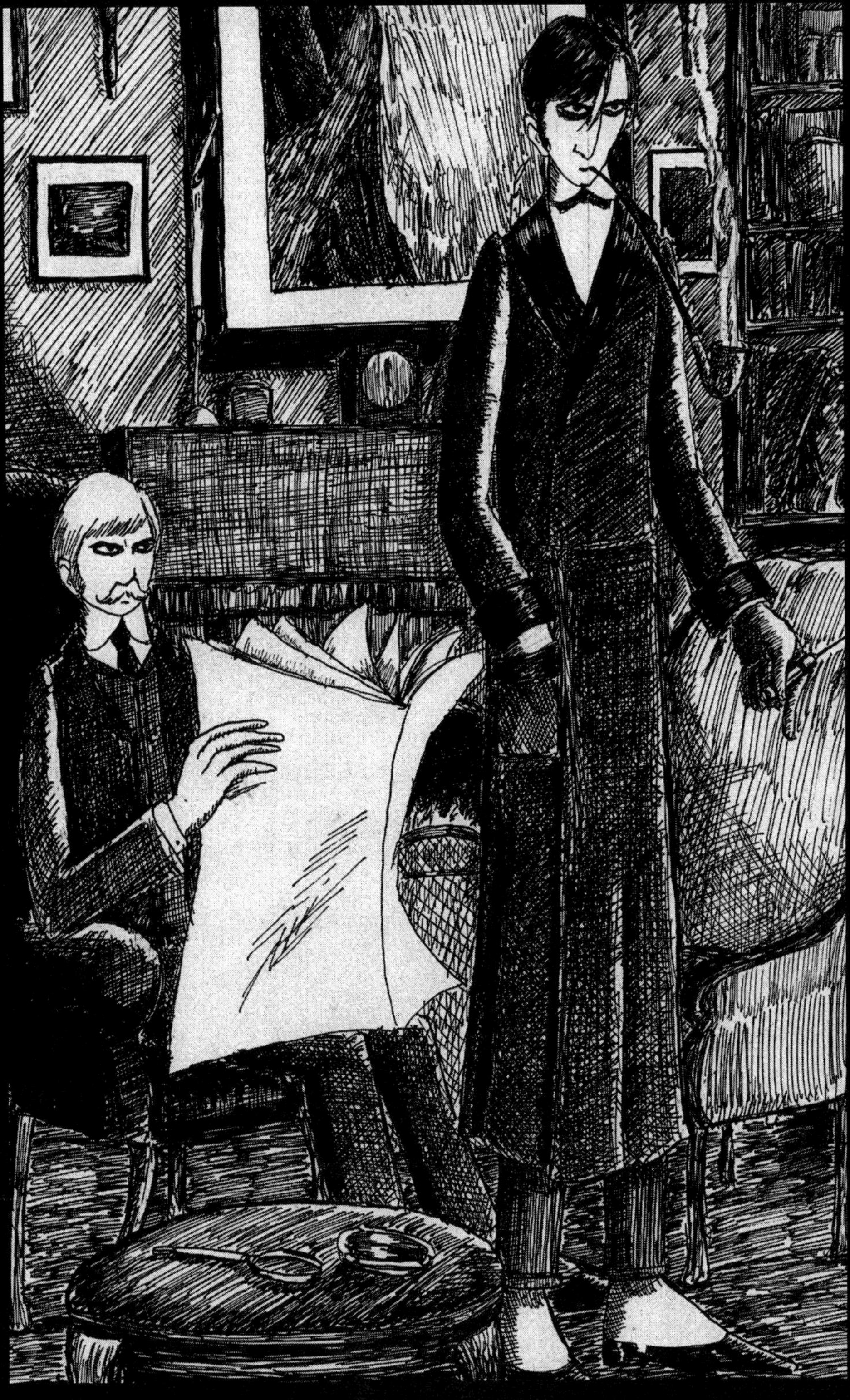

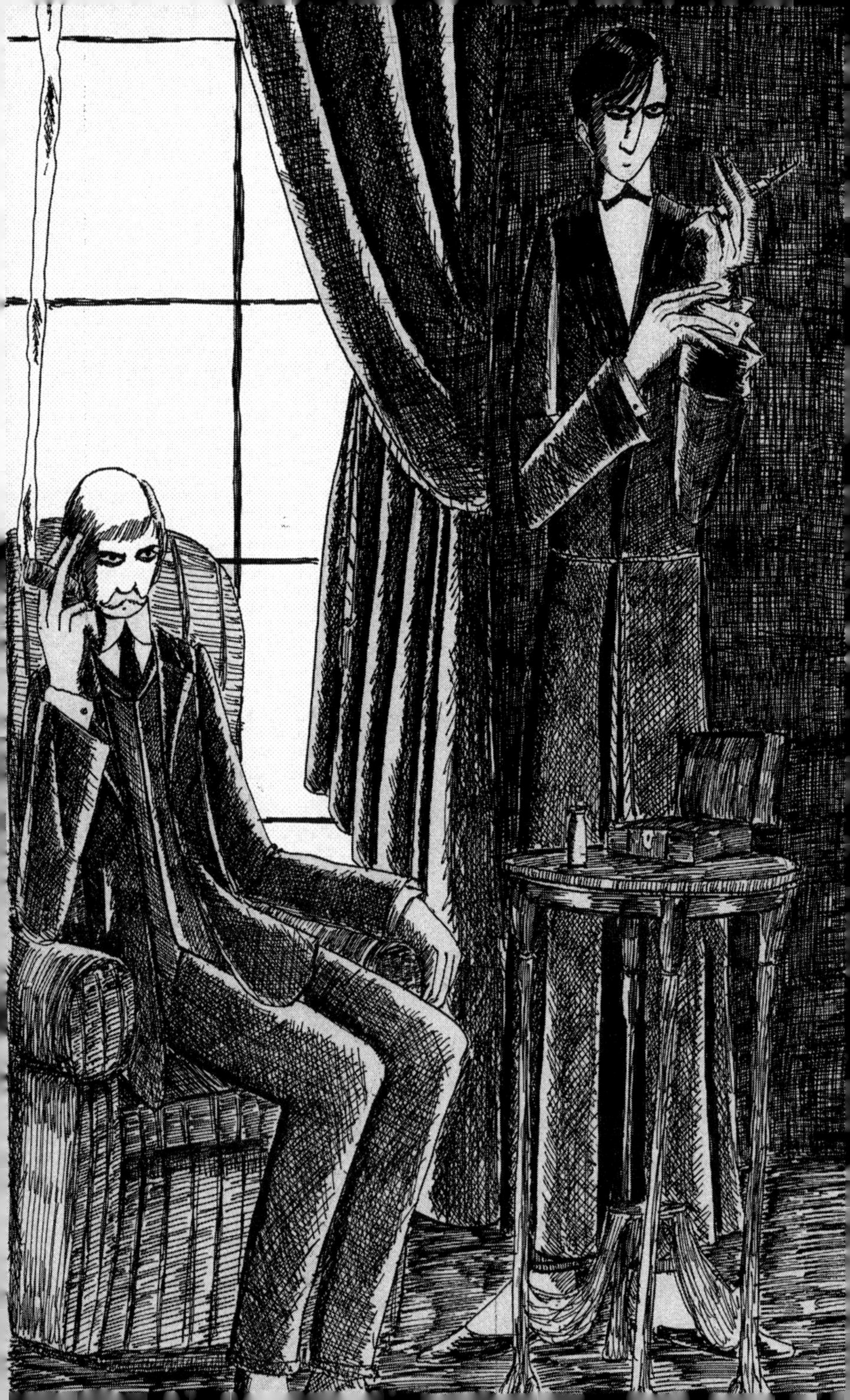

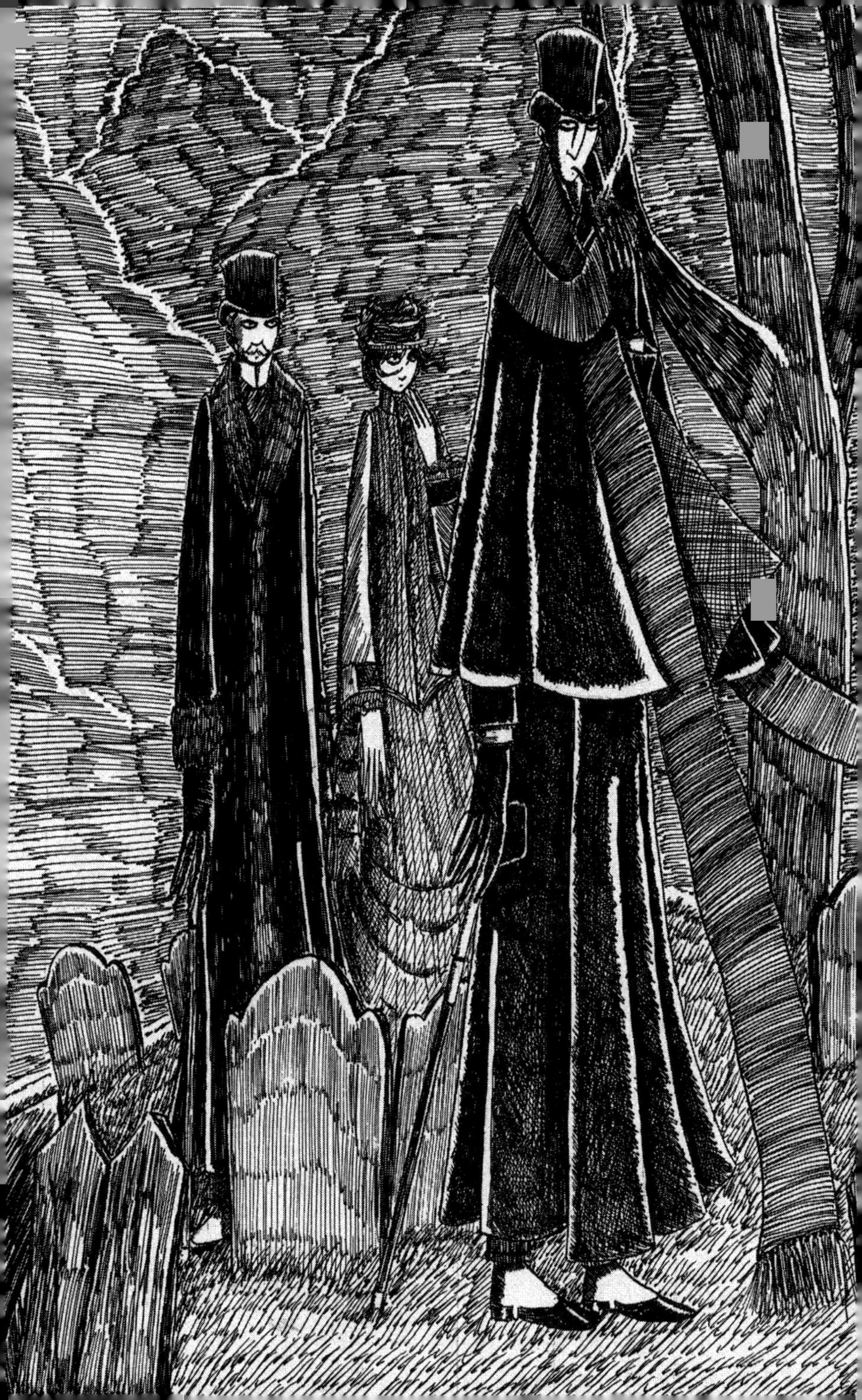

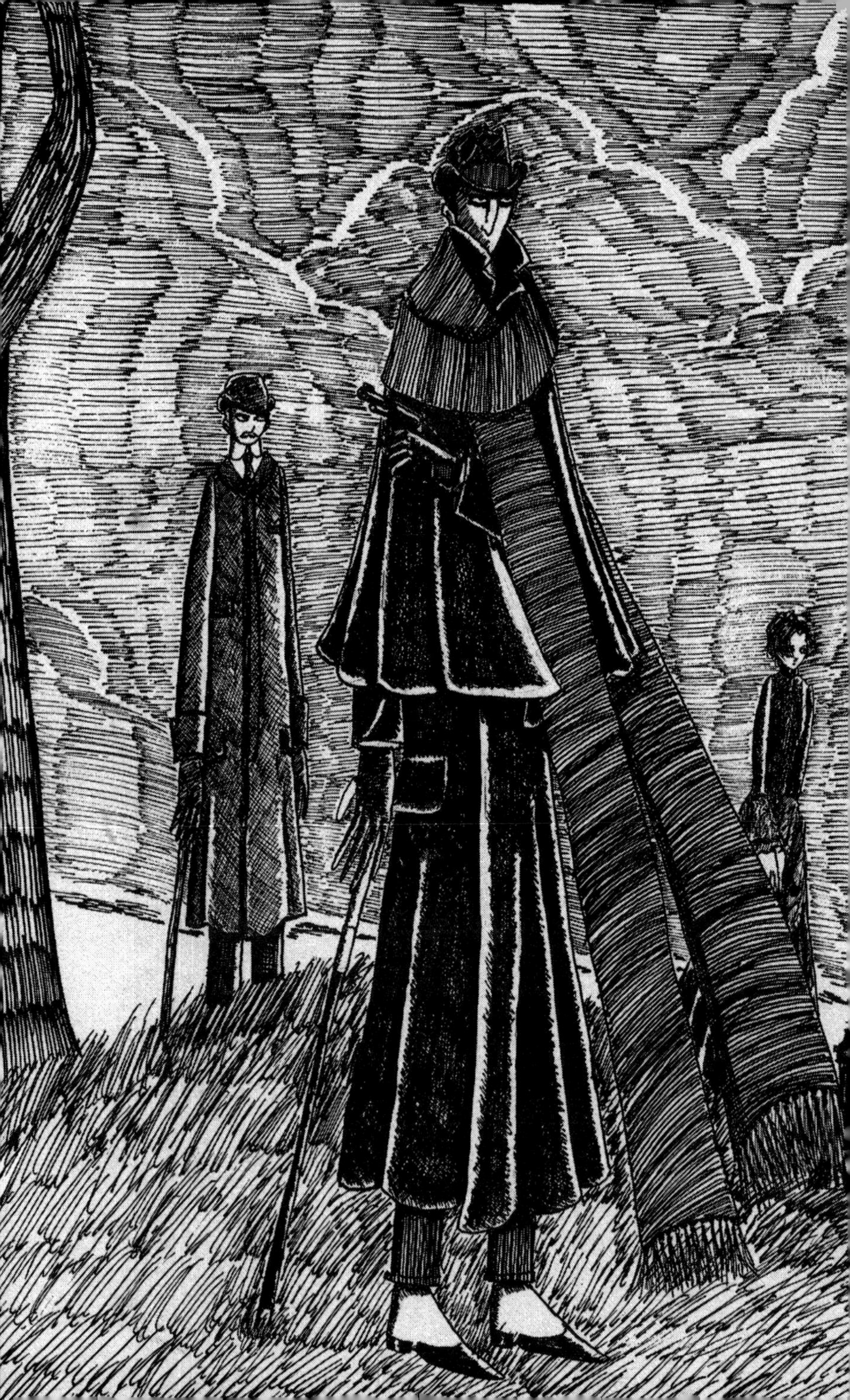

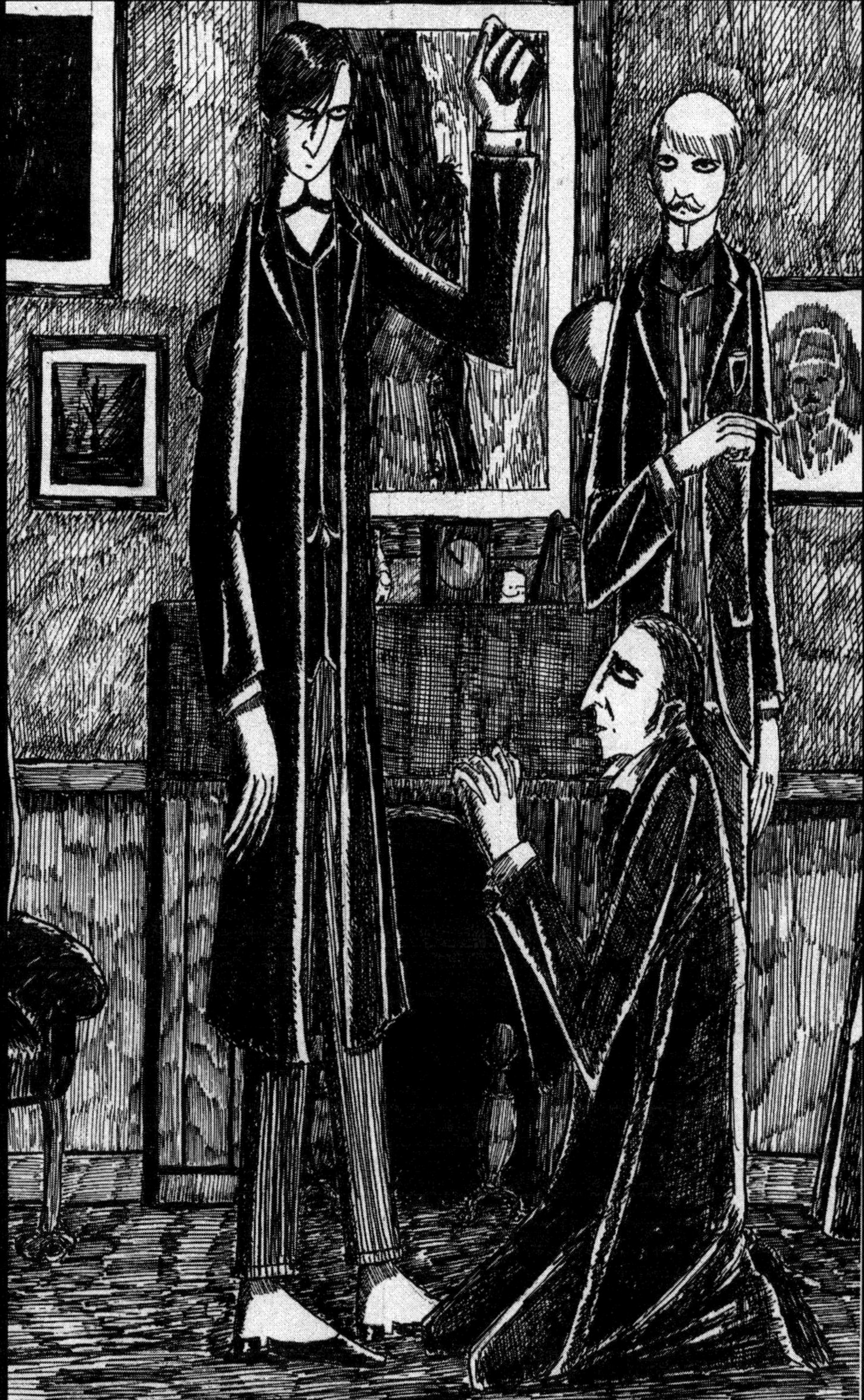

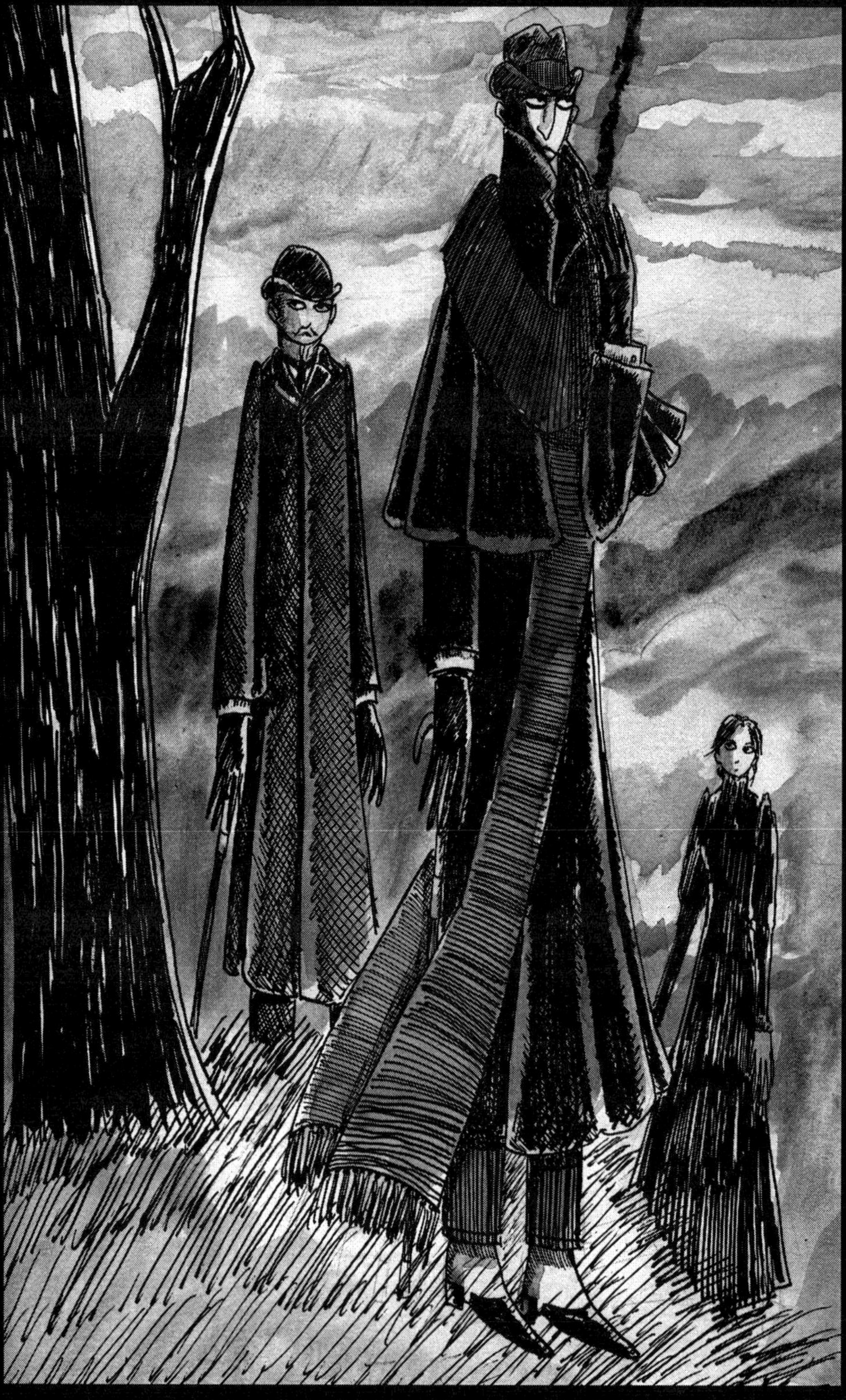

GILLETTE CASTLE

Taken on holiday in East Haddam, CT in August 2007

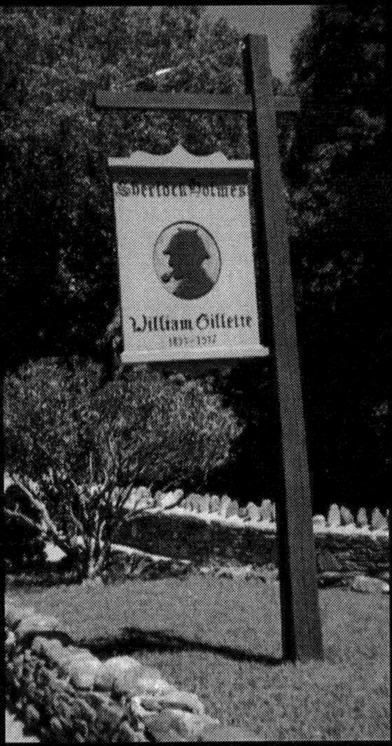
William Gillette

The home of Connecticut born actor/playwright William Hooker Gillette.

Originally christened Seven Sisters by Gillette himself, the fortress-like residence was later dubbed Gillette Castle after his. his death in 1937.
I based Edelweiss Lodge on GilletteCastle as a tribute to the man who first made the character ofSherlock Holmes famous on stage in the United States.

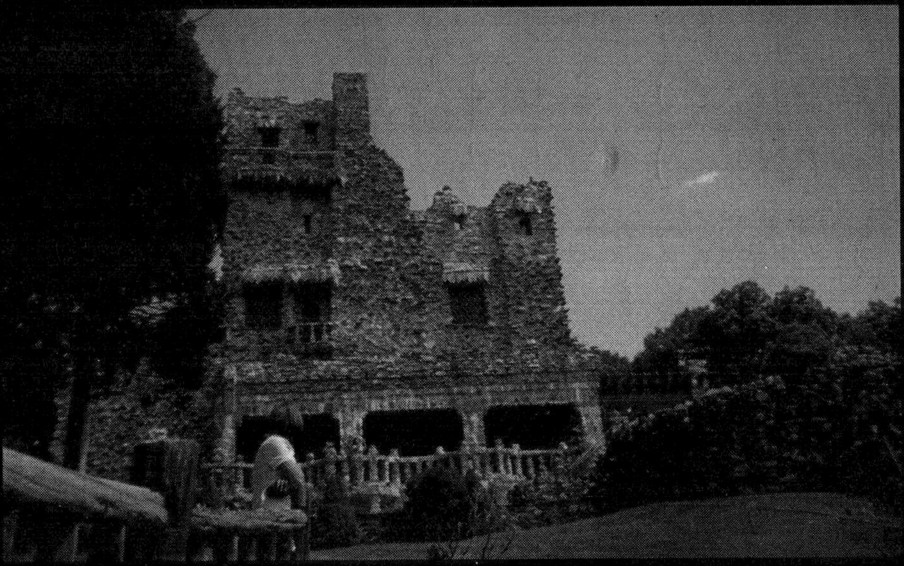

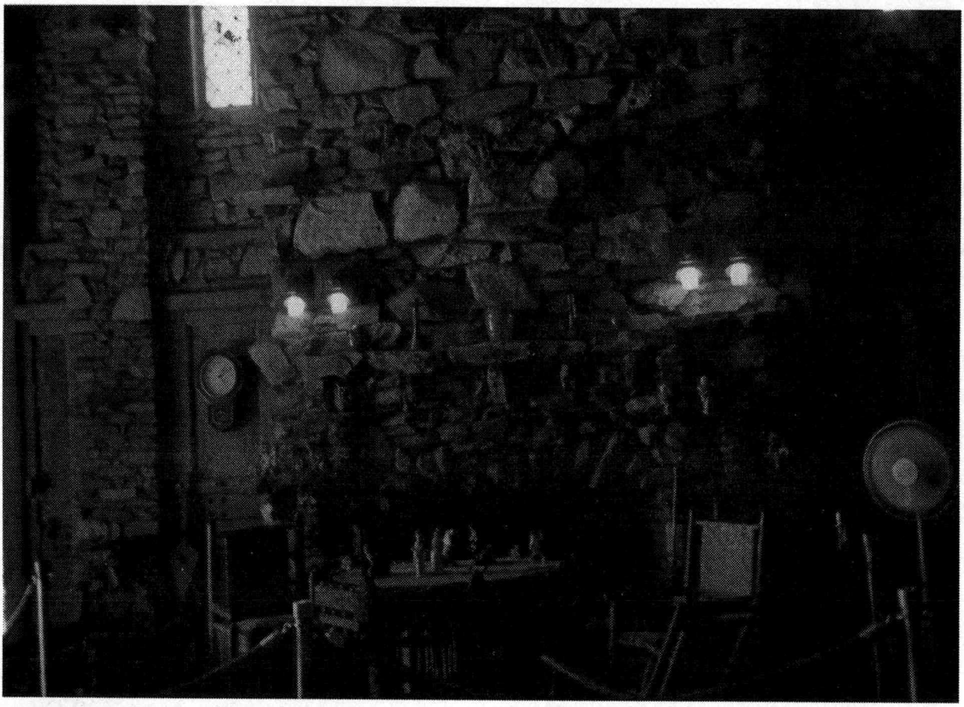

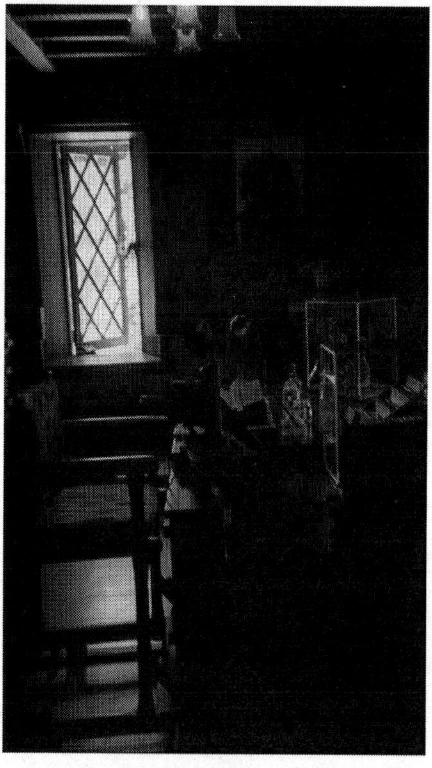

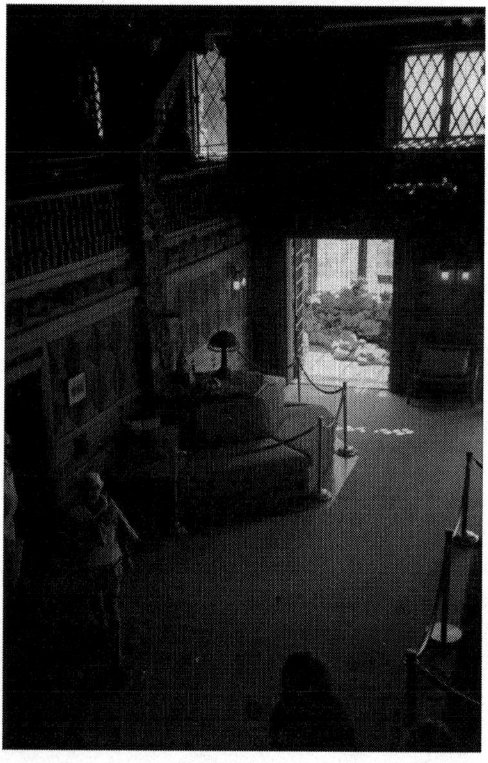

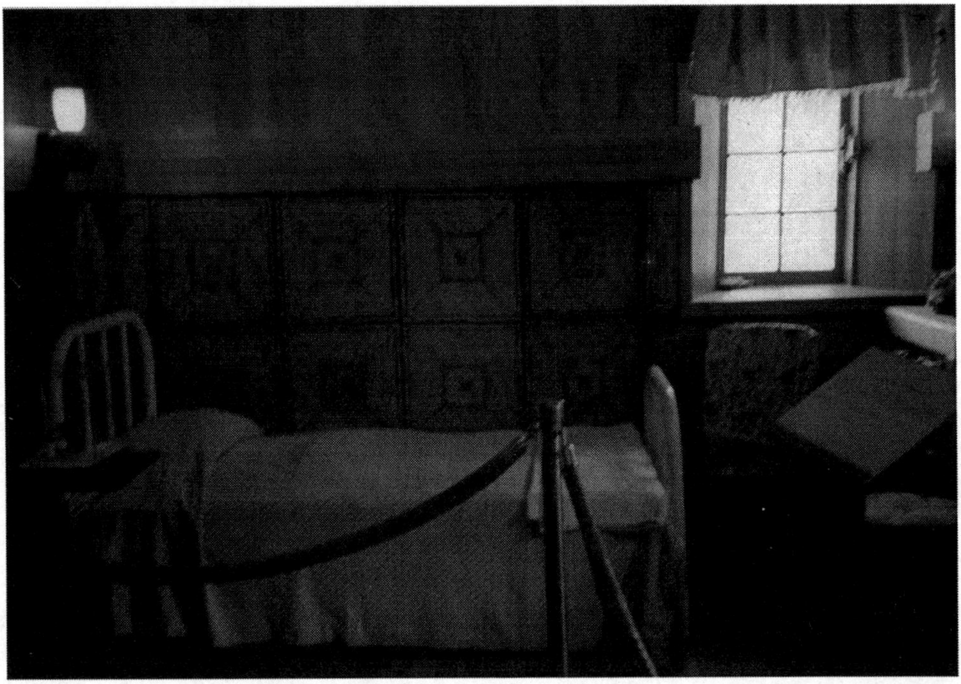

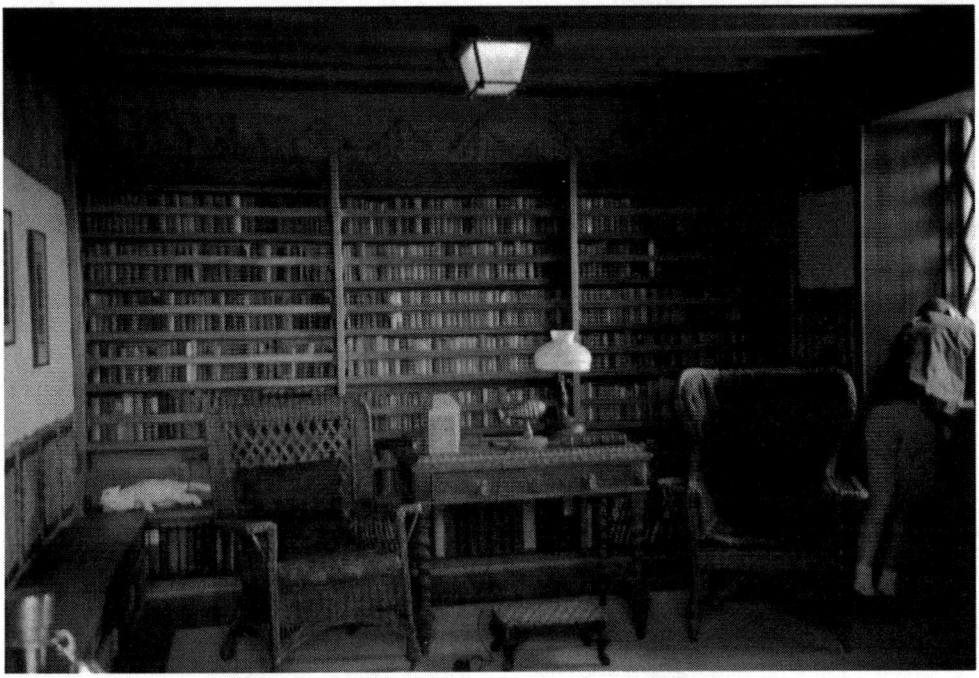

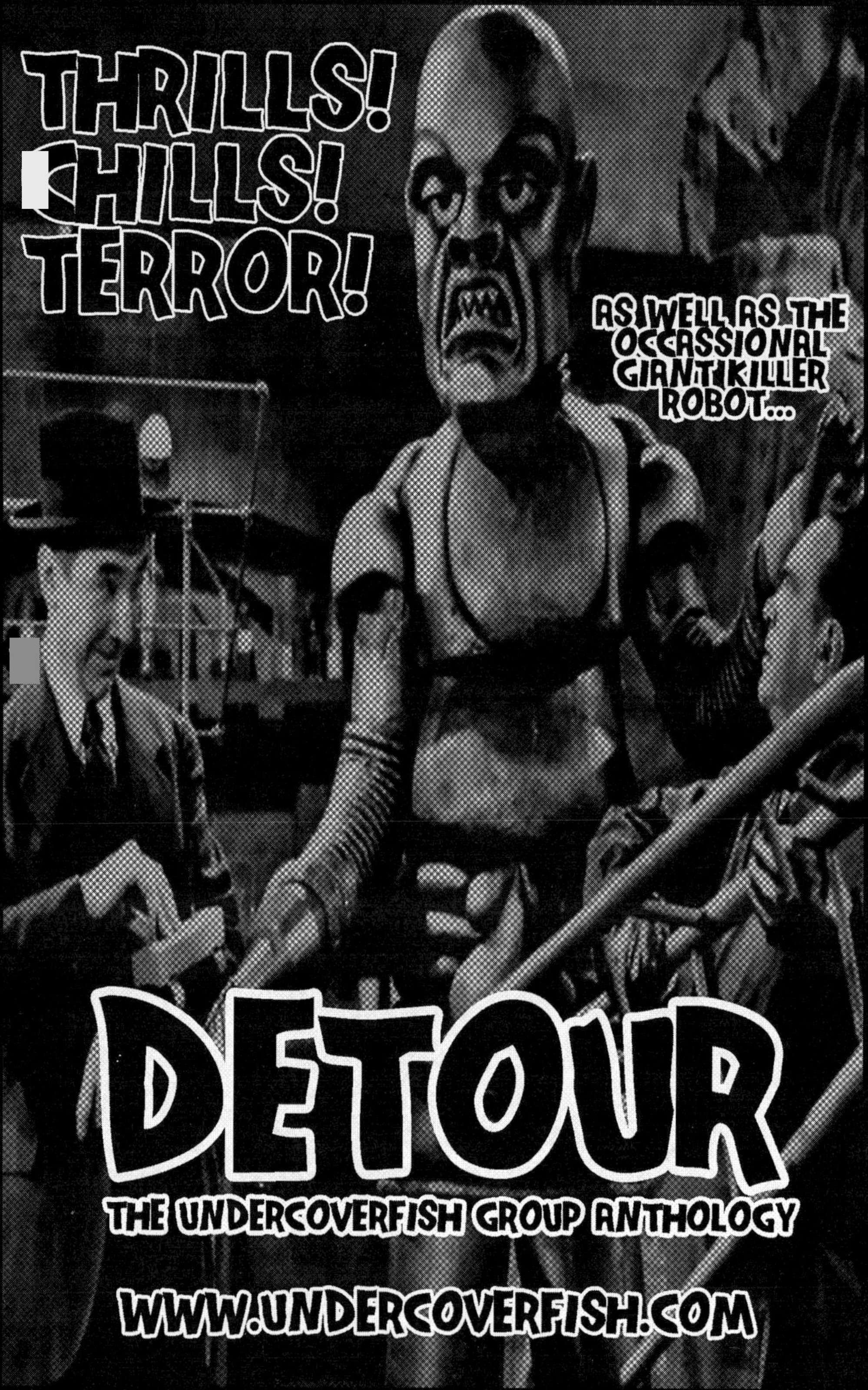
THRILLS!
CHILLS!
TERROR!
AS WELL AS THE OCCASSIONAL GIANT KILLER ROBOT...
DETOUR
THE UNDERCOVERFISH GROUP ANTHOLOGY
WWW.UNDERCOVERFISH.COM